I'VE
HAD
IT

*A Practical Guide
to Moving Abroad*

I'VE
HAD
IT

A PRACTICAL GUIDE
TO MOVING ABROAD

by Robert Hopkins

HOLT, RINEHART AND WINSTON
NEW YORK CHICAGO SAN FRANCISCO

Published simultaneously in Canada by Holt, Rinehart and Winston of Canada,
Limited.

Library of Congress Catalog Card: 77–155516

First Edition

ISBN: 0–03–086573–5

Designed by Carl Weiss

Printed in the United States of America

CONTENTS

AUTHOR'S NOTE

Very early in thinking about this book I talked with a soft-spoken black American named Bill Tutman, a former Peace Corps director in Tanzania. He told me about a trip he once made to the city of Marrakesh, and about some of the Americans he had met there.

"A lot of them came to Africa because they'd had it with America," he said. "But most of them didn't know where they were going or what they wanted to do. The saddest thing was that none of them had any idea what it really took to settle in an African country."

I was later to hear a similar comment from Americans living in Brazil, Argentina, Mexico, Australia, and New Zealand. Many Americans leave the United States to settle elsewhere with no real understanding of the enormity of what is involved.

Some go on the spur of the moment, others with grand illusions about life in distant countries, still others without enough money to give themselves a chance. Once living in a new environment, Americans invariably expect too much of themselves and their new place, and always too quickly.

Answering the question "What's really involved in a move to another country?" is the guiding aim throughout this book.

With the exception of Chapter 1, "A Quiet Exodus," the focus is on the practical problems an American moving abroad will surely encounter. In that first chapter I touch briefly upon some of the general reasons why Americans are willing to leave this country for another, and why there are more of them interested in moving abroad than at any other time in our history. According to a Gallup poll made in 1971, 12 percent of the U.S. population—some twenty-four million Americans—would emigrate to another country given the chance, a figure double that of a decade ago.

But as one migration theorist suggests, people on the move all have their own unique mix of private motives, the only similarity being that each has a starting point and a destination, and between them will encounter an unbelievable number of obstacles. The heart of this book is about those obstacles.

As of this writing, the United States recognizes some 136 independent nations and a number of other semiautonomous territories, dependent islands, city-states, and obscure principalities. I deal in varying detail with thirty-three, although a good many others are mentioned in passing.

Only six might be considered "people-seeking," though even then not without certain restrictions on whom they accept. Another half-dozen or so are amenable to foreign settlement if the foreigner has something to offer. Several of these countries—Australia and Canada most notably—have perhaps the last remaining geographic frontiers on earth.

I've also dealt with a number of countries that are attractive to Americans whether their presence is much desired or not—Britain and Mexico, for example. Occasionally I've had to choose representative countries, that is, those that have policies and procedures similar to those of a number of others. Once you understand the rationale behind Switzerland's caution in allowing foreign residence, you understand something about Austria and Denmark as well. Knowing the background to Mexico's restrictiveness makes it easier to understand why half a dozen other Latin-American countries are becoming more watchful.

In each chapter I've paid considerable attention to additional sources of information and advice. I've avoided reprinting information easily available from foreign consular officials. Despite my indebtedness to literally hundreds of people, I might well have titled this preface "There Are No Experts."

In the course of research, among other tidbits of misinformation, I've been given directly conflicting visa regulations by a country's embassy in Washington and its consulate general in New York; farming information six years out of date, which in the light of current economics might well have been sixty; and a dead-wrong assurance that a particular country made no income-tax claims whatsoever upon resident Americans.

The only occasion I've run afoul of the U.S. Internal Revenue Service while living abroad was the single time I relied without question on the advice of a tax "expert." There is in fact considerable information in this book paid for by the mistakes of Americans (myself and others) now living in foreign countries.

I've attempted to offer here a useful, workable primer on a subject that is in truth a whole new world. But you owe it to yourself and those dependent on you to take nothing for granted. It is *you* who must become the expert.

PART ONE

A QUIET EXODUS
Why and Where

AMERICANS EVERYWHERE

The first significant fact about Americans abroad is that there are more of them than ever before. By U.S. State Department accounting there were some 1,452,157 American civilians spread across the world as of 1971, with perhaps another half million overseas in military service.

Even during the most chronicled of expatriate eras—the 1920's—with Hemingway and others partaking of their moveable feast, there were never more than about 10 percent of the present number of Americans living in foreign countries.

The first impression therefore might be that America is suffering mass abandonment, while the rest of the world endures an American invasion. Nothing of the sort. The number of Americans moving abroad has never in any single year exceeded the number of other nationalities that immigrate to the United States. America remains an immigrant nation, though far from the great gatherer of the world's poor and suffering it once was. The fact to remember is that since 1967 America has become an emigrant as well as an immigrant nation for the first time since the end of the Civil War. Just why this is so, we'll come to in a moment.

As to our invasion of the rest of the world, the situation, much to the relief of a number of other countries, is not that dire. Of the civilian Americans abroad, more than one-third live in two countries, Canada and Mexico. In Canada they blend in almost invisibly; in Mexico, most live apart from the mainstream of national life.

Approximately another third live in Europe, with perhaps four-fifths of the total living in no more than 20 countries, although those countries are as widely separated geographically as Greece is from the Philippines. The remainder are scattered as though sporelike they were spread by the wind. The American who lives abroad is a selective creature, though the basis for his selection may be beyond our complete understanding. Small numbers of Americans can be found almost anywhere, not atypically in such obscure places as Rwanda, Gabon, Yap, and Mauritius.

AMERICANS ABROAD, 1971 — 15 COUNTRIES

(Excluding government employees, the military, and dependents)

	1969	1971	Net Change
Canada	172,134	240,500	+68,366
Mexico	86,867	98,381	+11,514
Italy	51,850	73,926	+22,076
Germany	50,676	64,416	+13,740
United Kingdom	38,620	44,111	+ 5,491
Israel	15,700	40,000	+24,300
Greece	20,835	29,650	+ 8,815
Australia	17,625	25,275	+ 7,650
Spain	20,093	24,000	+ 3,907
Japan	17,271	23,755	+ 6,484
Philippines	26,771	22,337	− 4,434
France	20,333	20,365	+ 32
Brazil	17,629	19,985	+ 2,356
Switzerland	19,400	19,300	− 100
Belgium	10,500	15,800	+ 5,300

Source: U.S. State Department

Where Americans abroad live and what they do, at least in general terms, is a matter of record. Why they live where they do is more difficult to determine.

A great number, of course, haven't chosen to live abroad voluntarily at all; the one half million servicemen, for example. Like them, a number of the civilian employees of the U.S. government live in foreign countries because they are assigned there. Not that most go reluctantly.

The 3,000 or so State Department Foreign Service officers, better known as the Diplomatic Corps, and their supporting staff at some 250 posts around the world are among the most highly privileged Americans living abroad, even if their privileges must often be enjoyed in places sometimes less than scenic or climatically ideal. They are in fact the smallest part of the U.S. government establishment in foreign countries.

The diplomats these days are often outnumbered in their own embassies by coveys of USIA publicists, World Bank economists, and AID technical consultants, all either agents of a propaganda machine or foreign-aid administration no longer workable or in fashion.

Temporarily though it may be, all live a highly subsidized American existence on foreign soil.

Add the Peace Corps, with some 8,000 staff and volunteers in some sixty-one developing countries, plus the more clandestine arms of American diplomacy, and the number of civilian government employees abroad still numbers less than 40,000.

While this figure has crept lower over the past few years, the number of other Americans abroad has shot upward. There are in fact a greater number of American missionaries living in foreign countries than government employees. They mainly administer schools, hospitals, and small-scale development programs, but seldom draw such a fine line on their activities. The Mennonites have a reputation as hearty settlers willing to pioneer regions other immigrants find inhospitable. The Mormons own large tracts of land in such far-flung places as Samoa and Argentina. The American Methodist Church in Rhodesia has been forced to claim the copper rights on its land to prevent outside commercial exploitation. While the Jehovah's Witnesses have been discreetly discouraged from spreading their word in Liberia, the rich voice of Garner Ted Armstrong remains one of the most persuasive forces in the English-speaking Caribbean.

Few people outside of their respective organizations realize the extent of activities by American missionaries abroad. They are influential, often powerful, and in many developing countries are the most numerous Americans likely to be found.

MOVERS AND THE MOVED

Beyond the Americans directly serving government or a higher order, there remains a large number of others who have had little say in the matter of settling in a foreign country. In any migration of people there are the movers and the moved.

The "moved" in this case consist mainly of the dependent wives and children of government personnel and the military, over a third of a million in 1971. The figure fluctuates in direct proportion to U.S. overseas military commitments, and is at the moment on a downward trend. The majority of dependents live in just five countries, all strongly aware of American military presence: Germany, Japan, the Philippines, Spain, and Portugal.

Subtracting government employees, missionaries, and dependent wives and children from the total, there are still more than a million

Americans abroad not yet accounted for. Presumably they have gone abroad voluntarily. Determining why anyone chooses to live in a country other than his own begins to get close to the heart of the matter.

Almost ninety years ago a British scholar, E. G. Ravenstein, was among the first to attempt to analyze the motives of people on the move. Observed Ravenstein:

> Bad or oppressive laws, heavy taxation, an unattractive climate, uncongenial social surroundings, and even compulsions . . . all have produced and are still producing currents of migration, but none of these currents can compare in volume with that which arises from the desire inherent in most men to better themselves in material respects.

In Ravenstein's time the future wandering of the military and their dependents was perhaps unforeseen. As were the machinations of twentieth-century politics, which would create large refugee populations, rearranging people over many parts of the globe. White Russians, Poles, Jews, Greeks, Ibos, Muslims, Hindus, Cubans have all ranged far from country of birth to escape the consequences of political change.

Though Ravenstein's theories lack a statistical basis, which modern social scientists would find unforgivable, most demographers feel that they have held up rather well. Particularly his awareness of the economic motive behind migration.

POWER OF THE DOLLAR

Economic reasons influence the greatest number of people on the move, and not least, many Americans. The search for dollar, lira, or peso is potent stimulus in pushing people from home, often family, in favor of unfamiliar environments.

At present, for example, nearly a million Spanish and Portuguese work in France because of higher wages, a quarter-million Turks in Germany for the same reason. Twenty-five thousand Filipinos, most of them professionals at home, migrated to the United States in 1970 and now work as clerks, secretaries, and waiters because they earn more money. Bolivians sneak across the border to work in Argentina, and young Argentines work illegally in New York City, both with the same object: to save enough money to go home comparatively wealthy. Years of economic depression in southern Italy have benefited Australian immigration immensely. Dutch go to New Zealand, Yugoslavs to Canada, Rhodesians to South Africa, Lebanese to Brazil—all moved by the idea that the money is a little greener in another country.

The so-called "brain drain" of the late 1960's is a demonstration that economic reasons motivate people at all levels of the wage scale.

Originally the label "brain drain" was attached to the migration of British engineers and scientists to high-paying jobs in the United States. It has now come to mean a more encompassing and potentially harmful phenomenon: the movement of many kinds of skilled people from places of poor economic opportunity to places of greater economic opportunity. Many underdeveloped countries suffer emigration of their most qualified and intelligent people, while the gain is made by a few already wealthy countries. Motivated strongly by economic and sometimes professional reasons, such people feel they have no way to go up except out.

Economic motives exert their share of influence on many Americans who leave to live elsewhere. In a broad sense their movement abroad has been related to the increasing presence of American business and industry in foreign countries, a direct investment approaching some 200 billion dollars. Perhaps one in four civilian Americans living outside the United States works for American-owned companies or is a dependent of those who do. Be it for Du Pont in Geneva, General Foods in São Paulo, or Ford in Johannesburg, many Americans earn more in real terms and live more luxuriously than they could holding equal positions in the United States. For those highly motivated by considerations best expressed in dollars and cents, there is probably no more comfortable existence than living in a foreign country while being paid an American salary, with perhaps an additional plus—not enjoyed even by diplomats—of exemption from paying full U.S. income tax. But like the diplomats, American businessmen living abroad can enjoy a high style of living. For many Americans, and a growing number of foreign nationals too, a position in the upper echelons of an American company abroad is the peak of attainment. As it is at any peak, however, there is precious little room for large numbers of people.

RETIRED AMERICANS ABROAD

Another group which has discovered the buying power of the dollar abroad, though on a less grand scale, is Americans who choose to retire in other countries. A Social Security check may certainly last longer in Portugal than in Chicago. The promise of sunny bargain paradises yearly lures many retired Americans, some who have never been outside the United States before, to spend their last years in less expensive but unfamiliar localities.

Many other retirees return to their countries of birth, drawn not purely by economic motives but by nostalgic memories of youth in Greece, Italy, Poland, Yugoslavia, Germany, or Ireland. There are some 150,000 retired Americans abroad. It should be noted that the shock of a foreign culture, or a forgotten one, seems to hit the retired more sharply than nearly any other group of Americans who choose to live in a foreign country.

AS MANY REASONS AS PEOPLE

Proceeding beyond the broad heading "economic motives," the reasons why people leave one country to live in another become ever more diffuse. For many new emigrants, economic motives for leaving the United States are almost nonexistent. In fact, economic motives are seldom the sole, undiluted reason people choose to live elsewhere.

Migration specialist Professor Everett Lee of the University of Georgia sees four general classes of factors that influence all migration: those factors associated with the country of origin; those with the country of destination; between the two countries, a very real set of physical obstacles; and influencing the decision throughout, a number of often powerful personal considerations.

The first two classes of factors—those associated with the countries of origin and destination—have often been called, slightly oversimplified, the "push" and "pull" factors influencing migration. More precisely, says Lee, each country has innumerable pluses and minuses all working on the mind of the prospective migrant at the same time.

Obviously the "push" factors, or negative factors, operating in the United States have had a large influence on recent emigration abroad. Following the 1968 Democratic Convention, with its attendant televised violence, inquiries to the Australian consulates in the United States jumped from a trickle to 8,000 in one month, and have continued to climb. In 1970 Australia alone received 120,000 requests for immigration information.

Many requests for information received by foreign consulates cite "social unrest," "fear of violence," "racial tensions," and the decline of moral standards in America as reasons for interest in settling elsewhere.

Undoubtedly American society is in very real crisis in many respects. The World Health Organization, for example, released a study in 1971 which estimated that New York City has had more homicides in recent years than Great Britain, Switzerland, Sweden, the Netherlands, Norway, Denmark, and Belgium combined. But as Professor Lee wisely points out, it isn't always the reality of factors at home and abroad that provokes people to emigrate, but rather what people *perceive* these factors to be.

THE ALIENATED

Whether the causes are real or imagined, dissatisfaction with aspects of life in the United States is a strong "push" factor among many people considering a move to another country. For some the push is less dissatisfaction than a rather pure form of political alienation. "Unilateral resignation" from the armed forces, avoidance of the draft, and vague general distrust of government have all pushed Americans abroad, not entirely willingly, or kept them from returning to the United States.

The exiled abroad are not an inconsiderable number. An estimated 35,000 deserters and draft-dodgers live in Canada, many illegally. A fair number of American medical students can be found studying in such widely separated places as Guadalajara, Bologna, and Brussels, as attracted by easy entrance requirements and draft deferment as by the idea of studying medicine in a foreign environment. Several hundred deserters remain in Sweden, Stokely Carmichael resides in Guinea, and countless other less vocal exiles populate small, closely knit, American exile communities from Istanbul to Monrovia to Vancouver.

Although physically present in a foreign country, the exiles might be considered outside the main current of present emigration. Their participation in the life of their country of residence invariably remains superficial, even if their stay stretches over a number of years. The truly alienated from any society are always spiritually bound to their country of origin for the nourishment of their alienation. In the capitals of Europe one can find Basque nationalists, Greek royalists, Guineans, Czechs, exiled South Africans, Cubans, Poles, and Spaniards who, with the politically alienated Americans, share the hope that things will change at home and they will return, ideologically vindicated. In the meantime, the exiles live in a mental climate that never allows them to embrace much of their country of residence; their eyes are always turned toward home.

Additionally, sociologists who have studied immigrants note that those who leave a country to escape what essentially are personal problems seldom succeed in their new environment. As Ernest Dunbar observed in his book *The Black Expatriates,* the early waves of alienated blacks who left the United States seemed to take their problems with them whether they went to Paris or Accra. Leaving America solved nothing.

Many of those who voluntarily leave the United States "turned off" by America often discover things in other countries they were unprepared for. Some find police more "fascist" than in America, bureaucrats as inefficient and thick-headed, and a middle class as money-grubbing as the one they left behind. A staggering array of prejudice can exist in other cultures, based on nuances of color, accent, and dress, that most Americans, black or white, would find unimaginable. The acceptance of "differentness" is not widespread, intolerance often masked by the superficial politeness some nationalities affect toward foreigners. Truly liberal societies are rare.

Many of the politically alienated people who leave America realize at some point that, as Tom Hayden suggested, the battle for them is back home. At least there the battleground is familiar. Invariably most exiles return home, if they can.

For the small percentage who remain, the alienation is either dissipated by the unexpected pleasures and demands of a new culture and language, or it hardens into a quiet bitterness and total rejection of everything American. Those who have given up totally on America are perhaps the least vocal of Americans abroad, often embarrassed by their remaining Americanness, but sincere and uncaring if their lives remain forever unchronicled by *Time* or *Life.* But all of the formerly alienated share a common experience. At some time they have been drawn into the appreciation of living in another country for its own sake, immigrants by default perhaps, but no longer willing to live the unsatisfying life of the political exile.

A QUIET EXODUS

Dissatisfaction with America, however, isn't necessarily the exclusive province of the young, the racially conscious, or the politicized. Among many of the new emigrants is a less vocal alienation of the middle class, a quiet exodus unheralded by public pronouncements, press conferences, slogans, or TV film clips.

In Australia's Ord river valley live cotton farmers from California, Arizona, Texas, and Louisiana. Many came to Australia because they felt they couldn't farm anymore in America. Soaring land prices, sheaves of government regulations, and expensive farm labor have become prohibitive.

A Nevada-based organization has put a proposal to the government of Rhodesia for the establishment of an autonomous state within Rhodesia's borders, to be developed along the theories of Ayn Rand and the economist Van Mises. The organization feels that "social meddlers" have put the rein on the ability of Americans who work hard to get ahead. They feel that such a "free-enterprise" endeavor is workable only outside of the United States.

For many others there is just a vague feeling of being "filled up to here" with the whole style of American life and society, often attended by a real discovery that elsewhere they have been able to take control of their lives again.

One such person is Janet Hanssen, a former Californian still in her twenties, whom one person described as the only American immigrant in South-West Africa. Jan admits that before she found something positive in her new life, she was pushed by the "I-didn't-likes" about Los Angeles: the social climbing, the cocktail parties, or

worrying about the neighbors, whether they can hear me brushing my teeth, or talking about their kids, their garbage disposals, their debts. . . .

I've been that route. I've had a modern suite of furniture, king-sized bed, stereo, wall-to-wall carpeting, garbage disposal, push-button stove. . . . But something was missing. I didn't know what then. I've found out since I've been here. People need something genuine to do. Not dribs and drabs to occupy time, but something basic. Here I raise stringbeans, chickens, children, and cacti. I have the time to watch my children grow, and here I'm not so busy worrying about the world that I can't watch a sunset. Here organization is not more important than a human being. . . . Yes, I suppose it is possible to find a haven in America. But for me it was easier to get completely away. To live forty miles from a town which is ten thousand miles from anywhere. I love it here.

PULL

Undeniably, a number of Americans who think about emigrating are pulled more than pushed. The attraction of Australia, Ghana, or

Israel in the mind of a prospective migrant can be phenomenal. The images of open space, racial or religious affinity, or the vision of a simpler, less hectic life all play their part in motivating people to take the step.

As often happens, a number of people most serious about settling elsewhere have little first-hand knowledge of their chosen country. The "pull" factors are more often a fantasized series of pluses, the "honey and sunshine visions," as one publisher termed them, often pushed to the brink of disbelief by slick travel promotion and the brilliant but odorless renderings of modern color photography.

Americans resident abroad know that many problems suffered in this country are experienced equally or worse in other places. Sydney has more serious industrial pollution than Chicago; Buenos Aires greater urban sprawl than Los Angeles; Lagos higher apartment rents than Honolulu; São Paulo more congested rush-hour traffic than New York City.

Not that these places are without compensating factors. But for a number of people considering emigration, the compensations are viewed exclusively, without realizing that America's problems have become the problems of a number of other places too.

A tendency to minimize or overlook the negative factors existing in any unknown country is immediately recognized by anyone who deals with prospective emigrants. One foreign consul nodded at the chair across from his desk. "When people sit there," he said, "they hear what they want to hear."

THE *NEW* EMIGRANT

For a fair number of others, the "pull" is not the pull of place but of ideal.

Perhaps this is the great distinguishing factor between people who leave other countries and Americans leaving the United States, even between those Americans who go abroad on assignment and the new American emigrant who leaves to settle in another country voluntarily.

These new emigrants often go in search of qualitative factors—for something beyond economic betterment, the acquiring of material things or "status." It may be a search for what Paul Goodman called the need to do "meaningful work." Among some young people there is a near-mystical interest in artisanship and working on the land. Among others it is a search for a fuller life or a more religious life, a search for something of value they are apparently not able to find in American society.

How many of these new emigrants there are in the total number of Americans living abroad is difficult to determine. The number of American civilians living outside of the United States increased by 194,000 persons between 1969 and 1971. About 100,000 of them settled abroad with some form of immigrant status, a figure treble the number of 1966 and 1967.

The ignoble paradox is that this sort of idealistic expatriation seems to be a rare by-product of American prosperity. Americans are perhaps the first people in history who have been able to afford the luxury of voluntary emigration unforced by famine, disease, imminent danger, religious intolerance, or the gnawing desire for economic betterment. By aiming to relieve the great majority of Americans from these threats, American society has apparently sharpened the sensibilities of a few beyond their capacity to endure it.

Thus the motives of even the new emigrants can't easily by summed up or classified. The "push" and "pull" factors seldom occur unalloyed in reality. All migration is influenced by an indistinguishable mixture of pluses and minuses, physical obstacles, and uncontrollable personal factors.

The most potent obstacle—as much of this book attests—may be obtaining permission to reside in another country. For many, the time and patience involved in gathering the necessary documents will cool the urgency of the moment, and the idea of emigrating may evaporate. Transportation, especially for a family, may be another obstacle, though certainly a lesser one in this age than ever before.

A WILLINGNESS TO MOVE

The obstacles, though real enough, may be overshadowed in the actual decision whether to emigrate or not by personal considerations.

For every new emigrant there are countless others with the will or desire who are prevented from moving by personal considerations beyond their control. A single man who would have tried farming in western Australia loses his taste for hardship when married. Families with teen-age children often feel caught in between—the children too old to adjust without problems to a new culture, and too young to be on their own. As in all things, timing plays a part.

Some personalities are resistant to change of any kind, which can keep a more adventurous partner in check. Still others need abrupt change in their lives, purely for the sake of change. It is well documented that people who have made one migration are more willing to take on another than those who have never moved at all. I spoke to a young woman who described herself as an "Army brat," growing up with a change of locale every few years as her father was reassigned. She confessed that the idea of settling anywhere permanently horrified her. Her willingness to move had been a key factor in her new husband's decision to sell his business and take a plunge into Argentina.

Even the accidental has its role to play. My generation, maturing as it did between Korea and Vietnam, is perhaps the only one of the past fifty years without its own personal war as part of the experience of coming of age. One cannot fail to find in any country touched by World War II, for example, Americans who discovered the country while serving there, and because the time was right, stayed on, or later returned.

I have met such men in Guam, Panama, and Samoa, businessmen now, married to nationals, and without exception moderately prosperous. They exist in the Philippines and throughout Europe. The Korean War created their counterparts in Japan and Korea, as will Vietnam among those who discover Australia, Hong Kong, or Thailand on leave.

As Professor Lee concludes: "The decision to migrate, therefore, is never completely rational, and for some persons the rational component is much less than the irrational."

THE LAST STRAW

A final example of the irrational aspect of migration is embodied in the so-called "last-straw theory," which might be more common than one suspects.

Here the idea of moving to another country may be in the back of the prospective emigrant's mind for years, sometimes unmentioned aloud. Then the price of beer goes up a few cents, the New York Central has one more breakdown, or the city decides that it's your kid's turn to be bused across town. Ties are cut and bags are packed in an amazingly short amount of time.

Unfortunately, almost every foreign consulate has experienced the fiery specter of the American who has sold his house, quit his job, and then decided to visit the consul, in the belief that permanent residence in a foreign country is a right to be had for the asking, given freely in a matter of hours.

Woe be to him.

RULES OF THE GAME

For Americans, travel is a right guaranteed by the Constitution. By Supreme Court affirmation (*Kent* v. *Dulles,* 357 U.S. 116,125, 1958) it is considered one of the personal liberties guaranteed by the Fifth Amendment, and therefore cannot be withheld without due process of law.

At the outset, however, we must make a distinction between travel as a tourist and travel with the intention of residence. Traveling worldwide as a tourist has never been easier. In the Western Hemisphere an American citizen can visit most countries with a tourist or visitor's card, easily obtained for him by airline or travel agent. Many countries, even in Asia and Africa, will allow a tourist to reside for several months with few formalities.

Entering a country as a tourist implies a gentlemen's agreement: that you have enough money to support yourself and those dependent upon you; that you will not work or otherwise involve yourself in the affairs of the host country; and that after a limited amount of time you will leave. For the purposes of this book the tourist is an evanescent breed seldom mentioned again.

While the tourist has had an easier time of it in recent years, taking up permanent residence abroad has become more difficult. Well into this century one could travel most of the world, settling at will, without so much as a document. Now a passport is one of the two primary items needed to travel and reside outside of the United States, the other being a visa issued by a foreign government.

PASSPORTS

A passport is two things. It is a polite request, on the part of the U.S. government to another government with whom the United States currently has diplomatic relations, to treat you well. It is also a guarantee that you can obtain certain modest assistance from an American consul abroad if things don't go so well.

More formally, a passport is "a document identifying a citizen, in effect requesting foreign powers to allow the bearer to enter and pass freely and safely, recognizing the right of the bearer to the *protection* and *good offices* of American consular offices." (*U.S.* v. *Laub,* as reported in the *Supreme Court Reporter.* Italics mine.) More about protection and good offices later.

There are three kinds of passports: diplomatic, official, and regular.

Diplomatic and official passports are issued to persons on U.S. government business. The regular passport is for the nonofficial citizen; it is a blue-green booklet measuring some four inches by six. Upon issue it will contain basic information about you or yourself and your family, an unflattering photo, and a number of blank pages that serve a definite purpose. Possession of a passport in another country is proof of American citizenship.

Passports may be obtained at any one of eleven centers in the United States (see list of addresses in Appendix), a growing number of post offices, and from nearly all American consulates abroad.

To obtain a passport you'll need to fill out an application, show proof of citizenship, have a pair of recent photos (at least $2\frac{1}{2}$ " $\times$ $2\frac{1}{2}$ " and not larger than 3 " $\times$ 3 "), and pay twelve dollars. It is wise when passport photos are taken to have two dozen extra prints made, and an equal number in profile. Applications for foreign visas sometimes require as many as a dozen, and you'll find that photos are required for licenses, identification cards, and a number of other items most people don't anticipate when passport photos are taken. Obtaining the passport is only the opening round.

Passports can be issued to individuals or to families, which includes you, your wife or husband, and minor children (under eighteen). Consider the idea of obtaining one passport each for husband and wife, putting the minor children on the wife's. This will allow each to travel separately, should the occasion arise.

If you are applying for a passport for the first time, you must apply in person. Passports are valid for five years.

In rare cases the State Department's Passport Office may attempt to withhold a passport. Passport applications are checked against a computerized list of people who have doubtful claim to American citizenship, or who the Passport Office feels ought not to leave the United States with the government's official good wishes.

Specifically, the Passport Office "bad" list includes defectors, persons wanted by a law-enforcement agency for criminal activity, and known Communists and subversives. It also includes expatriates in the legal sense of those who have formally lost or renounced citizenship, repatriates whose backgrounds demand further inquiry before a passport is issued, individuals involved in child-custody or desertion cases, and "delinquents in military obligation." A miscellaneous category includes many mental patients, criminal fugitives, and people who owe the government repayment for a previous indigent passage home.

Senator Samuel J. Ervin Jr.'s Subcommittee on Constitutional Rights claims the Passport Office has close to a quarter of a million names on its computerized list, many there without complete legal justification.

In any circumstance, a passport may not be withheld from an American citizen without due process of law, which in this case includes the right to appeal the Passport Office decision. Despite several categories on the "bad" list, passports may not be withheld because of a citizen's beliefs or associations.

VISAS

The other side of the travel coin is a visa issued by a foreign government. Technically, a visa is a request or authorization for you to cross a foreign frontier. *Tourist visas* are still required by many countries; but generally a visa implies another purpose.

There are *student visas* and *business visas*. Malta, Panama, Mexico, and Costa Rica now issue *retirement visas*. Then there is a thorny item called an *exit visa,* which isn't a true visa at all, but permission to leave, which some countries require. The most complicated and difficult visa to obtain, and the most important throughout this book, is the *residence or immigration visa.*

A visa is issued in the United States by a foreign consulate or visa office, often dependent upon the approval of the foreign ministry in the country's capital. In some cases the visa will be issued directly from the ministry, the consul acting only as a means of communication.

The visa itself may take the form of a stamp on one of those blank passport pages, or on a separate piece of paper. This is important: visas are usually issued prior to travel. Occasionally they may be given by an immigration officer at port of entry, as in England, for example, but then only on the basis of prior application or written request of a consul. Traveling to a country as a tourist and later obtaining residence is in most countries impossible. In some countries, Liberia for example, attempt to change status is met with immediate deportation.

The key point to remember about visas is that they are solely the responsibility of the foreign government. They can be withheld whimsically, and can sometimes be arranged outside the letter of the law. Obtaining a visa is a good first lesson in understanding that many of your rights and privileges as an American citizen cease at the border of the United States.

Obtaining a Visa. Requirements vary from country to country. They are discussed in some detail under each country further along in this book, but the rules can change suddenly. A new government can decide to close its borders, or regulations can be ignored. Tanzania, for example, has long-standing immigration regulations on its books, but now refuses to discuss them.

Generally, application for an immigrant or residence visa will require the following: (1) A valid U. S. passport, thereby proving you are a citizen. (2) A formal application, which may be one short page or four long ones. Most ask about various aspects of your personal status, that as a citizen remain with you no matter what country you reside in—marriage, divorce, financial obligation to dependent children, etc. (3) Passport-type photos, anywhere from six to a dozen, full-face and profile. Be sure to check size required by the consul; Argentina, for example, requires photos not larger than one inch square. (4) A police certificate, issued by local precinct or neighborhood station house, certifying to your good conduct. The police are familiar with these. Ask the consul if he requires a particular form. (5) A medical certificate saying you are healthy. Should include X ray, Wasserman blood test, urinalysis, and so forth. Ask the consul beforehand what is required. Some consuls require a certificate from physicians they approve; some use a standard form. Physicals can run from $35 to $75 per person. (6) A vaccination certificate. A yellow World Health Organization International Certificate of Vaccination can be picked up at the same time you acquire your passport. Certain inoculations may be to your advantage before traveling to some countries. Invariably, smallpox immunization is required.

The above is fairly standard. In addition, to obtain a *residence visa* you may have to furnish any or all of the following: (1) A work permit obtained for you by your future employer in the foreign country. (2)

Proof of economic responsibility—bank statement, letter from a banker, etc. (3) A certification of profession or trade. (4) A deposit of bond. (5) A notarized declaration of intention to deposit money in the national bank of that country (common in Latin America). (6) A personal interview. (7) Documents to support statements made in your formal application—marriage certificate, birth certificate, divorce decree, character references, etc.; either original document or certified copy; some countries require documents to be translated into their language.

In most cases you'll need to provide fewer items than this entire list. Let me expand on the *certification* of documents, since to most people such certification comes as a complete surprise, and at the least is a hassle.

Most countries will require the documents you supply to be original, in which case they will already have official seals and signatures. Or they will have to be true copies, legally testified to. A Xerox copy of your birth certificate doesn't count. Nor does a letter from your clergyman saying you are a good fellow. Both lack legal certification.

For documents you compile yourself, you will require at least the witness of a notary public.

Certification is essentially the job of acquiring legal seals on your documents. It is a bureaucratic procedure whereby a higher level of authority will certify that the stamp of a lower level on your document is valid, in force, and not a forgery.

It may mean that you have to acquire the seal of a county clerk certifying to the seal of the notary who just witnessed a letter from your banker. If you obtain a copy of your birth certificate from a county clerk, it may mean that *his* official seal must be certified by the Secretary of State in your state.

If a higher level of certification is needed, the state seal can be certified by the Documents section of the State Department. The Documents section has a safe full of facsimiles of official seals from all fifty states. Certification, right up to the State Department in Washington, can be done by mail but will take a couple of weeks.

Before you collect your needed documents, you must ask the foreign consul what he wants as proof of certification of the documents you supply. He may take it upon himself to certify, for a fee, the validity of even Xerox copies before he bundles them into an envelope with your visa application and sends them to his foreign ministry. Or he may ask you to go through the whole certification drill.

Remember, the demand for certified documents comes from the

country to which you are applying, not the United States, and they can be as demanding as they like.

An underlying intention of asking for these documents is to prove that you are who you *say* you are. And that you have the resources or talents to keep from becoming a burden on the community. The day of the drifter "on the beach," or citizen of the world living off the land, unfortunately for many of us, is very nearly at an end.

Gathering documents will take time, processing and approving them even more time. Visitor's visas and tourist cards take minutes to obtain; for residence visas, the wait seems endless. I know of no case less than two weeks. I spoke recently to a schoolteacher, met in the office of a consulate general, who had waited nine months. For the countries actively recruiting settlers, the average would be six to twelve weeks from acceptance of application (with all documents in order) to issuance of visa.

The whole process may seem unreasonable. Yet, in most cases, the requirements for Americans wishing to reside in a foreign country are less stringent than for foreigners wishing to reside here.

Once admitted to another country as anything other than a tourist, you may be required to obtain additional documents before residence is established.

This is common in even the most advanced countries. In England you need a *certificate of registration,* in France a *carte de séjour,* in Argentina a *cédula de identidad.*

Whatever their name, these documents are mainly for identification. They'll most likely have your photo and will state your occupation and your permanent address. They are usually issued by a local police station or by the alien section of the foreign ministry. The visa allows you to enter your new home; the I.D. card or residence permit allows you to go about living more or less as one of the natives.

As an American living in a foreign country, correctly visaed and duly registered, your status has now become *resident alien.*

WHOSE LAWS...

Despite the vaguely unsavory sound of the phrase, the status of *resident alien* (or *landed immigrant,* or *permanent resident*) invariably allows a number of the same rights as the citizenry in general. The most usual exception is voting. Most European countries consider aliens to have the same rights under the law as nationals, without discrimination. This tends to become more variable the less developed the country. Many countries allow an individual to own land, although here one may find reservations. In both Mexico and Panama a foreigner may not own land near a seacoast or border. Most Pacific islands absolutely refuse foreigners land ownership.

In a number of countries the *resident alien* has privileges locals do not, at least for a limited time. Portugal and Brazil allow customs-free import of household goods and belongings, provided you have had them for at least a year. Ecuador and Rhodesia offer liberal personal and business tax concessions, especially if you work in critical occupations (farming in Rhodesia, selected types of manufacturing in Ecuador).

With receiving the rights of a national you also obtain his obligations, such as paying local taxes and being subject to local laws.

In fact, as an American citizen resident in a foreign country you no longer have one great Uncle worrying about your behavior, but two. The concern usually manifests itself only at tax time, or when you run afoul of civil or criminal laws. But you must keep your eyes on what may well be two entirely different sets of rules.

LOSING AMERICAN CITIZENSHIP

Being an American resident in a foreign country does not deprive you of your American citizenship, nor put it in jeopardy.

Several Supreme Court decisions in recent years ruled on citizenship cases. The most far-reaching decision was the case of *Afroyim* v. *Rusk,* 387 U.S. 253 (1967). This decision makes it very difficult to lose American citizenship without voluntarily relinquishing it, either by formal act or by intent to renounce it.

Prior to 1967, American citizens abroad could lose citizenship by teaching school for a foreign government, by staying out of the country too long, or for a long list of other reasons derived from the Nationality Act of 1940 and the Immigration and Nationality Act of 1952. Between 1954 and 1964, 43,000 Americans had their citizenship plucked from them, many involuntarily.

Since *Afroyim,* the total number of Americans losing citizenship amounts to "a couple of thousand a year," according to the Passport Office. Many of these are former Americans who have had to renounce American citizenship as a requirement for citizenship in another country.

The *Afroyim* case itself, and the subsequent interpretation by the then Attorney General, Ramsey Clark, make several points worth remembering. (Opinion of the Attorney General. Expatriation. January 18, 1969.)

The petitioner, Beys Afroyim, was a naturalized American who went to Israel in 1950 and voted in an Israeli election a year later. In 1960, when Afroyim applied for renewal of his passport, the U.S. State Department refused to grant it. They contended that according to the Nationality Act of 1940, a U.S. citizen who votes in another country's political election loses his citizenship.

Afroyim appealed the judgment, eventually to the Supreme Court. The court ruled that under the Constitution, Congress had no right to pass laws depriving an American citizen of his right of citizenship unless he voluntarily relinquished it. Justice Hugo Black gave the opinion of the court. (*United States Law Week,* May 30, 1967.)

> The very nature of our free government makes it completely incongruous to have a rule of law under which a group of citizens temporarily in office can deprive another group of citizens of their citizenship. We hold that the Fourteenth Amendment was designed to, and does, protect every citizen of this Nation against a congressional forcible destruction of his citizenship, whatever his creed, color or race. Our holding does no more than to give to this citizen that which is his own, a constitutional right to remain a citizen in a free country unless he voluntarily relinquishes that citizenship.

Several vagaries of *Afroyim* will need subsequent cases before they are entirely defined. One loophole is the lack of a proper definition of what might be considered "voluntary relinquishment." The phrase is open to interpretation.

Attorney General Clark did offer some "guidelines" for "administrative purposes" that carry voluntary relinquishment beyond simple written renunciation. He implied that citizenship could be relinquished by "actions declared expatriative." But he made clear that the burden of proof would be on the party who asserts that loss of citizenship has occurred (i.e., the State Department). Clark said he would not normally consider either teaching in a foreign public school or serving in an allied country's army, both often-used criteria for depriving citizenship before *Afroyim,* as examples of acts that, of themselves, show an intent to give up citizenship. "But it is highly persuasive evidence, to say the least, of an intent to abandon U.S. citizenship if one enlists voluntarily in the armed forces of a foreign government engaged in hostilities against the United States."

The office most concerned with overseeing your citizenship is the

Foreign Operations division of the State Department's Passport Office.

In the wake of *Afroyim* and the Attorney General's statement, they have issued some "guidelines" of their own with the long title "Statement Concerning Loss of United States Nationality and the Afroyim Decision." It is a single sheet of paper available from American consular offices abroad and freely distributed by them "to all citizens abroad who have performed an expatriating act or are contemplating the performance of such an act."

This "Statement," in lieu of any recent Supreme Court decisions interpreting the loopholes in *Afroyim,* should be considered the operational document.

The "Statement" mentions four general acts that might be considered very persuasive evidence of intention to relinquish citizenship. Unless there was strong evidence to the contrary, an American citizen who performed one of these acts would most likely lose his citizenship: (1) Naturalization in a foreign state. (2) Taking a meaningful oath of allegiance to a foreign state. (3) Service in the armed forces of a foreign state engaged in hostilities against the United States. (4) Service in an important political post in a foreign government.

In the first instance, it should be noted that many foreign countries allow foreign-born aliens to qualify for citizenship. It is seldom obligatory. Usually citizenship involves a prior permanent residence of anywhere from two to twelve years and, often, examinations in the language of the country. More important, most countries require, as a condition of citizenship, formal renunciation of former citizenship. In this case, seeking the citizenship of another country would probably be considered evidence of intent to relinquish U.S. citizenship. Becoming a citizen of the Soviet Union does not require that you formally renounce American citizenship. But the act of applying for Soviet citizenship involves signing an oath of allegiance to the Soviet Union, which would probably result in the loss of American citizenship in any case.

In the last circumstance—serving in an important political post in a foreign government—even the State Department admits it is clearly impossible to give an exact definition of an "important political post." Generally they consider the following: chief of a foreign state or a significant subdivision; a cabinet member or high-level official of another country's executive; a mayor or chief officer of a city; a member of a legislature—national, provincial, or municipal; military or civilian chief of another country's armed services.

But even then, the overriding consideration is intent. To paraphrase the Passport Office's "Statement," no act can be made the basis for loss of nationality unless in the light of all circumstances, motives, and purposes, the individual's *intent* has been to transfer allegiance to a foreign state or abandon his allegiance to the United States.

Citizenship cannot be taken from an American citizen as punishment. It cannot be taken for refusing to report for induction to military service.

ON A MORE PRACTICAL LEVEL . . .

Citizenship doesn't derive from which country you claim; it derives from which country claims you.

Dual citizenship—when two or more nationalities have a claim on you—occurs because of the criteria by which different countries define citizenship. Some base citizenship on where you were born. Others base it on the nationality of your parents.

The United States, as do a number of other countries, plays it both ways. Anyone born in the United States has the right of citizenship, no matter the nationality of the parents, unless the child is of a foreign diplomat accredited to the United States. A child born of an American parent in another country also has the right of citizenship.

But the child may also have claims put upon him by the country of his birth. This is where trouble might begin. "Might," because in fact the problem is not as great as it once was. The United States has signed a number of reciprocal treaties, as it has with extradition and taxation, in an attempt to keep the individual from being caught 'twixt the machinery of two governments.

For the adult American citizen resident in another country, the alternatives are usually clear. Residence neither entitles you nor compels you to become a citizen of that country. For the child born abroad, the alternatives are less clear.

He may, for example, by the fact of birth on foreign soil, have options and rights unavailable to the parent, such as the right to acquire public land or hold political office, sometimes withheld from the foreign-born even though later naturalized. There may also be limits on how long a child may hold both the nationality of his parents and that of the country of his birth before declaring a single nationality, the decision point usually coinciding with legal coming of age.

Some countries consider anyone born within their borders a perpetual citizen, despite whatever nationality claims might later be put on him by other governments. Many retired Americans, particularly those born in Eastern Europe who later became naturalized U.S. citizens, have returned to the countries of their birth or youth, often to find legal claims put upon them, as though they were still citizens.

A most common situation for the American resident in a foreign country is the case of marrying a foreign national and having children.

If so desired, a child born abroad to an American parent married to a foreign national has the right of American citizenship if: (1) The American parent has been physically present at least ten years of his life in the United States prior to the child's birth. (2) Five of those years were after the parent was fourteen years of age.

Even then, there is another requirement. To retain citizenship, the child must spend at least five years within the United States between the ages of fourteen and twenty-eight.

(Note: At the time of publication, a case pending before the Supreme Court could liberalize the above.)

If you remain a United States citizen, as most Americans abroad seem to, residence in another country does not necessarily mean you are out from under the reach of Uncle Sam's long legal arm.

The days of bank president or gangster racing for a plane to Brazil to escape the Feds, bulging valise in hand, have all but disappeared. The United States has signed a number of extradition agreements with foreign countries. The agreements are signed separately with each country, and enumerate the crimes for which each will surrender the other's citizens for prosecution. Generally they deal with serious crimes against person or property, with piracy still very high on the list.

Notably absent are extradition treaties between the United States and the Soviet Union, Denmark, and the Philippines. The agreement with Cuba is generally ignored. A number of former colonial territories, now independent countries, have brought the former treaties up to date by the exchange of diplomatic notes; a number of others have not. Still other treaties have lapsed; the extradition treaty concerning what is now the United Arab Republic was signed between the United States and the former Ottoman empire in 1874. An extradition treaty with Brazil went into force in 1964.

There are several classes of crimes considered indictable by the U.S. Department of Justice, even though committed on foreign soil. Treasonable acts, for example, such as those committed by World War II's Tokyo Rose. Also a wide range of antitrust and tax-evasion violations. Trying to induce a foreign government to enact policies against the

United States is also included, and conceivably might include the work of activists trying to convince foreign governments to censure the United States and its policies.

MORE OBLIGATIONS

In a foreign country you'll be subject to civil and criminal laws as well. Another country's system of law may be derived from a philosophy quite different from that of the United States, which stems from English common law.

Many countries base their criminal code on the Napoleonic theory that it is the accused who must prove his innocence rather than the U.S. custom of the accuser having to prove guilt. Rights taken for granted under U.S. law may simply not exist. The right to a speedy trial, for example, bail, or *habeas corpus* (the right to inquire into the nature and validity of the charge). In many Latin-American countries, to be caught in the act—the so-called *en flagrante* violation— is virtually ironlike proof of guilt, excluding the possibility of extenuating circumstances. In some countries even minor automobile accidents are treated as criminal offenses.

Foreign narcotics laws, which have snared a growing number of young people, are usually more punishing than American ones, and their enforcement is becoming more stringent. In February 1969 there were some 121 Americans in foreign jails in twenty countries on drug violations. A year later there were more than 400, about one-third in Mexico alone.

Even in the countries that make a distinction between possession and trafficking of drugs—Britain, for example—the quantity of drugs distinguishing between the two can sometimes be quite small. In Britain, where a first offense for possession of narcotics might result in a warning and a fine, the first offense for a dealer may be five years.

Britain's laws are models of liberality compared with those of most Middle Eastern and Latin countries, where sentences of three to fifteen years for traffickers in narcotics are not uncommon. In November 1971 Iran executed by firing squad five convicted opium and heroin smugglers. One American college student in Turkey was sentenced to two and a half years for possession of a half-gram of hashish. An appeal was denied.

In Italy an American actor and his wife were arrested at a party in their own home and determined to be under the influence of drugs. Italy, as do a number of other countries, makes use of "detoxification asylums" for drug offenders, which usually means commitment to a hospital for the criminally insane. The actor was detained eight months before trial. His wife became ill, was operated on while in detention, and died. He was eventually found innocent.

Of the several hundred U.S. deserters in otherwise socially liberal Sweden, ten have been arrested on drug violations as of mid-1971, and two others have been deported for drug offenses.

What most Americans fail to realize is that where drugs are concerned there are few mitigating circumstances. Claiming U.S. citizenship, influential parents, just doing it for a lark, or carrying it for a friend means absolutely nothing to the authorities of many other countries. Whatever the eventual outcome of the trial, extended pretrial detention, often without bail, is the rule rather than the exception. Conditions of jails or hospitals are often medieval, to the extent of expecting the families of prisoners to provide food. When a person is caught abroad in a predicament involving drugs, there is little either the U.S. government or family in the States can do to help.

A more likely snare for the unwary is unfamiliar property and labor laws. Many Americans seem surprised when they discover that the way things are done at home isn't standard procedure for the rest of the world.

Britain, for example, has laws extremely protective to the occupants of dwellings rented—or "let," as the British say—unfurnished. Raising the rent or eviction by the landlord requires a long, complicated, well-justified case. Yet a tenant living in even sparsely furnished dwellings has no greater recourse for shoddy treatment or facilities in disrepair than a hotel guest.

In Italy, as in many countries, one chooses a maid, cook, or houseboy with great caution. Once hired, such employees come under the protection of rigid labor laws that make servants difficult and expensive to dismiss. In almost all Latin countries in Europe and Latin America, such "dependent" help receive the *aguinaldo* or its equivalent—a compulsory legal bonus amounting to a thirteenth month of wages, paid yearly.

Of course, an abundance of such advice and added warnings usually comes forth unsolicited from the American residents of any foreign country, unless they have lived there so long that such "peculiarities" of custom and law have become second nature. Unfortunately, a good portion of a newcomer's knowledge in any case is acquired by making mistakes. Everyone makes them. The idea is to avoid the costly and binding ones. Especially in the first months of living abroad, and particularly when negotiating lease or purchase arrangements, a lawyer one feels comfortable with is a great aid. As is a carefully cultivated ability to make haste slowly.

CITIZEN'S BEST FRIEND

Once you are a resident in a foreign country (with which the United States has diplomatic relations), your passport assures you of both the protection and good offices of the American consul.

A consul is an officer of the U.S. Foreign Service. He may serve in the consular section of an embassy; or, in areas away from a country's capital city, where there is a concentration of American interests, he will be part of a consulate or consulate general.

An embassy has a number of broad tasks—gathering intelligence and economic data, administering aid money, serving as communication between a foreign government and the United States—but the consul has one job. He is your man. His job is to provide Americans within his jurisdiction with both protection and his good offices.

Consuls are people too, and much of their own in-group humor revolves around the odd things American citizens abroad ask them to do. As it turns out, there is considerable misunderstanding about what his "good offices" might be. Americans commonly ask their consuls to please book a nice pair of tickets at the theater, or to acquire hotel and travel reservations—both categories of duty clearly outside a consul's brief. Calvin Trillin told in *The New Yorker* of the woman from Baltimore who wrote the American consul in London to please run over to Hyde Park and buy her a painting she had seen—"a picture of an antique automobile made entirely of watchworks."

The most common misunderstanding is the influence a consul may have in the affairs of another country's government. When an American citizen is arrested, for example, a consul cannot automatically arrange a jail door to be sprung, no matter how much foreign aid the United States has supplied that country in the past.

In the case of arrest, a consul will visit the detainee (if he learns of the arrest), inform him of his rights under that country's laws, provide him with a list of attorneys, and contact his family Stateside if the prisoner so wishes. He will attempt to use his influence to make sure an American is processed quickly, and may attempt, if possible, to improve the conditions of detention. But an American consul is limited by law and influence as to what he can achieve for an American who has violated local laws.

Another common misunderstanding is the idea that an American consul is a source of money. In dire cases a consul may offer a loan for "indigent repatriation"—that is, returning home broke. This requires proof that no relative can provide such funds, approval of the State Department in Washington, and a stamp in the debtor's passport requiring repayment before leaving the United States again.

In the normal course of business, *a consul can:* (1) Use his authority (as guaranteed by treaty) to help you if you are stranded, destitute, sick, or injured. This does not usually include giving you money. (2) At times of disaster, revolution, or civil commotion, provide you with protective measures or removal. (3) Offer you procedural guidance (though seldom advice) on programs administered by other U.S. government agencies, including Social Security, other governmental retirement systems, veterans' benefits, and Internal Revenue Service information. Also distribute government pension checks. (4) Offer you information on matters of citizenship for yourself and your children. (5) Issue passports to American citizens.

Occasionally, though not within the brief of the consul, he can give information on housing, schooling, and local background. This depends greatly on the particular consul himself.

A consul cannot: (1) Arrange a release from jail if you have violated civil or criminal laws of the host country. He will attempt to make sure your rights are respected (and if *he* is respected, can often do quite well). The rights themselves are those determined by the host country. (2) Serve as a legal adviser. In some cases American consulates can provide you with a list of local attorneys, but do so without liability. (3) Give you information regarding the host country's taxation policies. (4) Obtain local licenses, such as driver's licenses. (5) Lend you money. He may assist you in getting in touch with family or local organizations that lend money if the situation warrants it. (6) Act as a travel agent or help you find a job.

FINDING OUT MORE

The following are several helpful pamphlets:

"Information for Passport Applicants." Department of State. Passport Office. Washington, D.C. 20524. For sale by the Government Printing Office for ten cents, or available off the display rack in any Passport Office. The complete up-to-date information on what you need to obtain a passport.

"You and Your Passport." Department of State. Passport Office.

For some reason this brief pamphlet is not in general circulation. Ask for it when you get your passport.

"Fees Charged by Foreign Countries for the Visa of United States Passports." Same address as above. Available in Passport Offices free. Revised regularly with information mainly about tourist visas, but other kinds too. (Note the tremendous variation in visa costs and duration of validity.)

TAXES

You can't avoid death and taxes, so the saying goes. For the American living abroad, the former remains no less inevitable, while in certain cases the latter is indeed avoidable. Residence in a foreign country complicates both.

Three things to remember about taxes:

(1) If you are an American citizen living anywhere in the world, you have an obligation to the United States Internal Revenue Service (IRS), even if it turns out that you don't actually have to pay U.S. income taxes.

(2) You must file a yearly return with the IRS even if you are exempt from U.S. tax payment. The only exception is if your gross income fell below a statutory minimum. For the tax years beginning 1969 and before 1973, the minimums are as follows:

Single individual	$1,700
Single individual over 65	$2,300
Married couple, filing jointly	$2,300
Married couple, one spouse over 65	$2,900
Married couple, both over 65	$3,500

(3) Your tax obligation to the United States is separate from your tax obligation to your new country of residence. In a number of countries, treaties between the host country and the United States spare you from being taxed twice on the same money. Beyond this, a foreign country's tax laws, and how they collect them, is their affair and affects all residents, national and foreign alike.

OBLIGATION TO IRS

The basic rule of taxation for an American citizen is that the money you earn anywhere in the world is subject to U.S. taxes, unless you qualify under one of the exemption provisions.

In reality, a large portion of income earned abroad from the performance of personal services while resident in another country (salary from a job, for example) will be exempt from taxation by the United States. That is, unless you work for the U.S. government or one of its agencies. Government employees pay taxes as though living in the United States, no matter where they actually reside.

The Internal Revenue Code defines "earned income" as wages, salaries, professional fees, and other amounts received as compensation for personal services actually rendered. The law is not specific about what exactly constitutes "personal service."

To qualify for exemption on earned income, you must prove foreign residence.

The law stipulates two tests under which you qualify as a foreign resident. The so-called "bona-fide-residence-in-a-foreign-country" test, refers to actual residence in a foreign country for an uninterrupted period including a full calendar year (beginning January 1). Residence is demonstrable by having an abode, your family with you, a residence permit, and so forth.

Unaware of the full-calendar-year requirement, one American businessman delayed his transfer abroad until January 3 so he could watch the Bowl games on television, thereby losing an entire year of exemption from U.S. taxes.

You may also qualify under the "physical-presence" test. In this case you must be out of the United States for a minimum of 510 days (about seventeen months) in an eighteen-month period. You'll need to keep a record, supported by the entry and exit stamps in your passport.

In 1971, such proof entitled the resident abroad to exemption on the first $20,000 of earned income, or after three consecutive years of residence, the first $25,000.

There are no other ways to qualify for exemption from U.S. taxes on salary earned overseas. These residence tests apply only to the U.S. tax obligation.

Income other than for personal services, so-called unearned income, is taxed as though you are still resident in the United States, no matter where you live.

IRS includes as unearned income: dividends (from mutual funds or shares), interest, distributions from pensions or profit-sharing plans (when paid for solely by your former employer), income from rental property, capital gains and losses, and royalties.

One exception under royalties is helpful to writers who live permanently abroad. Where property which would normally produce royalty income is created for another (a book written for a publisher already contracted), payment received for this work can be considered income to the author. In other words, such money can qualify as earned income and therefore be exempt up to the exemption limits. This is usually assured by prior contractual arrangement with your publisher, and is accepted by IRS. The work must be written outside the United States.

The following kinds of income are exempt from U.S. tax obligations. You must still file a return if your income from other sources exceeds the minimum limits, but they are not required to be reported on those returns: (1) Life-insurance proceeds paid because of the death of the insured. (2) Gifts and inheritances. (3) Social Security and Railroad Retirement benefits. (4) Compensation for personal injuries. (5) Interest on state or municipal obligations. (6) Certain insurance payments received for living expenses as a result of casualty to residence.

U.S. citizens, when filing tax returns with the IRS, have until June 15 of the year following the tax year to file, if still resident outside of the United States.

OTHER COUNTRIES' TAXES

Whatever your tax obligation to the United States, your obligation in a new country of residence is another matter. How they tax you is entirely their business.

The U.S. Internal Revenue Service may be the most efficient organization of its kind in administering the world's most complicated income-tax system. But the IRS doesn't hold all the patents on ingenuity. Other countries may function without income taxes at all, making up for lost revenue by a long list of sales taxes, turnover taxes, value-added taxes, excise taxes, and the government's use of fees and stamps. The ways of extracting money from the citizenry are endless.

Systems of tax collection may be equally diverse. A number of European countries use a withholding-from-wages system such as that in the United States. Such schemes are often referred to as PAYE systems (pay as you earn). Other countries may cast an eye on your income once a year via tax inspection, at which time you are assessed a single lump sum. But even here, assessment systems vary.

Assessment may be based on some percentage of your previous year's income. In Switzerland, people who live on funds sent into

Switzerland from an indeterminate source are taxed some multiple of their apartment rental. Italy has an assessment system that seems to function by barter, although actual collection seldom functions better than erratically.

TAX RATES: A RELIABLE GUIDE?

Personal income-tax rates vary from country to country as much as tax systems. They can change drastically, often in midyear, to meet budget urgencies, as is common in France, for example, or Britain, where the Chancellor of the Exchequer's Budget Message each spring is awaited less than eagerly.

On even modest incomes Israel probably has the highest personal income taxes in the world, levied in combination with a stiff defense surcharge. In the United States a married man with two children would pay about $1,100 federal income tax on a taxable income of $10,000. In Canada he would pay slightly more, about $1,360. In Israel, a person with a taxable income equivalent to $10,000—an excellent salary by Israeli measure—would pay about $6,800 in taxes. There are extremely liberal family exemptions in Israel, however, which bring down considerably the taxable income a family would pay taxes on; there are also special tax exemptions for newcomers.

In general, after Israel the highest personal income-tax rates are in the Scandinavian countries and countries belonging to the British Commonwealth. The taxpayers in Sweden, Britain, Australia, and New Zealand generally pay a greater proportion of their earnings in income taxes than do either Americans or Canadians. In these countries the tax rates favor those at the lower end of the wage scale, are moderately heavy on mid-income people, reaching high maximum rates quickly, often at the equivalents of $10,000 or $12,000 a year, which would be considered a high wage.

In New Zealand, for example, a single taxpayer earning the equivalent of $6,800 per year would pay about $1,600 in taxes; married with two children he would pay about $1,400 on the same earned income. A single person earning the equivalent of about $11,000 a year would pay just under $4,000 of it in taxes.

At the opposite end of the scale are those countries which derive much of their government revenue from taxes on business and trade, to the benefit of those who pay personal income taxes. Panama taxes an income equivalent to $15,000 a year at about 7 percent. In Switzerland, the combined state and canton tax for a married man with a family of two living in Zurich with a taxable income equivalent to $10,000 a year is about 15 percent, or $1,500. South Africa has one of the lowest personal income-tax rates of any industrialized country, taxing a married man with two children about $950 on a taxable income of $10,000. Belgium, Singapore, Hong Kong, and Portugal all have modest income taxes, made up for in great part by various taxes on business and commerce.

A principal point to remember, however, is that one can never learn the whole tax picture of a country by only examining its personal income-tax rate.

In many countries, high personal income taxes may be offset in part by the social benefits the government bestows upon all residents, foreign and national alike. Sweden and New Zealand have among the highest personal income-tax rates in the world. Yet both have extensive national health care and insurance and pension programs that cushion a citizen's existence from birth to death.

Another often overlooked aspect of foreign taxes is the deductions from gross income that determine taxable income. Mortgage payments, insurance premiums, greater or lesser deductions for additional children—all may greatly reduce the actual amount upon which one would need to pay tax.

In still other countries the published tax rates are a fiction which few people would actually think of paying in any case. Brazil and Argentina were once both notoriously lax in their collection of taxes, to the joy of the taxpayer and the consternation of the government. Brazil actually resorted to the use of "fiscals," who were something between a tax inspector and a policeman, whose incentive to track down tax avoiders was a large percentage of the fine.

All that is changing. Beginning in the mid-sixties, both countries undertook massive tax reforms, with the aid of new computers and teams of consultants sent by the United States Internal Revenue Service. Income-tax collections now make up about 30 percent of the Brazilian government revenues, with the tax filing date a suspiciously familiar April 15.

In a lessening number of countries, tax evasion remains a way of life. In such countries it is serious business nonetheless, a constant battle between the hunter and the hunted, often between the government official whose salary is easily determinable and hence usually the first to be taxed successfully, and the wily entrepreneur armed with duplicate books, money invested in his wife's maiden name, cash transactions the profits of which are secreted or smuggled out of the country, and a list of tricks long enough to make complete discovery impossible.

THE EXIT VISA

One weapon in the hunter's bag that serves multiple purposes is the so-called *exit visa,* or *exit permit.* An exit visa is a permit to leave a country. Where used, it applies to any resident, either alien or national.

Obtaining an exit visa usually requires formal application to the appropriate ministry several weeks in advance of intended travel. After verification that the applicant owes no taxes (or in some countries is not wanted for a crime or is not a Communist), the passport is returned with its exit visa stamped in place, for presentation to the immigration officer at airport or ship. In countries that make use of an exit visa, there are always a number of citizens unable or unwilling to attempt travel from their country legally, lest application for an exit visa stir up already muddied financial or political water.

Another problem Americans moving to another country may encounter is determining exactly what a foreign country's tax laws define as income.

For example, pension payments that are already subject to U.S. taxation no matter where you live (excluding Social Security payments) may be considered taxable income by a foreign country, thereby requiring you to pay taxes twice. Some countries tax U.S. Social Security as income.

To ease the problem some, the United States has signed a number of "tax conventions" separately with twenty-eight countries to avoid dual taxation (that is, being taxed twice on the same money). The philosophy behind the "conventions" is to tax money in the country where it is derived. There are still many nations without tax treaties with the United States, leaving the tax matter up in the air in a large part of the world. Additionally, in those countries where a tax convention is in effect, the dual-taxation problem may be dealt with only in part.

Fortunately, even in those countries which tax income that is normally taxable by the U.S. Internal Revenue Service, the IRS now allows the foreign tax payment to be either deducted or credited against U.S. tax payments.

A FINE POINT: DOMICILE VERSUS RESIDENCE

There is a fine, technical difference between your domicile and your residence. The only time it will matter is in respect to some foreign countries' tax laws, or if you happen to die. In the latter case it won't matter to you, but to your heirs.

"Residence" is where you live. The IRS considers paying rent on an apartment or house that contains your own furniture and fittings, holding a residence permit, having your family with you, or being considered resident by a foreign government as good evidence that you are actually resident in a particular place. Other countries may have different definitions of residence, but they will be very close to this one.

"Domicile" may be a place other than where you are a resident. The IRS considers "domicile" a place where you for some time had a residence, where you remain, or where you intend to return. Your parents' address might qualify as a domicile. The United Kingdom considers a person's domicile to be his natural home, and that to which he intends to return.

For an American citizen abroad, it is fairly easy to establish someplace in the United States as a domicile. A basic principle of international taxation is that you will have tax obligations to your country of residence. But having a domicile elsewhere can in some cases allow you certain favorable considerations under foreign tax laws.

Persons residing in Britain, for example, but with a domicile elsewhere, are allowed to bring in capital funds without being taxed. With a domicile elsewhere, money you earn outside of the country is not subject to British taxes, as long as you don't have it remitted to you in Britain.

In the case of death, having a domicile outside of the country of residence can make things easier for your heirs. Portugal, for example, considers the law of estates of your country of domicile as the law to be applied. In the case of the United States, if your domicile was in California, California law would prevail in the handling of your estate, even though you died in Portugal.

It is wise for most Americans intending to retain their citizenship to establish a domicile in the United States before leaving. In the case of a married woman, domicile is considered that of the husband.

In this book some information about personal income taxes is included under each country. Beyond satisfying curiosity, such bits of information have little value, besides being subject to immediate change. Levying and collecting taxes is big business. Determining your tax obligation for both the United States and your new country of residence demands expert, up-to-date advice.

Even the experts, however, expect the taxpayer to have some idea of his problems. One international tax authority suggests that the more complete the taxpayer's understanding of the problems and alternatives, the easier it is to determine the best way to handle his taxes. Even if he doesn't have the answers, the taxpayer should at least know the questions.

HELP

There are three general sources of information about income tax. Printed sources (books, pamphlets, etc.); government sources (IRS and foreign-government counterparts); private sources.

A number of printed sources for tax information are listed in "Finding Out More," p. 42; several of these ought to be obtained *before* you leave the United States. They will help you find out what questions to ask, even if you decide finally to let someone else prepare your taxes for you.

Government Sources: The IRS. The Internal Revenue Service is concerned only with United States tax obligations. Once you are outside the United States, the overseer of your U.S. tax payments is the IRS Office of International Operations. They maintain tax consultants in U.S. embassies in London, Bonn, Rome, Paris, Ottawa, Tokyo, Manila, Mexico City, and the U.S. consulate general in São Paulo, Brazil. In addition, the OIO sends consultants abroad each year to brief consular staff on the simpler aspects of handling your U.S. income tax, and to hold seminars for American citizens in parts of the world where large concentrations of Americans live.

Objective tax people overseas consider the OIO competent, but not without a bias favoring the IRS in matters of interpretation. As any tax accountant knows, even under the most precise tax laws there are vagaries, tests, and loopholes that can be legally taken advantage of, to the benefit of the taxpayer. The OIO people naturally apply tax laws strictly, which should not come as a surprise. They will, however, answer any questions about your U.S. tax obligations when you are resident abroad, by mail. Write: Office of International Operations; CP: 10: 6; Internal Revenue Service; Washington, D.C. 20225.

In most cases, the IRS advisory help in their numerous Stateside offices know little about your U.S. tax obligations once you are abroad. Taxation of income earned overseas is an especially complex area of tax law, and their concern is primarily domestic. The experts are the OIO and to a lesser extent American consulates abroad.

Both, however, are forbidden from offering you tax help on your tax obligation to another country. Their job is U.S. taxes only.

In most cases they will suggest contacting the particular foreign-government office or bureau responsible for internal taxation in that country for advice and help on local taxes.

For all but the most informed, approaching a foreign country's tax office on your own is not advised. Tax laws, and actual administration and compliance, may bear little relation to each other. Perhaps the only sure rule in dealing with another country's tax office is "Never volunteer."

One tax adviser suggests that a starting point for separating law from reality is to discuss the matter with an American already living for some time in the country, paying his taxes in the accepted manner. One American living in southern Europe advises newcomers to ascribe to the local rule of thumb of "never doing anything official until cudgeled into it."

Even though such maxims may have the sound of wisdom, advice should be sought but never be accepted without verification.

Private Sources. These are probably your best bet for objective, informed tax advice for *both* United States tax obligation and foreign taxes.

The most reputable private sources are the large American-owned international accounting firms, found in an increasing number of foreign countries. There are about a half-dozen first-order ones, including Price Waterhouse, Arthur Andersen, and Arthur Young. The foreign offices of these large American firms, among other attributes, speak your language. Most have offices in major American cities.

Most international accounting firms specialize in corporate accounts and in work involving corporate personnel. They will take the private individual as a client. Fees generally range upward from $100 for filling out U.S. tax forms. With it you buy sound, expert advice. Reputable firms do not charge you for your initial visit if you are attempting honestly to find out if their service can benefit you.

Additionally, in each country there are reputable local firms and competent tax lawyers and accountants. Many American embassies will furnish you with lists, often of English-speaking nationals, which may be able to help you, but the embassies do so without obligation. The U.S. Department of Commerce maintains field offices in more than forty cities in the United States (see Appendix for addresses), which have lists of lawyers and accountants in many foreign countries. Such information is also available from American Chambers of Commerce which exist in several dozen countries around the world, although their information is usually given only to members.

Another source of information is banks. Most major banks offer business information and limited tax guidance. The largest American banks overseas—Chase Manhattan, First National City Bank of New York, Bank of America, First National Bank of Boston (particularly in Argentina and Brazil)—are all equipped to provide information to their customers.

If you are going abroad attached to an American company, you will have access to your corporate personnel and tax department, as well as to these outside sources of information. You should use all of them. Often there are steps that should be taken *before* you leave the United States that will prevent mistakes abroad. If you are a private citizen on his own, it is probably wise to pursue the matter of taxes before it becomes a problem. Most private citizens don't have the resources or corporate backing to afford mistakes.

AND DON'T FORGET . . . EXCHANGE CONTROL

Almost all countries have laws affecting the movement of their money in and out of the country. This exchange control is aimed at conserving that country's overseas funds and making sure that transactions involving their money have the knowledge and approval of the government.

In Western Europe, where the currencies are sound, there is little actual control; currencies are freely exchanged. Elsewhere, the movement of your dollars may be through a one-way valve, easier going in than coming out.

Developing countries in Africa and Latin America have strict regulations regarding the exchange of money in order to prevent speculation in their fluctuating currencies, and to prevent currency from being taken out stuffed in pockets or suitcases. Dollars are always welcome, either to be exchanged officially by banks (at official rates of exchange), or less officially at the rate dictated by the "parallel market," an accountant's phrase meaning what you can really exchange your dollars for if you look around.

Exchanging local currency into hard currencies—dollars, Swiss francs, German marks—is usually restricted, and even countries like Australia, New Zealand, and South Africa have exchange-control policies that change whenever there appears some economic necessity.

A country's exchange-control policy should be understood before transferring even moderate amounts of dollars from the United States.

FINDING OUT MORE

U.S. Taxes

Tax Guide for U.S. Citizens Abroad. Internal Revenue Service. Publication No. 54, 32 pages. This booklet, revised yearly, is a must for the average person going abroad to live in any capacity. Free from Internal Revenue Service, any office, or from IRS Technical Publications Branch, Washington, D.C. 20224. Also from American consulates abroad.

Foreign Tax Credit for U.S. Citizens and Resident Aliens. Internal Revenue Service. Publication No. 514, 12 pages. Not exactly a lucid document, but goes into more detail on the dovetailing of U.S. and foreign taxes. Free from any IRS office.

U.S. Taxation of Its Citizens Overseas. Arthur Andersen and Company. 101 pages. A comprehensive booklet prepared by a first-class international accounting firm. Available free. Requests written on business-letterhead stationery will usually get prompt response. Arthur Andersen and Company; 1345 Avenue of the Americas; New York, N.Y. 10019.

Information Guide for U.S. Citizens Abroad. Price Waterhouse and Company. Similar to the above. Available free. Write on letterhead. Price Waterhouse and Company; 60 Broad Street; New York, N.Y. 10005.

Foreign Taxes

Tax and Trade Guide (Various Countries). Arthur Andersen and Company; 1345 Avenue of the Americas; New York, N.Y. 10019. Guides written for a number of countries, revised fairly frequently. Probably the most helpful, up-to-date material available to the nonaccountant. Free. Write on letterhead. Arthur Andersen and Price Waterhouse have a number of guides on the same countries, but each has a few not covered by the other.

Information Guide for Doing Business (in Various Countries). Price

Waterhouse and Company. 60 Broad Street; New York, N.Y. 10005. Same as above.

Taxation Outside the United Kingdom. Board of Inland Revenue. Her Majesty's Stationery Office (HMSO). Eight volumes, paper-bound. Many tax experts feel this is the best series available. "Outside the United Kingdom" is a very British way of saying most of the rest of the world. Available in the United States from the British Information Service; Sales Section; 845 Third Avenue; New York, N.Y. 10022. The price is unfortunate at $57.60. Volumes not available separately. Worth a look if you can find them in a library.

THE CULTURE LEAP
Culture Shock and Beyond

Truth consists of the little things.

— RENAN

The legalities and regulations affecting a move to another country may be the smaller part of the battle. The less tangible adjustments an American must make consciously, subconsciously, and physically to live happily abroad are often more staggering.

Any dislocation from the environment we know takes its toll. Even a move from one part of the United States to another requires adjustment to a different climate, a change of physical landscape, a new set of regional mannerisms and etiquette. The reaction to such a minor dislocation may be a mild, fleeting homesickness or similar passing discomfort.

In *Daughter of Silence*, writer Morris West describes the not uncommon reaction to a different environment, a phenomenon he calls "travelers' malaise." An "acute melancholy, a sense of oppression by what is old and distaste for what is new . . . one is conscious of solitude and strangeness. The effort of communication in a foreign tongue becomes an intolerable burden. The food presents itself as a garbled mess. One longs for the thinnest wine of one's own country." As West noted, there is no remedy for such malaise, but seldom lasting harm either.

The effect of the leap into a totally different culture may not be so fleeting, especially if, unlike West's traveler, you are there to stay. At some point in time, cultural differences may affect a newcomer in a manner scarcely anticipated.

The term "culture shock" describes a common but sometimes rather severe reaction to cultural change. At some point in time culture shock catches up with the majority of Americans who move abroad. Though many Americans are familiar with the term, most are unprepared for what happens to them when the "shock" hits. At its extreme, the symptoms of culture shock amount to near-complete mental and physical debilitation, temporary though it may be.

44

Perhaps the only comforting thought is that some reaction to the culture leap is unavoidable. If not able to relax and enjoy it, as the old adage goes, it is at least possible to become acquainted with the phenomenon, for surprisingly, culture shock arrives in a fairly predictable way and affects a large number of people in the same manner.

AMERICAN TO THE CORE

By way of preparation, the first thing to recognize is that no matter how worldly and sophisticated you may be, you are incurably American, just as any adult Frenchman, Brazilian, or Japanese brought up in his culture is unalterably French, Brazilian, or Japanese. From birth we are all strapped bit by bit with a number of items of mental baggage from which we will never be completely unburdened, even if such unburdening were desirable. We are involuntary recipients of our unique culture, which anthropologists generally term as our sum of learned behavior patterns, our attitudes and material things. We are American from office pecking order to subculture rituals to the peculiar games we play. We are never going to be more American than in the moment we step from airplane or ship and put a first cautious foot on another country's soil. The phrase "we're all in the same boat" never had a more accurate meaning.

Yet no matter how different that country may be from our own, the first view most probably won't create shock at all. We've all been accustomed, thanks to Kodachrome and television, to the sight of rice paddies or rainforest or the urban congestion of Hong Kong or the squalor of a Caracas *barrio*.

The most usual initial reaction to a new place is elation, a delight at the difference, however great or slight it may be. The Norwegian sociologist Lysgaarde calls this the "spectator" phase. The "shock" will come later, when we can no longer remain spectators, but are forced to participate.

Initial elation is the first fairly predictable step in the long process of acculturation—that is, the process of adjusting your American self to the habits, traditions, customs, and language of a different culture. In all likelihood the process will stop somewhere short of complete assimilation, because of that baggage Americans carry with them. Somewhere in the process of acculturation an American may even discover just how American he is. It happened to one black American when he realized that the Swahili word for "outsider" was the same for him as for any white man. It happens to many American Jews in

Israel when they first encounter newly arrived Jews from Yemen or refugees from the Soviet Union.

The process of acculturation, it turns out, is less change than exchange. An American who has lived eleven years in Peru, married to a Lima girl, is amused at the idea of any American completely assimilating into a Latin culture. "You'll always be the gringo here."

Short of complete assimilation, the process of successful adjustment to another culture may take years.

SATISFACTION, IDENTIFICATION, ASSIMILATION

Australian psychologist Alan Richardson, on the basis of considerable experience among the large number of new settlers in Australia, clearly sees three stages in the process of acculturation: an initial stage in which the new settler seeks principally a few basic satisfactions in his life; a second stage in which the newcomer begins to identify with his new country and its people; a third stage in which the settler, or more likely his children, becomes indistinguishable from his countrymen.

The initial stage is the most critical. It is here that a new settler is made or broken. According to Richardson, it is absolutely necessary at some time during the first two or three years in a country to find some of the things that motivated the move to begin with. Usually it has much to do with finding a satisfying way of earning a living. But it can just as well be an inner satisfaction, peace of mind, or establishing a desired new life style. Conquering a new language, or the excitement of seeing children grow easily and naturally into bicultural human beings may provide sufficient satisfaction, if such aims were behind the initial decision to move.

Without such satisfactions during the first two or three years, most people aren't tenacious enough, especially if the move has been voluntary, to keep plugging away unsuccessfully at a way of life providing little joy. During this initial "satisfaction" stage there will be additional dangerous thresholds, such as getting past the effects of culture shock, which we'll come back to in a moment.

But if satisfactions are found, Richardson noticed that most settlers, no longer exactly new settlers, passed into another stage of the acculturation process—the "identification" stage.

In the stage of identification a number of things happen.

If the move has been to a country speaking a different language, the settler by now has at least mastered it to the point where it is no longer a vexation. The big change is in outlook. There is an increasing identification by the settler with the problems and goals of the new country. A study of British immigrants to Australia pointed out that during this period the pronoun "you" was often replaced by "our" and "we." If the settler is American, he is likely to still have a number of American friends. But unless he has chosen to exile himself in one of the super-American hiding places such as the Parioli or Via Cassia apartment complexes in Rome, or Ajijc near Guadalajara, or any of a number of expatriate enclaves found in almost any country, he'll now have a number of local friends as well. The roots will still be in America, and still cherished. But somewhere along the way the tug to take a visit "home" lessens. An American couple living in Rio noticed over the period of three or four years that the obligatory visit to New York, "home" for both, slowly gave way to a visit to Europe.

There are variables in all of this. Some Americans begin to identify with a new country of residence in a shorter time than others. This is especially true of those who have married a national. An American who had originally gone to Mexico with his American wife, and remarried a Mexican after his first wife's illness and death, said he realized then that he had never really been accepted before. An American woman in her twenties, married to an Afrikaner rancher, doubts that she would ever have learned the subtleties of local social life if she hadn't been married to a South African. An American businessman in Peru believes the secret "that gets you in" is marrying a Peruvian, as he has.

During the stage of identification the newcomer *feels* more like one of his new countrymen.

But as the wise American abroad notes, it's a long way from *feeling* to actually *being*.

Up to this point, a great many of the adjustments to a new culture have been forced on the newcomer by the physical or cultural environment. Learning to identify different cuts of meat available in the butcher shop, for example. Or wearing clothes to fit the climate. Few people cling to the habit of eating cornflakes for breakfast when they are imported at two dollars a box, and fresh milk a luxury reserved only for infant children.

During this stage of identification a new settler begins to adopt aspects of the culture because he recognizes now what is advantageous for him to acquire. Correctly speaking the language, for example, with all its polite forms of address. The accent may not be taken as native, but he knows the rules. Courtesies and manners are no longer an embarrassment to the settler or to his friends. During the identification stage the new settler becomes comfortable with life and is in control.

The last stage of the acculturation process—the stage of complete assimilation—is perhaps reserved for a new settler's children. That is, speaking and acting as one of the native-born, with all the nuances of style and naturalness of expression. The look, sound, dress, and movements of the native-born are difficult to acquire, short of birth.

What many Americans abroad fail to realize is that few societies, consciously or unconsciously, expect you to become a carbon copy. Having reached a level of adaptation, identifying successfully with a country and its people—little more is expected of the foreign resident. At this point it is perhaps wisest to sit back, resigned to the bits of Americanness that cling.

One example of the difficulty of trying to become completely native even in a culture similar to your own is the almost absolute certainty that you will fail, and embarrassingly so. Richardson noted that attempts of newcomers to imitate the accent, idiom, facial gestures and stance of a "dinkum Aussie" almost always caused resentment, or the feeling "what is he trying to prove?" As Richardson comments: "The deliberate attempt to take on the typical expressive qualities of host group members is likely to arouse suspicion of a British immigrant

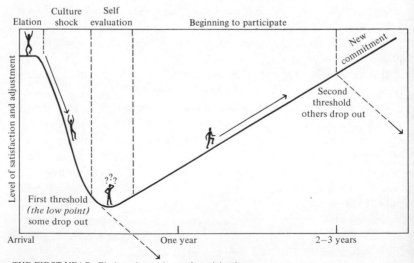

THE FIRST YEAR: Elation, depression and participation

who in so many other ways can pass as an Australian. It may appear to an Australian as a form of social forgery."

Passing beyond the identification stage of acculturation, the great obstacles have been scaled; what remains are a few hummocks and uneven spots in the terrain.

For Americans, as it is for all new settlers of whatever nationality, the first two or three years are the most difficult. It is in that initial "satisfaction-seeking" stage of trying to adjust that the real problems wait.

Let's take a closer look at those first few years.

THE DROP

Earlier it was pointed out that the most common first reaction to a new place is elation—the novelty of the situation, the feel of tropical warmth or perhaps the clear briskness of a northern autumn. Different aromas and sounds can be heady stuff, almost unfailing in their ability to make a person feel superior to the weaker souls left behind still slaving at their mundane little jobs, fighting the freeway, the 5:21, or a dozen other equivalents. The new settler is partly justified, of course. Actually, taking the step is no small thing.

But at this point a new settler's elation is little different from the thrill felt by a tourist or a sailor on liberty. The new settler has more in common with both of these than with his brethren who have gone before and successfully weathered the first critical period.

First of all, little is expected of a newcomer in a different society. Locals generally ignore the behavior of an obnoxious tourist or a disorderly G.I., who are not expected to know the rules; and neither is the new settler. This sense of social freedom is part of the reason behind the initial elation; the old social rules have been shed, like a snake wriggling out of its dead skin, and the newcomer isn't, as yet, being judged by new ones. For probably one of the few times in his life, a person has few commitments, no set habits, no precedents. For one fleeting moment, in a new country, he is free.

But if the newcomer is there to stay, the business of living soon settles upon him. No one can afford to live for long like a tourist, in a social sense or financially. With the need to put a house in order, find a job, and go about the business of living day to day, the newcomer is ripe for the drop. Sociologists commonly refer to it as the standard, recognized, "elation-depression syndrome." The depression is more commonly called "culture shock."

The effects are well known, because it strikes most people in much the same way, although not always at a predictable time.

A classic statement of what happens during culture shock was written by anthropologist Kalervo Oberg, who spent considerable time working for the American government in Brazil.

No matter how broadminded or full of good will you may be, a series of props have been knocked out from under you, followed by a feeling of frustration and anxiety. People react to the frustration in much the same way. First, they reject the environment which causes the discomfort: "the ways of the host country are bad because they make us feel bad." When Americans or other foreigners in a strange land get together to grouse about the host country and its people—you can be sure they are suffering from culture shock. Another phase of culture shock is regression. The home environment suddenly assumes a tremendous importance. To an American everything American becomes irrationally glorified. All the difficulties and problems are forgotten and only the good things back home are remembered. It usually takes a trip home to bring one back to reality.

Some of the symptoms of culture shock are: excessive washing of hands; excessive concern over drinking water, food, dishes, and bedding; fear of physical contact with attendants or servants; the absentminded, far-away stare (sometimes called the tropical stare); a feeling of helplessness and a desire for dependence on long-term residents of one's own nationality; fits of anger over delays and other minor frustrations; excessive fear of being cheated, robbed or injured; great concern over minor pains and eruptions of the skin; and finally, that terrible longing to be back home, to be able to have a good cup of coffee and a piece of apple pie, to walk into that corner drugstore, to visit one's relatives and in general, to talk to people who really make sense. . . .

THE CAUSES OF CULTURE SHOCK

The essential cause of culture shock is the meeting, head-on, of your American self with the habits, attitudes, and behavior patterns of another culture. The unavoidability of the clash is embodied in the comments of an American businessman who has lived for many years in a rapidly changing South American country, and in his words: "seen Americans come and seen them go."

He put it this way:

The most difficult thing for any American here is the fact that he suddenly comes up against a way of living he has never seen before, or has anything comparable to in the United States. Most don't know how to handle it. The tremendous bureaucracy, poor utilities, high costs, the differences in class structure, and almost no middle class as we think of it. No one gets anything done here without friends, influence, or push, and the newcomer has none of these.

An American in his mid-twenties who lived and taught for two years on the Caribbean island of St. Lucia believes firmly that the "cultural arrogance" most Americans bring with them to a new place makes them ripe for culture shock. "Most Americans really believe there is no better way to live or to do things than the way it's done in America. When they find out there are other ways, other attitudes toward life, and some of those alternatives pretty satisfactory, the shock hits."

Just how soon after arrival culture shock will happen depends on the individual and his circumstances. It occurs when he suddenly discovers how much more there is to it, and how far there is to go before he'll have it made in a different place and culture. That realization may occur in a few weeks, but most certainly in the first six or eight months. For a few rare individuals, seldom identifiable beforehand, culture shock may not happen at all.

Often the onslaught of culture shock can be caused by the mundane. Sociologists John and Jeanne Gullahorn studied the adjustment problems of American students in Paris, and tell of shock being brought on in a graduate student with a single year to research and write his dissertation suddenly being confronted with the agonizingly slow operating procedures of the Bibliothèque Nationale.

In Rome, an American housewife's accumulated dread of daily buying a chicken, because it was the only thing she could recognize, was worsened by having to deal with its intact feathers, head, feet, and entrails. The thought of touching those feet became nearly more than she could stand, forcing her into spells of crying. A more experienced American wife told her later that the poulterer would have cleaned and jointed the chicken for her if only she had asked.

As Oberg points out, two major components of culture shock are nostalgia, often accompanied by idealization of the home country, and a feeling that the locals "are out to get me"—if not physically, in a social sense. The specific manifestations can be as varied as people themselves.

Once in downtown Tokyo I was going with an American publisher living in Japan to see Japanese Nobel prizewinner in physics Hideki Yukawa. My acquaintance flagged a cab and gave the driver what sounded like fluent instructions in Japanese. Americans abroad usually master taxi fluency in a language shortly after restaurant fluency. But in this case apparently, the taxi driver didn't understand a word. He asked a single question. There was a brief heavy silence before my countryman flew into a rage, leaped from the taxi, and stomped away shouting ethnic slurs, while I sat being watched carefully by the cab driver. Finally he gave me a universal shrug, and I humbly went the way of my friend.

I described the incident later to a Japanese friend of mine, who predicted a hard road ahead for the publisher if he continued to act that way. (He did, and later lost his job.) He explained that the Japanese lose respect for anyone who can't hold their temper. They have a proverb that sums it up: *tanki wa sonki.* A short temper means a lost spirit.

One of the most common crutches for the American abroad nostalgically hungry for things American is *Time* magazine. For those caught in culture shock, its weekly arrival may be awaited with open anticipation.

Once in the American embassy in Rio, a woman finishing her sixth month of an AID contract bent my ear in honest rage at the incompetence of the Brazilian postal service. They had failed in their delivery of *Time* on its usual Thursday afternoon, a half-day ahead of its appearance on newsstands. Rather than endure the wait until the next afternoon's delivery, she had sent her driver to wait at the newsstand until the magazine appeared. They had already received *theirs,* she hissed at me.

For many people caught in culture shock the structuring of time becomes an overwhelming burden. In this instance women may be more susceptible than men. Men at least have their work. The woman of the house, even if living modestly, may for the first time in her life have a servant or two to relieve her of the time-filling task of housework and cooking.

In *The Blue of Capricorn* the late Eugene Burdick told of a fairly typical young woman named Sarah who had married her college sweetheart and moved with him abroad, eventually to fall into a rather classic syndrome:

> In the morning she no longer played tennis, but leafed through the Sears Roebuck catalogue and almost invariably ordered something . . . a portable electric hair dryer, a transistor radio, a copper chafing dish. . . .
> Sarah also began to order American magazines. At first she ordered a

few avant-garde magazines and then *Life* and *Time* and then movie magazines. Finally she ordered the little magazines on "how to do it;" magazines
full of mechanical ingenuity. By the time she had been on_____a year she
subscribed to over fifty American magazines.

Filling great spaces of time with a blur of idle reading is a fairly
typical reaction to culture shock. Another, for those with unstruc-
tured time on their hands, is seeking the extraordinary reassurance of
a familiar environment: bed.

Most experienced Peace Corps volunteers recognize the phenomenon—the new volunteer who isn't seen for several days on the job or
at the usual volunteer haunts and must often be literally dragged from
bed back into action.

But unless a person makes no attempt to adjust to a new culture,
or is isolated by money or position, some effect of trying to cope with
the unfamiliar will sooner or later catch up. It is a natural part of the
process of acculturation.

The standard advice for avoiding culture shock is to keep busy,
which may be akin to advising a drowning man to swim for it. Research by the Army's OSS assessment staff found that the support of
a peer group can often be one of the most effective bolsters to sinking
morale during the period of cultural adjustment.

Unfortunately, organizations of Americans outside of the United
States are few in number, but where they do exist they can be valuable
in this capacity, especially during the first few months of settling in.
The Association of Americans and Canadians in Israel has been par-
ticularly effective in taking the woman of the house under their wing
during the hectic first days after arriving in Israel. The American
Families Association of Queensland (Australia) and the American
Society in Brazil both provide information and "insiders' " advice on
settling into their respective countries, and the camaraderie of fellow
Americans abroad when needed.

Some of the most effective organizations, though not widespread,
are the small semiformal women's organizations often built around
the almost missionary efforts of a few individual American women
abroad. There is an American Women's Club in Paris, a small newcomer's group in São Paulo, and a small effective organization of
American women in Lusaka, Zambia. When they can be found (or
started), they are invaluable for Americans in the initial stages of
adjusting to a foreign culture.

Many people find that the ear of someone knowledgeable about the situation can help in getting past culture shock, as many of the Peace Corps doctors assigned overseas can attest. One young woman in Africa felt that having a person back in the States to "pour it all out to" without regard to personal sensitivities was essential.

Implicit in her remark is one of the real dangers to the American caught in the throes of culture shock—the tendency to criticize.

Until a newcomer gains a measure of acceptance, he may be under a good deal of scrutiny by his new countrymen. They may be openly envious of his material well-being, or curious why anyone would leave so rich a country as America to live in their own. Perhaps because of this, foreign nationals are supersensitive to appraisals of their country, especially by foreigners they have less than accepted. And in the midst of culture shock the temptation to criticize and compare is overwhelming.

Here are a few highly subjective suggestions that might be kept in mind during those first months in a new country. Once accepted by your neighbors and new friends, you'll find many of these generalizations will bend. It is wise to keep in mind the advice one American offered a newcomer when asked how a person would know when he had been accepted. "If you are in doubt, you haven't."

(1) Don't tell people how to run their country, solve their traffic problems, or get the working man to be more efficient. "Candid" or "frank" criticisms, which Americans relish, are seldom appreciated in other countries, especially from foreigners. Most people prefer to be direct, obliquely. Thirty-day experts aren't appreciated anywhere, especially when as a nation we have a few unsolved problems ourselves.

(2) Don't preface your remarks with "Back home we always . . ." Cultural arrogance and insensitivity are the most common criticisms of Americans abroad. Such comparisons seldom appear to favor the here and now.

(3) Don't overflatter or gush compliments because you think other people will like you for it. False sincerity is seldom rewarded with friendship. American women, particularly beware. If you have the uncontrollable urge to compliment or flatter people, find something simple and honest. If you look around, it is usually not difficult.

(4) Watch the objects of your humor. Dirty jokes and double-entendres based on sex as an attempt to break social ice will most often be embarrassing or misunderstood. Few cultures have the same basis for humor or sources of amusement that we do. Sarcasm and the ability to laugh at oneself is a limited commodity. Latins especially

have an unwillingness to be laughed at or ridiculed, particularly by strangers.

(5) Don't wisecrack in public because you think no one speaks English. Invariably the few people in a country who do will be close by.

(6) Respect other people's currency. It may be filthy, held together with Scotch tape, have too many zeros in it, and be diminished in value by inflation. But references to "funny money" or "monopoly money" seldom amuse others.

(7) Be polite, and speak softly. You may be mistaken for a Canadian, but it's worth it. Reserve is more often considered a sign of strength and status than of weakness.

(8) Try to speak the language (you'll never learn otherwise). Most people will appreciate it and try to help, the French a possible exception.

(9) Remember what anthropologists have learned: there are no superior or inferior cultures. Only different ones.

A DECISION POINT

In addition to the temptation to criticize, the other great danger is that, caught in culture shock, many Americans consider returning home. Arriving at this first threshold of decision is not peculiar to Americans, but common to all settlers new to a foreign country. For those who do give up, the justifications and hardships endured can often be greatly magnified.

Australian demographer W. T. Appleyard once made a study of a shipload of former settlers on their way home. He pointed out that once aboard ship the actual failure itself seemed to bother people little. Most were occupied with trying to develop plausible stories to tell friends and relatives when they got back home. A follow-up study of the same group a year later found that the reasons they gave then for their failure were radically different from the original reasons cited aboard ship. The truth about failure is apparently seldom to be had for the asking.

At this decision point, the peculiar independence of Americans is likely to be a disadvantage. Unlike Cortez' strategy for getting his soldiers to move forward (he burned the boats they landed in), most Americans when they go to a new country don't burn their boats, their bridges, or anything else, and wisely so.

An American Jew, an attractive dark woman in her late thirties,

who holds Israeli as well as American citizenship, said: "Our generation will always keep a foot in each camp just as long as we can. That's
why I keep the passport. I know I can always go back if things don't
work out, or if something goes wrong. That could always happen
here."

Even faced with less volatile environments, most Americans keep
a ready reserve of justifications pretty close to the surface, "in case
things don't work out." But migration specialist Professor William
Barnard of Brooklyn College believes this reserved commitment may
hinder the successful settlement of many Americans in other countries:

> Most Americans, unlike Yugoslavs or Greeks, have a few thousand
> dollars tucked away somewhere. When the first crunch comes, instead of
> taking a breath, catching their second wind, and pressing on, there is a
> greater temptation for Americans to toss it in. Just buy an airplane ticket
> and take off.

REASSESSMENT

Provided the person caught by culture shock can successfully move
past this first threshold of decision, at some point the depression will
"bottom out," followed by a several-month period of, if not the agony
and disorientation of culture shock, at least painful difficulty.

Sociologist and former Peace Corps staff member Maurice Sill
studied what happens to Peace Corps volunteers after their low point.
Sill noted that in most Peace Corps volunteers it occurred at an
average time of four months. It was followed by a several-month
period of realignment.

During this period of realignment a person reassesses himself totally. His skills, his expectations, his values, all come under scrutiny,
even if the scrutiny is less than formal. Most Peace Corps volunteers,
as do most Americans new to a country, tend to overvalue what they
can do or contribute in a given amount of time. They expect too much
of themselves.

This period of reassessment is the slow turning upward from the
depths of culture shock. It is still a period of frustration and setbacks,
probably the most difficult time in any country.

But Sill found about the eighth month that volunteers' work seemed
to take on new value, and they slowly began to participate in life.
Satisfaction with life in a new country seems to increase once the
period of culture shock is passed.

SECOND TIME AROUND

Sometime between two and three years abroad most Americans observe a second threshold of decision. It is more subtle than the plunge into culture shock. The resultant soul-searching may be more probing than earlier. For by this time there are few novelties about living abroad. There are new routines, new obligations. The question now becomes: Do we really want to stick it out? For a businessman or technician, the growing realization that he may be "out of touch" with his profession or with life in America nags at this point. The feeling of never being able to fit in again in the United States "if we don't go back soon" troubles some families considerably. If the earlier expectations are unrealized, the language improperly learned, the temptation to return is maximized. Often the decision point is emphasized by the expiration of an overseas-assignment contract. At this second threshold of decision, many Americans return home, wiser and with a broader outlook, only to experience the initial elation-depression syndrome brought on by being back in America.

A very successful American in his mid-thirties, former vice-president of a London advertising firm, went through an almost classic progression of thoughts. "When we first arrived in London we were tremendously excited. The whole idea of being here—the architecture, the quaintness, the theater, the night life. Then after a few months it began to wear off. We began to see the seediness. And the weather really is terrible. Just after we were here two years I felt a pressure inside to make a decision. We had grown very accustomed to London by this time, but there was this pull to go back. I finally looked it in the face, decided we were going to go back eventually anyway, and it might as well be now."

People who don't go back to the United States at this second threshold generally experience some sort of a recommitment, either to their work or to their adopted country, and plunge deeper into the identity stage of acculturation.

Skip Leavitt, an American, gave up managing Don the Beachcomber's in Honolulu to take a sight-unseen job managing a safari lodge in Tanzania. The sound of it would be hard for anyone to resist, but Skip found himself in for several tough years of isolation and loneliness. When the second threshold of doubt came, Skip was lucky enough to have the choice made for him.

It was marvelous fun for a while, but a couple of years ago the bush began to lose its attraction, and I wanted out. However, I was in so deep that I couldn't get out without taking a blow. So the only thing I could do was try to expand. . . . My partner and I found an old abandoned German fort in the middle of nowhere. I forgot about the yen for civilization and poured myself into that fort . . . it cost twice as much as planned and took twice as long to build as forecast. But we are open. Just. Out here you are standing on your own two feet, and no fooling about it. You aren't having a salary socked away in the USA by AID or Aramco or Benevolence Inc. You make a mistake, and too bad. Nobody but nobody is going to send you a Social Security check. That's half the kick. Doing it on your own.

When an American begins talking that way, acculturation may not be complete, but there are few surprises left for which he is unprepared.

FINDING OUT MORE

Edward T. Hall. *The Silent Language*. Doubleday, 1959. Not about language at all, but about the whole subject of culture. Examples from foreign countries and American Indians. Hall, an anthropologist, was director of training for the State Department's Point Four Program during the 1950's. Available in a Fawcett Premier paperback.

Clyde Kluckhohn. *Mirror for Man: Anthropology for Modern Life*. McGraw-Hill, 1949. An easy-to-read primer about some of the aspects of culture anyone going abroad will face—customs, race, language, and personality.

Charles Wagley. *The Latin American Tradition*. Columbia University, 1968. Professor Wagley, an anthropologist who heads Columbia's Institute of Latin-American Studies, calls this a book of essays on Latin-American culture. He is modest. Along with Frank Tannenbaum's earlier work, *Ten Keys to Latin America,* Wagley has identified and discussed a number of the different elements of culture that can be found in any Latin country, such as the role of the church, the place of the rising middle class, and so forth. A good first book about Latin America.

Ernest Dunbar. *The Black Expatriates*. Dutton, 1968. Interviews with sixteen black Americans living in Europe and Africa. More than a book about acculturation problems for black Americans, it deals with many of the nuances of cultural difference that strike any American living in another culture.

John Bainbridge. *Another Way of Living*. Holt, 1968. *Playboy*-like interviews with a number of Americans living in Europe, the majority at the high end of the scale. Most of the interviews are with an older breed of American abroad, but worthwhile for anyone, especially those thinking of moving to Europe.

John Ney. *The European Surrender.* Little, Brown, 1970. Ney has written a witty, sharp, sarcastic book using as a "departure point," as he would call it, the idea that all Europe has surrendered culturally and economically to America. Lots of snippets of how other cultures react to American and Americans, and some of the things that irritate Americans abroad who can never forget their cultural "superiority."

Ludovic Kennedy. *Very Lovely People.* Simon and Schuster, 1969. A British writer, Kennedy subtitles his book "A Personal Look at Some Americans Living Abroad." Not exactly an exposé à la *The Ugly American,* but his anecdotal look at Americans living in Asia, the Far East, and Africa at least takes us off the well-worn "look-at-Americans-in-Europe" track.

MINOR ADJUSTMENTS
Time, Weather, and Climate

TIME

In a move to a new place, the reaction to time change is fleeting. It will usually affect only your first few days in a place, seldom more than a week.

If you travel by ship, the adjustment to time change is more or less automatic, your mental clock resetting itself with the comparative slowness of the ship's movement. Even long hops north and south by jet cause little reaction, since you remain in a single band of time. Board a plane at 8:00 P.M. in New York, fly south for ten hours to Lima, and you would step out of your plane at 9:00 A.M. without resetting your watch; dinner in New York, breakfast in Peru without a break in the rhythm of your day.

Some people find that this quickness of stepping from one culture to another has other disconcerting effects. One State Department staff officer, a woman in her mid-fifties, said she always preferred to move to a new assignment by the ambling slowness of ship. "It gives my mind a chance to slip the hold of the former country and begin preparing for the new," she said.

The most jarring time changes occur in jet flights east and west. Here one crosses time zones with impunity. Flying west, you race along with the sun, clock time scarcely advancing at all while your body ticks along at the time of your departure point. Fly east, and the sun is left rapidly behind (or you move rapidly toward it), and you find that night or day appears before you are physically or mentally prepared for it.

Long jumps east or west set your body out of phase with the clock time of your new locale. Experienced jet travelers recognize this "jet lag," which leaves you wide-eyed and staring at 3:00 A.M. and yawning at afternoon tea. Some people experience more difficulty flying east, since you arise those first few days at an absurdly early hour as far as your body and mind are concerned. Flying west, it is simply a problem of keeping your eyes open later in the evening, which for most people is the preferable choice.

There is no way to prevent some reaction to time change. The single trick of the long-distance air traveler is this: immediately upon boarding the aircraft, set your watch to the time of the place you are going. For some inexplicable reason, the mind begins to accept that time, adjusting itself to the new rhythm of night and day.

A possible problem associated with time change is the distortion in judgment and perception that often attends lack of sleep, the exhaustion that seems to accompany long-distance jet travel, and the possible temptation to drink too much when tired or tense.

One top-level sales engineer for McDonald-Douglas who spends much of his time visiting clients around the world has a firm rule he adheres to, no matter the temptation: put off making any important decisions for the first forty-eight hours in a place. Things never look as urgent after two days as they do during the first two hours.

Added to the probability that your perceptions of a place will change during the first few days is the tendency most people have in a new locale to push themselves harder than is really necessary. The urge to "get things moving" is hard to resist. One man in his early fifties with a long string of government assignments abroad to his record said it took him many years to realize that he didn't have to solve *all* his problems in his first few days on a new assignment.

The best advice for dealing with time change is to plan on giving yourself two or three days of doing nothing in a new place when you arrive. Walk a lot, since there is no better way to get the "feel" of a place, and sleep as much as you can. It's a nice way to begin.

GETTING USED TO THE WEATHER

Until the mid-1940's, when the scientific research engendered by World War II proved otherwise, a wide range of doctors, scientists, historians, and engineers believed that climate and weather had an ironlike grip on where man lived on earth and how.

During the early part of the century a cascade of books and articles was published as variations on the theme of climate and evolution, or climate and history, even an article about the effects of climate on the Lincoln-Douglas debates titled "Weather as Destiny." S. F. Markham's *Climate and the Energy of Nations,* published in 1941, went through two best-selling editions in England. Ellsworth Huntington's intriguing book *Mainsprings of Civilization* was one of the last great testaments to these "climatic determinists' " point of view—that climate and weather were the determining influences on the activities of man. "If it is a life of indolent ease he desires [a man] should head for tropical heat where that kind of existence prevails naturally." This kindly advice might well have been offered in 1842, instead of a hundred years later by a widely read climatic determinist, Dr. Willis Miles (M.D.), whose books can be found in many libraries today. What Dr. Miles would have said, had he been caught in the midday rush in downtown Singapore or Panama City, is hard to imagine.

While the climatic determinists stated their case, the Marxist geographers were busy proving the other extreme—that climate and weather are always subordinate to science and man—even while they did note that it was easier to grow tomatoes in the Ukraine than north of the arctic circle.

Both schools of thought have their measure of truth. Climate and weather do affect man, though not nearly as absolutely as once thought. And undoubtedly technology has allowed man to live and be active in climatic environments thought uninhabitable a hundred years ago, as is evidenced by the usefulness of air-conditioning, irrigation that has turned desert into lush agricultural areas, and new blends of fabrics that have made man better able to endure heat or cold.

The single overwhelming fact about human adjustment to radically different physical environments is this: physiologists have demonstrated that the healthy human body adjusts itself rather efficiently to changes in heat, cold, and altitude.

Such acclimatization eventually requires adjustment in the functioning of nearly all the body's systems, primarily the endocrine, circulatory, respiratory, and nervous systems. While the adjustment is taking place, the individual is likely to be in for one or more discomforts that may include constipation or diarrhea, shortness of breath, uncommon thirst, profuse perspiring, drowsiness, decreased or increased appetite, mental depression or anxiety, and a number of other minor symptoms that vary with the individual.

But the adjustments the body makes begin immediately in a new climatic environment, and proceed automatically. There are some people who are "weather sensitive" and physiologically cannot adjust to drastic changes in their physical environment. In such cases, "I can't take the heat" or "I'll never get used to this cold weather" are physiologically honest appraisals rather than simply nagging complaints.

For most other newcomers, all they need do is be patient, knowing that their immediate discomfort is transient. For most people, acclimatization is only a matter of time.

TAKING THE HEAT

The human body adjusts most easily to heat. In a hot climate the process of acclimatization is well under way in from four to six days, even if the individual is exposed to the heat for only a few hours a day, which might be the case with people living and working in air-conditioned surroundings.

A number of things happen to the body: the blood vessels dilate so that more blood is exposed to the cooling power of the air; the sweat glands become more active; there is a slow increase in the total blood supply of the body, while the body, having less need to heat itself, consumes less oxygen. But within two weeks these adjustments are virtually complete. The critical period is the first three days, when people tend to overextend themselves in any case. Physiologists have proved that drinking large quantities of water to avoid dehydration and taking salt both help the body acclimate itself.

Contrary to myth, physiologists (Blum and others) have noted that black people do not adapt more easily to hot environments than white people. The increased amount of melanin pigment in their skin makes dark-skinned people less susceptible to sunburn and skin cancer. But the functioning of the body systems during the acclimatization process are the same.

Physical comfort in a hot climate is a function of what climatologists call "sensible temperature." This is how a place feels to you, rather than what the thermometer indicates it should feel. Anyone who has spent time in the desert has sooner or later experienced the shock of looking at a thermometer nudging 100 while feeling surprisingly comfortable. The reverse phenomenon is the muggy spring day with temperatures in the mid-seventies when you never felt more uncomfortable.

Since your body's cooling system depends principally on the evaporation of perspiration from your skin, a low "sensible temperature" depends on how well that system is able to work. In places of high humidity, evaporation works slowly; in dry areas it works more efficiently. The expression "it isn't the heat, it's the humidity" is closer to truth than falsehood. A high humidity combined with a high temperature puts you in real physical discomfort.

On the basis of "sensible temperature" alone, some climatic areas are more pleasant to live in than others, at least at certain times of the year. The pleasantness of the Hawaiian Islands and a number of other tropical and semitropical environments is due in large part to the prevailing trade winds, which aid the body's cooling, keeping the "sensible temperature" low. Desert areas tend to have lower "sensible temperatures" than their high summer temperatures might indicate. The point is that there is more to the comfort of a climate than just high or low temperatures. But relative comfort has little to do with acclimatization; your body makes its "neurotropic" changes in any case.

COLD

It takes the human body longer to adjust to cold than to heat, but not much. Adjusting completely to a cold climate can take anywhere from two weeks to two months, depending on the individual. A number of things that the body did to acclimate itself to heat now go through the reverse process. Blood vessels constrict, and the blood thickens and moves more slowly. To provide more body heat, the appetite may increase and the consumption of oxygen grow; shivering is an attempt the body makes to produce more heat.

Newcomers to a cold climate should pay attention also to the "chill factor" created by wind. Essentially, each mile per hour of wind speed has the effect on the human body of an appreciable drop in temperature below that registered by the thermometer. For example, the chill factor of a 45-mph wind at a temperature of 20 F. has the effect of dropping the apparent temperature to about -20 F.

During acclimatization, special attention should be paid to clothing and dress. It is difficult to dress too warmly. Dampness of shoes or clothing should be avoided, since there is a tendency among those unacclimatized to cold to be slightly more susceptible to respiratory infection.

ALTITUDE

Adjustments to altitude take the longest time. Complete acclimatization may take up to six months. The physiologists Jungmann and Halhuber have noted that the body adjusts to altitude in fits and starts, moving from one level of equilibrium to another, with periods of time in between.

Adjusting to altitude has bothered people for centuries. The Spanish founded their first capital in the New World logically enough near their great silver discovery at Potosí, high in the Bolivian Andes, at an altitude of almost 14,000 feet. In addition to dizziness, shortness of breath, and odd tricks played by their digestion, the Spanish found that after their first year not a single child had been born. Leaving the mines to overseers and highland Indian slaves, they beat a course immediately for the more amenable site of Lima at sea level, where life returned to normal.

For most people there are few problems acclimating to altitudes below about 6,000 feet. At these levels most of the body's adjustments occur in the first month, although complete comfort still requires six months or so.

Above 6,000 feet, acclimatization is a longer, more difficult process. The greatest danger of adjustment to high altitude is likely to be for those with heart trouble. At high altitudes there is a slow increase in the hemoglobin content of the blood. The blood becomes thicker. With the body's need to take in more air and process it through the lungs to take needed oxygen into the blood, the heart may find itself abnormally busy. Anyone considering residence or prolonged travel in countries with even modest altitudes should take the precaution of having a thorough physical, with special attention to the condition of the heart. There are four capital cities in the Western Hemisphere at elevations more than 6,000 feet: Mexico City, Quito, La Paz, and Bogotá.

Over about 12,000 feet the unacclimated body goes through a struggle. There are no permanent human habitations at all above 18,000 feet; many Andean Indians work regularly at altitudes of 14,000 and 15,000 feet, although they have the advantage of a lifetime of acclimatization.

Above 12,000 feet even the most simple acts, such as climbing a flight of stairs, are enervating, and there is a good chance of some form of mountain sickness occurring. In his classic work on altitude sicknesses, the Ecuadorian doctor Carlos Monge noted that they were all directly due to the deficiency of oxygen at high altitudes. Monge called such mountain sickenss *"la enfermedad de los Andes."*

Americans who move to places of moderately high altitude find by necessity a change in the rhythm of their lives. Most learn to control their physical activities to prevent exhaustion, most important during the early months of residence. Most tend to drink less alcohol than they used to because of the rapidity with which it enters the bloodstream and reaches the brain. At 10,000 feet a single bottle of beer is

likely to bring on giddiness. Digestion proceeds at a slower rate with
an increase in altitude, and Americans even in Mexico City generally
adopt the habit of eating the major meal in the middle of the day and
a light snack for dinner.

ADJUSTING TO A DIFFERENT CLIMATE

The physiological adjustments our body makes to acclimatize itself to
a new environment fortunately happen without our conscious effort.
A little more attention to eating regularly, getting enough exercise
without overdoing it, and proper rest, and the human body adjusts
itself. The discomforts in any case are, for most of us, passing.

The mental adjustment to an entirely different climatic setting is
less automatic, and is for many people the more serious challenge. The
thing to keep in mind is that most people can adjust to living in a new
climatic environment, even as radically different as Alaska from Hong
Kong, with no mental or physical ill effect. The solution is wanting
to.

Initially, the mental adjustment to a new climate may be bound up
in the general problem of cultural adjustment and culture shock.

The Swedes, for example, have noted that the southern Europeans
who have moved to Sweden to take high-paying factory jobs seem to
experience trouble getting used to Sweden's long dark winters, when
there may be only a few hours of full sunlight during the day. Yet few
Italians or Greeks give up the higher wages and other delights of
Sweden to return home.

In England I've talked to newly arrived Americans, especially those
from the western United States, and Australians, who become terribly
depressed by their first damp, gray English winter. The depression is
sometimes caused equally by culture shock, but a drab winter can
seem to compound every problem. The harm is seldom lasting. The
Americans that choose to remain in England eventually become very
much like the British in at least one respect; they talk about the
weather constantly but seldom really pay much attention to it.

Invariably the nostalgia for things American that accompanies culture shock involves remembrances of the climate or weather of the
former locale. In this respect, there is no single climate in the world
that is "better" than any other. Some may have more sunshine, softer
yearly temperature changes, more or less rain, or even stimulating
extreme daily changes. But it's the weather we're used to that counts,
as odious to outsiders as it may appear.

One American on the lush tropical island of Ponape in the Caroline Islands told me, while relaxing in one of the most idyllic tropical environments I'd ever seen, that he missed his native eastern Pennsylvania. He missed the yearly change in the seasons more than anything else in the United States. Sometimes it is not strictly the weather and climate of a place that cause adjustment problems, but other aspects associated with temperature, humidity, and rainfall.

One American housewife in Panama said she couldn't stand the place because of the weather. Between mid-December and the first of May, Panama City experiences a warm, clear, breezy season that most Americans find quite pleasant. It is followed by seven or eight months of rain for a period each day, totaling some eighty inches a year. On closer questioning, however, it turned out that the housewife was bothered most by the stale mustiness of clothing and linens during the rainy season, and the forming of mildew on shoes in the closet.

Once I heard a Peace Corps desk officer remark, only half in jest, that he had a suggestion for the screening of staff prior to assignment to any tropical post. He proposed a test to see how people reacted to cockroaches, rats, and a variety of other "creepy-crawlies," adding: "That's really what bothers them the most, the wives especially. All those things that crawl around."

A great deal of research on adjustment to tropical environments has been made by the U.S. Army. One of the first things that must be pointed out is that tropical regions are no more physically unhealthy than any other region. Certain classes of diseases are associated with hot climates, dry climates, and cold climates, but with proper immunization the overriding considerations are a person's own susceptibilities, diet, and personal contacts. A doctor on Yap, originally from Indiana, said he believed as a whole that the people were healthier than in his home town. They suffered a little tuberculosis, he said, and almost universally from intestinal worms because of their bad health habits. But there was no trace of degenerative heart disease, nor did he often find the need to perform major surgical operations.

The myth of mental decay in the tropics has been around for a long time, thanks in part to the climatic determinists, partly to a number of writers who have found decay marketable (as are tropical settings), and partly because some people do "go around the bend" in hot places, as they do in cold ones. After extensive research on Americans living in tropical environments, about the only conclusion the U.S. Army came to was that people who had prior problems—mental, marital, or whatever—find that they tend to become more intensified in tropical environments.

Of course, many of these tropical environments also have the added temptation of inexpensive alcohol or the liabilities of a confining social environment, and sometimes an absolute limit of space. "Island fever" is a fairly common experience of many Americans, especially those who have spent long periods of time on atolls. At some point, people feel a need to get out. Strictly speaking, however, maladjustments can't be blamed on the weather.

As a general rule, adjustments to climate, weather, and their attendant irritations tend to become critical only when other aspects of life in a country are going poorly.

Then five days of steady rain, two weeks of staring at the same cloudy sky, or mice-sized cockroaches skittering across a kitchen floor are apt to drive even the most even-tempered of Americans abroad to curse themselves, their situation, and everyone within reach. If it happens to you, go ahead. It's probably good therapy, and you're not the first.

FINDING OUT MORE

About places

There is no substitute for the perceptions of place gathered first-hand. It is possible to get an inkling about what a place is like via books, maps, and atlases. Maps particularly have the capacity to conjure up visions of places that even well-written novels sometimes fail to do. I say beware on this particular score because I have been more susceptible to the lure of maps than most.

R. R. Bowker. *Reference Guide for Travelers.* A guide to other travel guides. An expensive book, best used in a library. May be found in a librarian's own personal collection of reference books. Generally, because of their bias toward entertaining, travel books may not be the ideal source of information about any country. The single guide I can recommend without reservation is:

Andrew Marshall. *The South American Handbook.* An English publication revised yearly. Available in the United States at many bookstores and by mail from: the Hammond Map Store, 1 East 43rd Street, New York, N.Y. 10017. Price $6.95; add postage. They are also distributors of the top-quality Michelin road maps of Europe and Africa, and also the superior Swiss Hallwag road maps of Europe.

They will mail anywhere in the United States and have catalogs available.

The most impressive vendor of maps in the world is Stanfords, a London firm who will send maps by mail order to the United States. An initial query letter is recommended, stating the area you want and the intended purpose of the map. They will answer the query with a list of maps available and quote a price. First-class selection. Conscientious. Stanfords, 12–14 Long Acre, London W.C.2, England.

Another source of maps is: American Geographical Society, Broadway at 156th Street, New York, N.Y. 10032. They publish a number of flat maps of the world, and distribute sheets of the International Map of the World project for Hispanic America, at a scale of 1:1,000,000 (about one inch on the map to sixteen miles on the earth). A useful series if you know exactly where you are going and want to understand the lay of the land. Ask the A.G.S. for the catalog "List of Publications." They also publish a monthly bulletin, *Focus,* which treats separately in each issue a country of current interest, mainly the geographic and historic background. A good introduction to a country. Back issues available. Subscription is $3.50 per year.

Also: National Geographic Society, Washington, D.C. 20036. The society produces a number of regional maps measuring 25 " × 19" for a dollar each, postpaid, and a number of wall maps of specific countries for two dollars, plus another dollar if an index is desired. Write for their "Publication Order List."

About Climate and Weather

David Blumenstock. *The Ocean of Air.* Rutgers University Press, 1959. Popular introductions to climatology, which is essentially the study of the effect of climate and weather on man. Blumenstock's book is perhaps the most readable, with clear explanations about what causes different climates, and some of the influences of climate on man's activities.

Glenn Trewartha. *Introduction to Climate.* McGraw-Hill, 1964. A standard introductory textbook on the subject—more on the scientific nature of climate than its effect on man. Trewartha has also written an outline on climates called *Climates of the World* in a newspaper-sized format and priced under a dollar. It deals mainly with the different types of climate around the world and their characteristics. Useful.

Howard Critchfield. *General Climatology.* Prentice-Hall, 1966. Another introductory textbook, but with a good deal more information about weather and about the effects of climate and weather on man.

Professor Trewartha has also edited *Goodes World Atlas,* published by Rand McNally. Better atlases have maps that do more than show you where a place is. They have maps that show the shape of the land through shading or color, and that show patterns of climate and vegetation. Using such maps you can begin to pin down what a place is really like. I mention *Goodes World Atlas* because it is one of the less expensive quality atlases available, under $10. Rand McNally also publishes an abridged version of the *Goodes Atlas* with a selection of maps from the larger edition, selling for a few dollars. For years I've carried one in my suitcase when traveling.

About Health

R. T. Atkins and J. Atkins. *The World Traveler's Medical Guide.* Simon and Schuster, 1958. The most popular of the books about how to keep healthy in other parts of the world, including names and addresses of places where you can get medical help in each country. The textual sections can be relied upon, but the names and addresses are dated.

Patrick Doyle and James Banta. *How to Travel the World and Stay Healthy.* Acropolis Books, 1969. Not as comprehensive as the above, but the style and racy format make it easier to read.

Health Hints for the Tropics. The American Society of Tropical Medicine and Hygiene. Available from: The Editor, Tropical Medicine and Hygiene News, National Institute of Health, Bethesda, Maryland 20014. Price fifty cents. Currently in its sixth edition, this thirty-page pamphlet is up-to-date on the latest information on the expanding field of tropical medicine. Good sections on skin diseases and stomach problems.

Intermedic Inc. 777 Third Avenue, New York, N.Y. 10017. An organization that has capitalized on one of those questions that gnaw at Americans going abroad, but which they seldom do anything about: What happens if I get sick? Intermedic publishes a directory of participating physicians in 100 cities in 55 countries who are well-qualified, speak English, will respond to your call, and will charge a guaranteed fee for an initial visit. The directory and a yearly membership is available for $5 personal membership, $9 family membership. Write to them directly for a brochure.

Kevin M. Cahill. *Medical Advice for the Traveler.* Holt, Rinehart and Winston, 1970. Cahill's book is brief (eighty pages), sensible, and makes a neat, lazy man's introduction to medical problems abroad. Strong emphasis on the special health problems of the tropics. Has the most reasonable suggested list of medicines for a traveler to take along.

James P. Carter, M.D., and Elenora de Antonio West. *Keeping Your Family Healthy Overseas.* Lippincott, 1971. Two people with considerable experience living abroad have put together probably the best book of its type. Strays a little far from the straight medical problems into mental health, cultural adjustment, schooling, and so forth. Talks about such realistic problems as "what do I do about getting the Pill?" Good sections on food, hygiene.

LIVING ABROAD AMERICAN STYLE
What Will It Cost Me?

We may be boxed in by the spurious precision of numbers.

— WILBUR ZELINSKY

One well-known American trait further complicates settling easily into another culture. Most Americans tend to measure their standard of living purely in concrete terms. The size of a house instead of its physical comfort. Their automobiles, clothes, appliances, as proof of the quality of their life. A job's salary instead of the nature of the work.

Our preoccupation with material things as the measure of standard of living frustrates many foreigners who deal with Americans.

"It's the hardest thing to explain," said one foreign consular officer. "People come here wanting to know about my country. The first thing they ask is how much everything costs, a new car or a washing machine, for example. When I tell them, they look surprised because they're so expensive. I try to explain that many things you have here we do without, and it makes no difference. Most Americans don't really understand that."

A Brazilian girl returning to Rio after two years in the United States admitted the kitchens in America impressed her the most. In Brazil she had seen such kitchens only in the apartments of the very rich. She adored the kitchens in America. But she was going back to Rio because she missed its excitement. In the United States life was *chata,* life was dull.

Measuring our standard of living in terms of objects prevails. The American Institute of Public Opinion (the Gallup poll) measures standard of living by "what people can buy and do," using as indicators the ownership of material goods such as television sets, radios, automobiles, and washing machines. A 1970 feature article in *Time* magazine warned Americans moving abroad to be prepared for a 10 percent drop in standard of living, then went on to define standard of living mainly as the cost of consumer goods.

We remain the one nation on earth that most thoroughly confuses the price of things and their ownership with how well people live. Seldom do we consider that a high standard of living might be based on the qualitative aspects of life as well.

AN EXPENSIVE WAY TO LIVE

Pursuit of an American-style standard of living turns out to be extraordinarily expensive in most other countries.

Outside of the United States, with perhaps the single exception of Canada, manufactured goods we take for granted are often considered luxury items. New automobiles, TV sets, giant refrigerators, garbage disposals, even inexpensive ready-made clothing. A British consular official living in the United States thought an electric toothbrush quite an unusual "necessity."

We are the most dependent of any nation upon the automobile. The planners of mass transit in this country recognize that most Americans are reluctant to sacrifice independence of movement in their own auto despite the prospect of faster, less expensive, effortless transport by bus, monorail, or train. The term "mass transit" itself rings of travel as part of the herd. Behind the wheel of our own car at least we retain control of a portion of our destiny; and sacrifice it by choice —never. But our love of the automobile is spreading. Drive on the Continent during August, and it seems as though all Europe is motorized, returning lemminglike to the shores of the Mediterranean. Despite this impression, few Europeans would consider a new automobile anything but a luxury. In the United Kingdom, only four families in ten have an automobile; in Uruguay, only one in ten. In such countries the idea of a car for the wife and perhaps another for a teen-age son for most people would be an unthinkable waste of money.

For good reason. In proportion to income, automobiles outside of the United States are prohibitively expensive. Auto prices in Brazil are the lowest in South America, yet a Brazilian-made Volkswagen is half again the price of an imported Volkswagen in the United States. In Chile, a three-year-old Chevrolet in average condition might be worth the equivalent of $7,000. In many countries it is not uncommon to find automobiles fifteen and twenty years old in near-mint condition, well maintained because people realize that they could never afford a new one.

In Bombay a successful salesman told me how lucky he had been to find a twelve-year-old Ford Anglia for sale. Price—$800, about four months' wages. Even in Australia automobiles and large appliances cost more than in the United States. One American wrote from Australia that the overall cost of living was lower, "but not as 'lower' as it ought to be." In comparison with wages, it wasn't lower at all.

In England the British watch the "telly" as much as most Americans. Yet the price of a TV set in London is about double that in New York City, and seldom would a family consider more than one a necessity.

For an American moving abroad, finding a house or apartment to match an American-style "standard of living" is exceedingly difficult. High rent may be only the first shock.

Renting is not a widespread practice outside the United States. It is a phenomenon seemingly popular only in a society mobile enough to move itself around every two or three years, a luxury many other cultures have yet to experience.

In an inflationary economy, renting is bad economics, unless you are a landlord. Most people buy houses or apartments or even automobiles as a hedge against inflation, knowing their price is likely to rise.

The most difficult places in the world to obtain American-style apartments are the boom towns of developing countries: Conakry, Lagos, Caracas, São Paulo, and a dozen other cities. Cities with large numbers of new immigrants share the rental pinch—Sydney, for example, or Salisbury (Rhodesia), or Jerusalem.

In Australia and New Zealand the difficulty in finding a place to rent is created by the custom of most people buying their own homes. In Australia, buying a home is something aimed at shortly after marriage. About 70 percent of Australians own their own homes or are paying them off with the help of mortgages or hire-purchase, the Commonwealth equivalent of installment buying.

In major cities, where renting is more available, the prices may be out of all proportion to other costs within the country. Most people in other countries expect to spend a higher proportion of their income on housing than do Americans, not uncommonly a third to a half.

A survey prepared by *Business Week* warned businessmen moving abroad of what it might cost to equal their Stateside accommodations. A two-bedroom unfurnished apartment in a first-class neighborhood that might cost $200 per month in Houston, Texas, might run as follows: Milan—$325; São Paulo—$450; Paris—$400; Tokyo—$850.

Caterpillar Tractor Company, after going into partnership with a Japanese company, found the going market rate for apartments so unbelievably expensive, at $1,000 to $1,200 per month, that they bought and furnished their own apartment unit for their executives, renting them back to them below the market value.

Apartments appointed to American standard are rare at any price. In England and the Continent, most apartments are rented not only unfurnished, but plucked clean—bare floorboards, no light fixtures, and fittings protruding from kitchen walls instead of a stove and refrigerator.

American Jews immigrating to Israel encounter a similar problem. If able to find an apartment at all, many are surprised by the smallness of what Israelis consider standard: three small bedrooms, plus kitchen and dining room and small bathroom, totaling perhaps one thousand square feet of floor space. Americans who plan far enough ahead to have apartments built for them find Israeli architects still unable to grasp the idea of building more than one bathroom or adding built-in closets.

Often there are additional costs beyond rent. In Paris there is frequently a demand for "key money," a lump cash payment often of several thousand dollars for the privilege of renting a particular apartment at all. Londoners are used to paying "rates" on top of rent, a combination of borough tax and fee for cold water. In any Latin country, a building or a cluster of private homes will have a *portero,* something between a handyman and a guard. His salary will officially be paid by all tenants who share his services. Unofficially, an additional periodic gratuity is needed to assure vigilance or, since he sees all, perhaps his continued discretion.

In most places telephones are a definite luxury. The thought of being able to request a telephone and have it installed in a few days' time for a modest fee is strictly an American luxury. Rio de Janciro for example, a city approaching four million people, has less than a half-million telephones. Even commercial enterprises may share their phone line with two, four, or even a half-dozen other customers. In Rio, a common misdemeanor is the tenant equipped with his own telephone and phone wire tapping into another person's phone connection and using it to make calls. Telephone numbers are sold or traded like apartments or houses.

As a general rule, renting accommodations of American standard in any major city in the world will cost more than the equivalent Stateside.

DIPS AND BUSINESSMEN

Perhaps the most persistent in seeking to reproduce American-style living outside of the United States are the employees of the U.S. government assigned abroad (with the exception of Peace Corps volunteers) and top-level American businessmen, often on two- and three-year assignments.

For the benefit of the State Department and American business, the U.S. Department of Labor each year in October prepares an index rating what it costs, in their words, to "transplant" an "American pattern of living" to a number of foreign cities.

The index figures given each city are based on the comparative cost of food, clothing, furniture, medical care, and recreation, but excluding the cost of housing and schooling. Also taken into account as necessary to transplant an American abroad are such factors as the need to hire domestic help, buying "additional food because of spoilage from humid weather or unsanitary handling," and the purchase of additional clothing to replace those articles ruined by harsh drycleaning methods.

According to the Department of Labor's index, of the ten most expensive cities in the world for an American to transplant his pattern of living, seven were capitals of black African countries, with Conakry, Guinea, at the top of the list. Using Washington, D.C., as the standard, with an index number of 100, Conakry was pegged at 170.

Only two European capitals were in the top ten, Paris and Stockholm, although the Department of Labor considered quite a number of cities abroad more expensive for an American to live in than Washington D.C.

LIVING LIKE AN AMERICAN ABROAD:
The Comparative Cost in Some Selected Cities

Paris	145	Montreal	103
Nice	127	WASHINGTON, D.C.	100
Stockholm	127	Salisbury	98
Tokyo	121	Lisbon	98
Caracas	119	Canberra	97
Copenhagen	119	Manila	97
Monrovia	119	Singapore	97
Milan	117	Buenos Aires	95
Brussels	115	Hong Kong	95
Madrid	115	Johannesburg	94
Rome	115	Dublin	92
Geneva	110	San José	91
Tel Aviv	110	Rio de Janeiro	89
London	108	Mexico City	88
Kingston	106	Istanbul	81
Athens	105	Wellington	79

Source: U.S. Department of Labor

Using the Department of Labor's calculations, the cost of living American-style in another country ranged from nowhere less than about 75 percent of what it would cost to live in Washington, D.C., up to 70 percent more in the case of Conakry.

As a side note, the United Nations compiles a similar index for assigning pay differentials to U.N. officials sent around the world. This U.N. index also rated Conakry as the most expensive city for a foreigner to live in, but only about 15 percent more expensive than Washington, D.C.

The United Nations finds Paris no more expensive for a U.N. official than Washington, both receiving the exact same rating on the U.N. index. Both were considered much less costly than trying to live in New York City. Additionally, the U.N. classified Athens, London, Nairobi, Beirut, and Bangkok all less expensive for U.N. personnel than living in Washington D.C. The Department of Labor thought Americans living in each would spend considerably more.

A conclusion that might be drawn is that it costs more to transplant an American who intends to take his "pattern of living" with him to many foreign countries than it does a Swede, Swiss, or Turk. A corollary of this is often that the poorer the country, the more expensive it is to reproduce an American-style standard of living.

LIVING POOR

Of course, Americans can make a downward adjustment in what it costs them to live abroad. Peace Corps volunteers are a good example. The idea that Peace Corps volunteers are all young people fresh out of college living around the world in mud huts is an image the public-affairs division of the Peace Corps has been trying to eliminate for years. An increasing number of volunteers aren't recent college grads at all, but experienced teachers, businessmen, and skilled workers, running the gamut of age up into the sixty-year-olds.

Volunteers are supposed to live at the level of the people they work with, which for a schoolteacher in East Africa or a graduate MBA on assignment in Venezuela might be quite comfortable, though never extravagant.

The Peace Corps has considerable experience in accurately budgeting the costs for an American to live in local circumstances. Volunteers receive no salary while in the field; a cost-of-living allowance is paid them according to local needs. From this allowance volunteers are expected to pay for housing, food, clothing, and the miscellaneous costs of living (of which dry cleaning is seldom considered a necessity).

In fifty of the sixty-three countries where volunteers were assigned in mid-1970, the cost-of-living allowances were between $100 and $200 per month. In only two countries did they exceed $200 per month; in eleven others volunteers lived comfortably at the level of the people on less than $100 per month.

At perhaps a happy medium between diplomat and Peace Corps volunteer, the American Institute of Public Opinion has long been interested in what it costs the average family to live in the United States and abroad. A recent poll in the United States determined the needs of a family of four living modestly ranged from $126 to $148 per week. In Brazil, a local family of four needed the equivalent of $77 per week; in Great Britain, $66; in Greece, $56; in the Netherlands, $51; in Uruguay, $53; in West Germany, $82.

One reason families live cheaper abroad is that, in each country, balancing high costs for hard goods, automobiles, and housing, are

WHAT AN AMERICAN CAN EXPECT TO PAY ABROAD
(Expense of items compared with average cost in the United States)

Will Cost More	Will Cost Less
Automobiles	Fresh foods: local fruits, vegetables, meat, and fish (In some places, dairy products an exception)
Household appliances	
Canned and frozen foods	
Ready-made clothing	
Schooling fees	Public transportation
Rents	Public entertainment: movies, theaters, sporting events
Mortgage interest rates	
Imported alcoholic beverages, cigarettes	Tailoring and hand-made clothing
	Domestic help
Radio and TV sets, stereo equipment, phonograph records, and tapes	Auto repairs
	Neighborhood restaurants
	Domestically produced beer, wine, and spirits
Gasoline, oil, and tires	Holidays and vacations
Dry cleaning	Medical and dental fees (also drugs and medicines)
	Books, magazines, newspapers
	Personal services: shoe repairs, plumbers, carpentry, electricians, barbers, and beauticians

usually a number of bargains. With Scandinavia an exception, food usually costs less. In Australia, first-grade lamb chops sell for the equivalent of twenty-nine cents a pound. In Brazil, locally distilled Beefeater gin is about $1.30 a liter (larger than our quart). In Costa Rica, a full-time maid is paid $30 a month. The only rule of thumb most Americans living abroad learn quickly is, if it is imported it will be expensive.

In Mexico, French wines bought in a *supermercado* start at about $8 per bottle. Imported Scotch whisky in Japan retails for about $25 a fifth. A box of American cornflakes in Guam costs $1.50.

A MATTER OF ATTITUDE

Another reason people in other countries live more cheaply is by virtue of different attitudes toward life and money. Each society has its own social-status system, but it is seldom based strictly on money or the acquiring of material things. At one extreme, perhaps, is the attitude of Pacific islanders, who, though no longer living in moneyless subsistence economies, have still refused to accept possession of the dollar as the key to social success. The late Eugene Burdick, coauthor of *The Ugly American*, who knew Tahiti and the rest of the Society Islands well, once wrote of the system of status there: "It is nothing like an American knows. It rests on qualities of patience, ability to sing and dance, to cook well, to be understanding with children. An American's wealth and family position count for nothing. . . ." The Tahitians have a saying that sums up much of their attitude in a phrase: *ai'ta pupa, ai'ta mai-tai,* which roughly translated means if you're not a good lover you're worthless.

Americans who adjust most successfully to life in other countries are those doing something worthwhile, and who have slowly given up pursuit of a standard of living measured strictly in American terms.

Sometimes this adjustment in attitude involves a very real shrinking back of expenditure. An increasing number of Americans living abroad have neither high salaries nor highly subsidized ways of life. Those working for foreign employers, living in the foreign economy, learn to use their earnings more carefully, as have many retired persons in the United States. They cultivate a new attitude toward money.

A Frenchman once told me what he thought was the main difference between Americans and Europeans. An American, he said, spends his time worrying about earning money and little about how he spends it. A European ponders cautiously how he spends it, and cares less how he earns it.

One businessman in São Paulo, Brazil, now struggling with his own manufacturing company, went through a change of attitude not uncommon among Americans who live long overseas.

He had gone to Brazil as head of an American-owned beverage company at a dollar salary high in five figures. When he started his own company, he was barely able to take out one-tenth his former salary to live on, and he had the addition of a wife and new child. He still found his new life preferable to the old. "Suddenly I was forced to live like a Brazilian, which has its comforts. Before, I was an American living in Brazil. There's a difference."

An adjustment in viewpoint seldom means that such Americans must give up pursuit of a good life. Other nationalities enjoy life too, some almost embarrassingly so. A Japanese businessman frequently mixes business and pleasure, transacting as much business in the presence of food, good music, and the attendance of young ladies (all considered valid business expenses by the Japanese tax people) as he does in an office. Even then he may not separate the two. Once in Tokyo I was received by an energetic entrepreneur who ushered me to one corner of his office, which had been transformed into a rock garden with a small fountain, green plants, and low overstuffed furniture. The subtle mixture of the elements was instantly soothing. He admitted he often spent hours sitting in the garden listening to the water bubbling from the fountain, and that he often had his best ideas in such an environment.

Anyone who has lived in Spain has adjusted to the daily rhythm of a morning of work followed by four hours of food, rest, and the pleasures one enjoys in the middle of the day, then a few more hours of work, capped by a late meal. One invariably falls into bed aware of having lived a full day, one designed for people rather than commerce.

Nor does an adjustment in viewpoint mean that people in other countries forgo all things material. A Flemish bank clerk or a Venezuelan insurance salesman might give us all a demonstration in the energetic pursuit of material things. It means only that most Americans living in other countries for long periods of time no longer rely on numbers and objects as the sole measure of standard of living.

The qualitative aspects of life take on a new significance. The words *umbiente, joie de vivre,* and "flash" are all words without quantitative equivalents, yet to an Italian, Frenchman, or St. Lucian they are very real expressions about an attitude toward life.

Most Australians firmly believe their equable climate and life oriented to the out-of-doors is worth more than a mad scramble for a dollar, and they will tell you so.

An American living in Mexico, who considers himself lucky to have found work locally and a measure of acceptance, said: "The total hours I work are longer, and the pay is lower than I would earn in the United States. But people don't watch the clock here, either. And the style of living, for me, is superior . . . you spend all you earn, but you live well."

Learning to live well outside of the measures of an American-style standard of living is perhaps, next to learning the language, the most trying aspect of an American's move to another society.

LEARNING THE LANGUAGE

HOW FAR CAN I GO WITH ENGLISH?

As a language useful worldwide, English serves as well as any. With it you can happily travel most of the planet, sticking to well-worn trails. You can live comfortably in most European capitals and get along in countries once part of the vast British empire, including many in Asia and Africa.

English serves admirably in more than a dozen African countries, including Kenya, Nigeria, Tanzania, Ghana, Uganda, Malawi, Gambia, and Zambia, although in each there are numerous tribal languages and dialects spoken too.

In India, which someday proposes to use Hindi as a national language, English persists as the only *lingua franca* which speakers of the fourteen separate national languages can use to talk with each other. One can island-hop much of the Pacific through Micronesia, the Cook Islands, Samoa, and Fiji; or the Caribbean islands—Jamaica, Antigua, Grenada, Barbados, and Trinidad—knowing English and nothing else. English is a co-official language in such unlikely places as Singapore and the Philippines.

Of the thirty-five foreign countries where 90 percent of the Americans abroad live, English is the official or co-official language in eleven. Part of the appeal of Canada, Australia, Britain, Ireland, South Africa, Rhodesia, and New Zealand to Americans is the comforting knowledge that language won't be a problem. There may be momentary confusions over differences of accent, or regions where a second language may be favored—French in parts of Canada, Afrikaans in South Africa. But for Americans considering these countries, the stumbling block of learning a foreign language is virtually nonexistent.

A knowledge of French or Spanish will serve in an additional fourteen of the thirty-five countries Americans prefer, as well as in many other countries. As the language of France, French is also spoken in the French overseas possessions in the Caribbean and the Pacific—Martinique, Guadeloupe, French Polynesia, and New Caledonia. In Europe, French is the official language of Luxembourg and Monaco, and is co-official with Flemish in Belgium, and with Italian and German in Switzerland. French is spoken widely throughout Europe, and probably remains the equal of English as the most valuable language for a globetrotter.

French is clung to rather tenaciously by the African countries once part of France's colonial empire. It is the official language of twelve African countries, co-official in six others, and widely spoken in Morocco, Tunisia, Egypt, Ethiopia, and Ghana. Knowing either English or French, one could live comfortably in almost any African country, if language were the sole consideration.

A knowledge of French will also stand you in good stead in Jordan, Lebanon, and Syria, countries whose primary language is Arabic, very difficult for most Americans to learn. French would help you get by in Turkey or in the separate countries of former French Indochina now known as North and South Vietnam, Cambodia, and Laos.

Among many groups of people the world over, the French language still has high status or utility. The Brazilian, Mexican, or Greek super-rich are more likely to converse with one another in French than in English, and refugee aristocrats from Hungary or pre-Revolutionary Russia would find it easier to communicate in French than in any other language. Its breadth and expressiveness, like English, also make it a favorite of diplomats.

Spanish is the most widespread language in Latin America, although the single largest country, Brazil, uses Portuguese, which in practice is quite different. Even in Latin America one can find places where no one speaks Spanish or Portuguese, favoring the Indian languages such as Quechua or Guarani, or even rather pure Japanese or German spoken by immigrants who have never learned another language. But a command of Spanish would make easily accessible some eighteen countries from the Rio Grande to Tierra del Fuego, not forgetting Spain itself and a number of its attractive islands in the Atlantic and Mediterranean.

The American who does choose to live in Latin America has perhaps the greatest necessity of learning the language. Except among the culturally elite, English has made less of an inroad than one might expect.

The Peace Corps once studied volunteers around the world in an attempt to find out how important it was to know the local language to work effectively in a country. In Latin America 90 percent of the volunteers said fluency in Spanish or Portuguese was absolutely essential. Many Americans going to Latin America for the first time are often surprised when they discover dignified, cultured people who speak no English at all, and haven't the least interest in learning it.

Of the ten remaining countries of the thirty-five where English, French, or Spanish is not used officially, a person could probably communicate using one of them in all but three countries—Japan, Thailand, and Saudi Arabia. In Holland, for example, English is widely used in commerce, and as a nation the Dutch may be the most multilingual of any. Certainly, in Scandinavia, anyone speaking either English or French would be understood by someone. Italians have little trouble communicating with Spaniards, and Greeks seem to understand everybody, perhaps due more to their nature than a specific linguistic ability.

Even in some countries where English is ostensibly the official or co-official language, one can run into an occasional snag. Hong Kong has been a British Crown Colony for centuries, yet only an estimated 10 percent of the population speak English. In the Philippines, which were once an American territory, English is an official language of instruction in secondary schools, yet only about 40 percent of the people have any command of the language.

In light of the linguistic complexity of the planet, it is surprising that knowing English, French, or Spanish serves one as well as it does. The Modern Language Association estimates there are some 3,500 languages spoken in the world today, approximately 140 having more than a million speakers each. On the basis of absolute number of speakers, linguist Mario Pei adds to English, French, and Spanish as important languages: Russian, German, Chinese, Italian, Portuguese, Arabic, Hindi-Urdu, Bengali, Japanese, and Indonesian-Malay. In addition to English, French, and Spanish, the United Nations uses Russian and Chinese as co-official languages, calculating apparently that sooner or later everybody will know one of them.

For Americans speaking only English and choosing to live in other than the English-speaking heartlands, the utility of the language fades rapidly. As a rule of thumb in non-English-speaking countries, English becomes less useful in direct proportion to distance from capital city or tourist enclave, as one moves from top to bottom of the social scale, or in attempting to understand the people and their culture.

LANGUAGE IS THE KEY

If there is a single key to happiness in a non-English-speaking culture, it is learning the language. Anthropologists and sociologists have long recognized that language and successful cultural adjustment are intertwined. This fact has been acknowledged by several governments as well.

The Israeli Ministry of Absorption, for example, is yearly faced with the task of assimilating newly arrived Jews from Eastern Europe, Africa, South America, the United States, and Canada, all bringing not only radically different cultural traits but also mutually unintelligible languages. Despite their religious bond, the new arrivals cannot talk to each other, which adds immeasurably to whatever other problems may be involved in the culture leap. The Israeli government enrolls many new arrivals immediately in state-run adjustment centers called *ulpanim,* where they study Hebrew five hours a day, six days a week, for a month.

Australia has a similar scheme of sponsored language training for the large number of newly arrived southern and Eastern European migrants. The Australian government has found that, more than anything else, language instruction has helped the migrants to assimilate quickly into the mainstream of Australian society; without learning English they tended to end up in national ghettos, following for many years patterns of life much like those in the country they had left.

More immediate for the American hoping to live in a non-English-speaking country is the hard reality that knowing the local language is a near-absolute requirement for employment.

A Swedish businessman shakes his head slowly when asked how difficult it would be for an American to find work in Sweden knowing only English. "About as difficult as it would be for a Swede in the United States speaking only Swedish."

A Swiss government official comments almost apologetically that without a knowledge of one of their three official languages—German, Italian, or French—the chance of working in his country is practically nil.

An American living in Mexico City states flatly that without Spanish an American is worth less than a local, whatever his skill, if he can find a job at all.

In Brazil, both the American Chamber of Commerce in Rio and

the director of a major personnel-consultant firm preface their remarks on work with: "Of course you must speak Portuguese."

A director of his own New York-based executive-search organization observes that language capability is second only to topnotch professional skills for obtaining a high-level management position in an American-owned company abroad.

A recruiter of technical advisers for the United Nations Secretariat says simply, "We take languages for granted."

Finding yourself in a non-English-speaking country without the language, and needing to work, there is perhaps a single occupation open to you: the classic expatriate profession of teaching English privately. But in these increasingly restrictive times, in many countries even that is illegal without a work permit.

Occasionally abroad one can still find the American, Englishman, or German who has lived long in a foreign country, never learned the language, and damn well never will. Once in talking with a wizened and most successful soft-goods dealer in New York's garment district I was surprised to find that he had spent three months in Mexico each year of the last twenty and by his own account had never breathed a *buenos días*. He was surprised I thought it odd. He explained flatly that his money had always done the talking. But such people are a waning breed.

For an American moving abroad, I think the choice is clear. Either settle in an English-speaking country or go determined to endure the long, painful, mistake-ridden process of mastering a language other than your own. "The magnificent conquest," one American advertising man in Buenos Aires said of learning Spanish. An American in a non-English-speaking country already wears the not necessarily unflattering label "foreigner"; without the language, he is doomed to be an outsider as well.

In his book *The Summing Up*, Somerset Maugham, who was quite fluent in French and German, reflected that most people could never learn a language to perfection in any circumstance, and it was futile to try. The object of language was communication.

There are, of course, various levels of communication, ranging from making yourself understood to an impatient waiter to the sustained daily use of a language in a variety of settings. Learning a language in all its complexity can be a lifelong task if one wants to approach it in that way. Consciously or unconsciously, learning to use even our own language is a process continuing throughout our entire lifetime. If your objective is in rough agreement with Mr. Maugham—that language is important primarily for useful communication—then it might not take a lifetime to learn after all.

Linguists and language teachers cite a long list of factors that affect what it really takes to learn a foreign language. Most agree that *aptitude* and *motivation* play a large part.

APTITUDE

The arguments "I don't have the aptitude" or "I'm not smart enough" and even "I'm too old to learn anything new" are all less valid reasons for failing to learn a foreign language than too little application to the task or a poor course of instruction.

It is true that we are not all born equal in our ability to learn languages. But an aptitude for language learning is more cultural than biological. Some cultures *learn* to learn languages as a habit—the Dutch, for example, who have always had to look beyond their borders for commerce and trade. Or the Swiss, with three official languages and international business important to their economy.

Dr. Paul Pimsleur, director of Ohio State University's Listening Center, cites two other aspects of language aptitude in addition to motivation. What he calls "verbal intelligence"—the knowledge of words and the ability to reason analytically in using verbal materials. And auditory ability—the ability to receive and process information through the ear.

Dr. John Carroll of the Educational Testing Service in Princeton approaches language aptitude differently. His conclusion is that aptitude is essentially a function of the time required for learning. A person with a high aptitude for learning a language may reach a certain level of proficiency in a shorter length of time than a person with a mediocre or poor aptitude, given the same kind of instruction.

Carroll believes that age has little to do with aptitude. When people get older their aptitude probably declines slightly, but there is little evidence that older people can't learn languages. Young people up to about the age of eleven or twelve pick up languages with disconcerting ease when plunked down in formal instruction, or in a new country. Once past twelve, we are all in the same category, and age by itself is no excuse for failing to learn a language.

Furthermore, language aptitude apparently has little to do with general intelligence. William Moulton in the introduction to his book *A Linguistic Guide to Language Learning* suggests that learning a language is hardly an intellectual activity at all, presuming the mind of about a five-year-old child. "A great intellect is perhaps necessary before one can say anything worth listening to; but mere talking, as well as learning how to talk, apparently requires little in the way of intellectual capacity."

Moulton points out several reasons why young children, whatever their nationality of birth, have so little trouble picking up languages around them. A child doesn't "fight" the language; he merely copies what he hears and says what he is told to say without worrying whether it is logical or not. Adults, evidently, have all sorts of preconceived ideas about language. "One of which," says Moulton, "is that every language should be 'logical' and that there must be a 'reason' for the way everything is said. Not so the child. He couldn't care less. He simply mimics what he hears and refuses to worry about such adult problems as 'logic' and 'reason.' And this, apparently, is the attitude which any language learner ought to take. . . ."

Beyond aptitude, your motivation and the manner in which you are taught may be equally important factors in learning a language.

MOTIVATION

There is a pool players' adage that says you learn only if you play for money, and evidently it is much the same with learning a foreign language. Needing to learn a language for food on the table or social survival can be a factor overriding other aspects of language learning.

In Fiji I met a missionary couple who had spent most of their lives building a college of what was then some 800 students fifty miles north of Suva, the capital, country once considered the bush. They had arrived as newlyweds from Australia, fresh, untrained in languages, and scared to death. Six weeks later the missionary gave his first sermon in Fijian. Rudimentary Fijian, he told me, but Fijian. It was a matter of reaching the people in their own language or never reaching them at all.

With enough pressure, a language can be picked up without formal study, as the missionary demonstrated. A Dutch salesman in Mexico once told me he could learn any language in a month, and then went on to chatter at me in a dozen or so different languages. His range was impressive—even if they did all come out with the same unmistakably Dutch intonation.

But for most people getting ready to tackle a new language, the idea that you'll pick it up once you arrive in a country is a dangerous assumption. If done at all, it will be under great mental stress. At best, haphazard language learning has its greatest expense in lost time.

An added danger is that you'll learn the language wrongly to begin with. One expert points out that unguided language learning "consists predominantly of learning to substitute foreign words for English ones in structures which are basically English and which presupposes semantic discriminations which are characteristically English, e.g., singular versus plural, past versus present, definite versus indefinite. In a word he learns to talk English using French, Hausa or Korean words."

There are several other aspects of learning a language that have a bearing on how fast you learn: the method of instruction; the length of the instruction period; the size of the class (which has a relation to how much time is spent on *you*); how often you have instruction; and the total hours spent.

Time and perseverance have always been a part of language learning. But many of the new methods and ideas for teaching languages coming into wider use today evolved (at least in the United States) from the experience of the Army Language School in Monterey, California, during World War II, and more recently the experience of the State Department's Foreign Service Institute and the Peace Corps.

All three shared a single objective in their language teaching. They weren't trying to produce scholars. They wanted people who could use a language in practical situations.

The "standard" FSI language course is usually a minimum of 300 class hours for the so-called "easy languages," and up to 550 introductory hours for "hard" languages.

Languages vary in difficulty for speakers of English, or for anyone, for that matter. The difficulty is a function of the difference from the learner's native language—its grammar, sounds, vocabulary, and the way it is written, including the shape of the alphabet. For speakers of English, Mandarin Chinese is therefore not only hard to speak but also extremely difficult to write.

For speakers of English, the easiest languages to learn are the Romance languages—Spanish, Italian, Portuguese, French—and German. The most difficult are Korean, Thai, Arabic, Turkish, Amharic (the main language of Ethiopia), Farsi (the official language of Iran), Hindi, Swahili, Somali, the languages of Micronesia, and Indonesian-Malay, as well as Chinese.

Somewhere in between would be Hebrew, Russian, the Slavic languages of Central and Eastern Europe, Swedish, Finnish, Norwegian, Icelandic, and Danish.

In the FSI 300-hour-minimum course, the foreign language is taught in four-hour-long instruction periods each day over a three-month period. The basic method is an "intensified audiolingual approach," which means using a combination of a skilled teacher trained in linguistics, native speakers as language informants, practice in dialogue and pattern drills, and a language lab to provide you with the horror of your own tape-recorded voice as it slowly tries to imitate the pronunciation of native speakers. The FSI usually limits class size to six.

One study showed that the typical result of such a basic 300- to 550-hour course of instruction was an oral proficiency about equal to university language majors in their final year of study.

For readers over thirty who groped their way through years of grammar-oriented language instruction and are still unable to utter a correct sentence, this may seem something of a miracle.

It is none of that. The example serves only to prove that during the last decade teachers of language have learned that the rudiments of a foreign language can be taught in a short period of time.

Both the FSI and the Peace Corps, as have a number of universities and private institutions, have experimented with a wide range of "accelerated" and "intensive" or so-called "immersion" courses (differentiated mainly by the number of hours of instruction a day). Sometimes they crammed the standard three-month course into eight hours a day, six days a week, with special attention to varying instruction, even to the point of changing classrooms.

One recent experiment in basic Russian taught at the University of British Columbia ran for six weeks from 8:30 in the morning until 9:00 at night, with no English spoken after the first day. Students ate meals, heard news broadcasts, attended a wide variety of cultural events together, all in Russian. Again no miracles. But people respond well to saturation or intensive methods because they can actually see a change in their ability to speak a language.

Some researchers feel that the results of accelerated courses are in the long run more lasting than superintensive courses. Linguist John DeFrancis makes a case that ten hours of instruction a week (two hours a day five days a week) is more effective because of his belief that people's learning rates, and the speed with which teachers can cover the material, just can't cope with the superintensive courses.

Such courses also allow for a student to study on his own, outside of formal class hours.

But the "Experiment in International Living," a nonprofit Vermont foundation with three decades of language-teaching experience, offers a number of language courses pared down to bare essentials. They pack an intense ninety hours of language study into sixteen days. According to their results, this is said to impart a basic survival knowledge of the langauge as well as confidence that you can "get by." This quickie course has been particularly successful with students prior to several months of living with a family in a foreign country. Again, knowing you are actually going to use a language is a powerful force in the ability to learn quickly.

One shortcoming of miracle offers to learn a language quickly, be they records, programmed materials, or so-called pure audiolingual courses administered by professionals, is that most overstress vocabulary, since word learning is fairly easily measured. The FSI type of course functions on the idea that language training should provide a firm foundation for continued learning. Research has found that once in a country people tend to pick up new words and increased speed pretty much on their own. But pronunciation, intonation, and mastery of a language's structure remain static. Optimally, part of language instruction should stress the distinctive character of a language. Wrote one researcher: "To exclude the value of form is simply not to teach language."

Of course, there is quite a distance between a survival knowledge of a language and fluency. Very early in its thinking about language proficiency, the Foreign Service Institute devised a proficiency scale that has come into wide use.

The FSI scale has five categories, plus gradations in the four less-than-fluent categories. For the light they may shed on your own language requirements, they are listed here in some detail.

S-1 ELEMENTARY PROFICIENCY

Able to satisfy routine needs and minimum courtesy requirements. He is able to ask and answer questions on topics very familiar to him; within the scope of his very limited language experience, he can understand simple questions and statements if they are repeated at a slower rate than normal speech.

Speaking vocabulary is inadequate to express anything but the most elementary needs. Errors in pronunciation and grammar are frequent, but can be understood by native speakers used to dealing with foreigners; should be able to order a simple meal, ask for a room in a hotel, ask and give street directions, tell time, handle travel requirements and basic courtesy requirements. Normally his grammar is so weak he cannot cope with social conversation . . . he frequently says things he does not intend to say. Pronunciation and comprehension are generally poor. Accuracy limited to set expressions, almost no control of syntax; often conveys wrong information. Adequate only for survival travel . . . except for memorized expressions, every utterance requires enormous effort.

S-2 LIMITED WORKING PROFICIENCY

Able to satisfy routine social demands and limited work requirements with confidence but not with facility . . . beyond routine conversation the speaker is usually hesitant, often forced to silence by limitations of grammar and vocabulary; in general understands nontechnical speech directed at him but sometimes misinterprets, or needs utterances reworded; usually cannot follow conversation between native speakers.

S-3 MINIMUM PROFESSIONAL PROFICIENCY

Able to speak the language with sufficient structural accuracy and vocabulary to satisfy all normal social and work requirements and to handle professional discussions within a special field. Rarely hesitant; always able to sustain conversation through circumlocution. Understands most of what is said to him . . . and most conversations between native speakers, but not in great detail.

S-4 FULL PROFESSIONAL PROFICIENCY

Able to use the language fluently and accurately at all levels pertinent to professional needs. Can handle informal interpreting from and into the language.

S-5 NATIVE OR BILINGUAL SPEAKER

Speaking proficiency equivalent to that of an educated native speaker.

In their basic course (300 to 550 hours), both the Peace Corps and the Foreign Service Institute aim at a language proficiency of S-2 or slightly higher. Considering the number of people trained, they have moderate success, especially in the easier Romance languages.

A study of Peace Corps language trainees over a two-year period showed that 63 percent of all trainees (all ages, sexes, aptitudes) reached an S-2 level of proficiency in training. Students in the hard languages fared more poorly, with 80 to 90 percent below S-2 level. Other government organizations often give as much as 2,000 hours of the hard languages before moderate proficiency is reached.

When it is remembered that our previously mentioned five-year-old "practiced" about 10,000 hours to acquire a basic control over phonology and syntax of his language, these amounts of time may not appear so exceedingly large. But of course they generally don't produce quite the competency of the five-year-old in some respects, either.

The desire to bring language trainees to a minimum of S-2 is not merely an arbitrary objective. Educational Testing Service's John Carroll studied what happened to a number of language trainees once they were actually in the country. Even with an S-2 Carroll pointed out that a couple of months were needed before they could hear words spoken by native speakers as separate. But in periods ranging from four to seven months, S-2 speakers gained working proficiency of the language. They were to the point where their language learning could "take off."

Trainees that went into the field with lower language proficiencies took a disproportionately longer time to come to grips with the language.

The point made is that several months of intensive language training can greatly shorten the total time before you become functional in a language.

BUT HOW DO I LEARN THE LANGUAGE?

Admittedly, few people have the funds or opportunity to study a language in the manner it is taught by the Foreign Service Institute or to Peace Corps volunteers. There are a number of alternatives remaining; all have good points and drawbacks, depending on the money you have to spend, pressure of time, and your access to language-teaching facilities. At one time or another in the not entirely successful pursuit of three languages (Italian, Spanish, and Portuguese) I have sampled a number of them. Of the opinions that follow, my own are decidedly the least objective.

In-country. Undoubtedly the fastest way to learn a language is to study formally, full time, in the country itself. Both the Peace Corps and the FSI have had marked and rapid success with so-called "in-country training," especially with rather esoteric languages with few developed teaching materials and native speakers available outside of the country itself—Tongan, Yapese, and Fijian, for example. The Experiment in International Living has a number of programs that combine language and cultural studies actually in a foreign country; especially among young people, often a few months can show tremendous results.

If time and funds were no problem, which is seldom the case, there would be no more ideal introduction to a country than four to six months' study of the language, unencumbered by the need to make a living. Often admission to foreign universities allows you to enter the country on a student visa, which sometimes has its advantages; also, in many countries students in their mid-thirties or older are common, so self-consciousness about age is unjustified.

There are several ways to find out about language study abroad. There is a section in the Appendix called "Study Abroad," which lists a number of organizations and schools available to Americans for the study of language abroad. Second, particularly for the countries of Europe and Latin America, the cultural section of the appropriate embassy, and frequently its consulate general as well, have information about language study in their country. See addresses under each country in "Part Two."

For French or Spanish, one doesn't need to go to France or Spain (or Argentina, or seventeen other countries). You can study both in native settings on this continent, in Canada and Mexico. The language-teaching facilities in Mexico are more modern and less expensive than in any other Latin American country I know of. An intensive three months of study, over a summer, say, of either French or Spanish would be a big step toward learning each.

The drawbacks to studying the language in-country are as obvious as the advantages. First of all, most of us can't afford it, or don't have the time. Some of the difficulties stem from the country itself. With the exception of Europe, Mexico, and Canada, it is sometimes extremely difficult to find competent teachers and modern language-teaching facilities. One organization in Brazil made a brave attempt to capitalize on the need of the large American population to learn the language. They developed a syllabus with Americans in mind, advertised persistently, and offered instruction at a moderate price. They were finally defeated by their inability to keep the tape recorders in their language lab in repair.

Facing a lack of proper language-study facilities, most Americans turn to tutors or students. Neither, without stubborn encouragement, will usually give enough time to the task, and many, surprisingly, know little about teaching their own language to someone else. Just think for a moment how you would make a start teaching someone else English. Then there is always the chance that's what you'll end up doing: teaching your newly acquired student-teacher English, instead of learning enough of their language to be of permanent value.

It's an ulterior motive many have for teaching Americans to begin with.

To get the most out of a tutor or student, or to learn from your maid or housekeeper, you must know exactly what you want. In essence, you must design the instruction they give you. It is not as difficult as it sounds, if you have ever studied a foreign language. Learning the first language makes learning others easy, because you have already had to think about how language goes together, or rather how it might be taken apart. Some of the books that follow in "Finding Out More" will help you learn how to teach yourself with the help of others.

Another danger of putting off learning the language until you are actually in a country, especially if you know a little of the language already, is habituation.

Everyone new to a country, after the first elation, tends to slip quickly into a set of comfortable routines, taking the path of least resistance. An American businessman with a high-level job in an American-owned company has the greatest temptations to put off learning the language. His routine is quickly set for him. He deals with his driver, his colleagues (if not American, bilingual), and an occasional waiter. Invariably people are around to relieve the burden of speaking in another language.

His wife may be living on the brink of chaos trying to communicate with the maid and the tradesmen, but at least she is in a position to learn, if only born of frustration. But for the businessman, his pattern becomes set, and learning the language is always to start next week. In the end, as Graham Greene observed, a man may spend his time in a place knowing a city only as a few familiar streets.

When studying the language in a foreign country, there is one sure sign of growing competence. When people *stop* complimenting you on how well you speak their language, you'll know you are beginning to make progress.

While Still at Home. For most people, the most practical way to begin learning a language is formal study before departure. Often those several months of waiting for the issuance of a resident visa can best be spent making a start on learning the language. At this point you'll have motivation, which is the main reason you didn't learn Spanish or French or German sitting in that high-school or college classroom.

Probably the most expensive road to language learning is the private language schools, Berlitz, the American Express-owned Institute of Modern Languages, and a number of other lesser known, equally competent organizations that exist in most major cities.

The U.S. government in its language training programs attempts to spend no more than $3 per student per hour on instruction. That is essentially the cost figure for modern, topnotch language instruction. Since the language schools are businesses, they don't sell their service at cost. Most charge two or four times the above figure per hour for private language instruction. They usually require you to contract for a block of study, perhaps thirty or forty hours at a time.

Most of the professional language schools use variations of the same method—an emphasis on speaking and imitating the speech of native speakers. Individual or small classes of instruction force you into using the language aloud. These schools are hard-working, flexible in arranging study to your convenience, and they do of course compliment your successes, which is good for you and for them.

With the problem of the businessman in mind, Berlitz and a growing number of other language schools offer "immersion courses," which subject the individual in a matter of several weeks to a linguistic brainwashing, and are said to be very effective in many cases. The only person I ever talked to who had taken an "immersion course" was a slow-speaking engineer from Texas, working in France. He said he still went blank the first time a Frenchman spoke to him, but he thought later that the immersion course "hadn't done him any harm."

But seldom can such a crash course be thought of as any more than a partial solution for having put off learning the language until the last minute. Such courses must be followed by continued study, preferably in the country itself, to make it worth the cost and effort.

I once had a crack at Spanish via Berlitz. I'm perfectly willing to admit that the lack of success I had was more my doing than theirs. I was working at the time for the international division of a company in New York and was unwilling to devote the time each week that Berlitz preferred—or enough cumulative hours, a mistake on two counts. I ended by studying four and a half hours a week and a total of fifty hours. I also found myself aching for some structure on which to hang all the words and phrases I was learning, since formal instruction in grammar is much the lesser part of the professional language schools' method of instruction.

Later I found a tutor, a gracious Peruvian girl who was not only a good teacher but was also willing to explain some of the logic behind the language, and the connections between Spanish and Latin American culture. We also decided that I needed to spend more time on the language if I was serious about learning it, something my friends at Berlitz had been trying to tell me all along. The sessions eventually got up to about two and a half hours every other day, at a time when I was also making short business trips to Mexico, Central America, and western South America. Six months of this routine, and I became competent, though not fluent.

Probably the best value for money is the language courses taught in many colleges and universities. Here again the problem is to get enough exposure to the language fast enough. It does little effective good to have ninety hours of language instruction spread over an entire year. An increasing number of colleges and universities are offering intensified, audiolingual courses in languages.

For those geographically distant from any language-teaching facilities, correspondence instruction may be an answer. Some two dozen universities around the United States offer correspondence courses in twenty-one different foreign languages, from Arabic to Icelandic to Serbo-Croatian, as well as the more popular "easy" and "hard" languages. (See "Finding Out More.")

Most university correspondence courses provide you with a text, the language assignments, and language records. The total cost per course seldom exceeds $75. The strength of the correspondence courses is also their weakness. You can choose your own time to study, but the method severely tests the willpower. When you are your own teacher, there is a tremendous temptation to dismiss class early and not be overly hard on a student doing poorly.

A word about records and tapes: There is a growing number of fairly inexpensive high-quality recordings available that will aid proper pronunciation of the language—RCA Victor's *Modern French by Sound,* the World Publishing Company's *Foreign Language Record Series* and *Living Language Course.* The publishers of this book, Holt, Rinehart and Winston, inherited many of the fine foreign-language-teaching materials from Henry Holt and Co., developed originally by the U.S. Army. Other publishers who not only publish books but also other foreign-language materials are Harcourt, Brace and Jovanovich; Crowell, Collier and Macmillan; American Book Company; and McGraw-Hill. Generally, the reputation of a publisher is a good guide to the quality of the foreign-language-learning materials.

The designers of reputable tapes and records seldom claim that they will absolutely and surely teach you the language of themselves. They are designed as an aid, usually to formal classroom instruction, and are always meant to be used with parallel books and printed materials.

I once received promotion material through the mail from an organization that offered to find me the dream job I had always wanted overseas (where I could live like a king or queen on my high dollar salary), all for a slight fee, naturally. To sweeten the offer, they advised me that once I had sent in my fee and had been subsequently offered a job, they would at no extra cost send me a record of the appropriate foreign language so that I could learn the language fluently in the few weeks I had to kill before I boarded the plane.

Such promises of quick, painless learning of a language should make one instantly beware. There are no shortcuts to learning another language.

In summary, the points to consider when judging the suitability of any course of language instruction are as follows:

(1) At least initially, you should have qualified formal instruction. Unless faced with no alternative, don't try to teach yourself.

(2) It should be audiolingual in method—that is, should stress speaking and understanding. It should emphasize the structure of the language as well as vocabulary. Native speakers or language laboratories are a must.

(3) The course should be intensive or accelerated. Ideally it should approach 300 hours of total instruction, with something near 100 hours as a bare minimum. Class instruction should be daily.

(4) Classes should be no larger than nine or ten persons.

(5) Perhaps the primary criterion in selecting a language course is whether it offers the opportunity for a large amount of active use of the language—both speaking and understanding—in situations that are similar to real-life ones.

FINDING OUT MORE

There is, unfortunately, no easy way to assess your own aptitude, or to find out how long it will take you to learn a particular language. Dr. John Carroll (with S. M. Sapon) has developed a widely used language-aptitude test called the Modern Language Aptitude Test (MLAT). It can be taken at a number of universities, either in their testing center or student-counseling center. The test in its long form can be administered in an hour. A short form, without tape recordings, takes half that time.

The chief advantage of the MLAT test is that it has been in use over a long period of time, and a great deal of data has been gathered about its predictive ability.

The MLAT does not predict whether an individual can learn a foreign language if he is given enough time and opportunity to do so. It *does* predict, with pretty fair certainty, how well and how rapidly he can learn a foreign language given a prescribed course, in a given period of time.

For this reason, the MLAT is finding increased use by businesses (it is already used considerably by the government) to find out whether certain individuals are worth the time and expense of foreign-language training.

Mario Pei. *How to Learn Languages and What Languages to Learn.* Harper & Row, 1966. Not as great a problem-solver as its title implies. Has sections on the particular problems of learning the Romance languages, German, Russian, and so forth. Also tips on language learning.

Eugene A. Nida. *Learning a Foreign Language.* The Friendship Press, 1957. Originally designed for the use of missionaries going into areas for which there were no language materials available. Valuable.

Edwin T. Cornelius. *How to Learn a Foreign Language.* Thomas Y. Crowell, 1955. One of the surprisingly few books devoted to language learning from the student's point of view rather than the teacher's.

M. Kraft and C. Kraft. *Where Do I Go from Here? A Handbook for Continuing Language Study in the Field.* U.S. Peace Corps, 1966. This is a seventy-nine-page booklet containing suggestions on how to organize your own language study after you have finished the basic course. Once these were given away in great numbers by the Peace Corps to volunteers. It is still in print and still held in large stocks by the Peace Corps in Washington. Worth a try to write to them directly. Peace Corps, Division of Language Training, Washington, D.C. 20254.

A Guide to Independent Study (Through Correspondence Instruction). National University Extention Association, Suite 360, 1 Dupont Circle, Washington, D.C. 20036. Price fifty cents. Under separate subject headings, the guide lets you find out which universities offer correspondence courses. Big section on languages.

The Experiment in International Living. Putney, Vermont 05346. An established, reliable organization that among its specialties arranges language study and home-study programs abroad for people between the ages of sixteen and thirty. Regional offices in New York City; Washington, D.C.; Chattanooga; Highland Park, Ill.; and San Francisco.

The following are available from the Materials Center of the Modern Language Association, 62 Fifth Avenue, New York, N.Y. 10011:

William G. Moulton. *A Linguistic Guide to Language Learning.* Second Edition. Modern Language Association, 1970. Price $1.50 (include another fifty cents for postage). A fairly straightforward explanation to the language learner of the linguistic approach to learning. Learning *how* to learn a language is a large part of the problem. This book helps, even though it does become a bit too technical in some parts to understand from cover to cover.

Advice to the Language Learner. Modern Language Association. Actually a reprint of an article from the M.L.A. *Journal* in May of 1966. A short statement, and probably the most concise in print of what's involved in learning a language.

YOUR CHILD'S LEARNING

As Harland Cleveland and his coauthors noted in *The Overseas Americans* (published in 1960), an earlier generation of Americans abroad often had a seemingly abnormal preoccupation with "American-style" schooling for their children.

Especially among Americans abroad for a short term, the preference still exists. As one American businessman said, the rigidity of the system at home, the pressure to attend college, and the necessity of taking College Boards gives the parent, anxious to do right by his children, little choice. American companies searching for technical people to staff overseas projects must usually guarantee the availability of American-style schooling, "so the kids won't lose out," in order to find qualified people willing to spend two to three years outside of the United States.

To a fair number of new emigrants, American-style schooling is less than a prerequisite. Many couldn't care less. For some, the promise of liberation from the values of American education profoundly influenced the desire to move to another country. Among younger families going abroad, there is often a feeling that their own education was wasted, unfulfilling, "irrelevant" if you will. They feel what Ivan Illich termed one of the most critically needed principles of educational reform—that the initiative and accountability for learning must be put back into the hands of the learner or his most immediate tutor (or parent). That somehow the shift must be made from "schooling" to "learning," from "getting an education" to acquiring something of value.

Whether it is a family looking for this perhaps-mythical, more satisfying environment for learning, or a hard-pressed search to find more traditional schooling abroad, the children's education remains a prime thinking point for a family considering emigration. Because the decisions impinge on so many other aspects of the move, it often turns out to be the critical go or stay factor.

In most countries there exist a number of radically different alternatives, each with its attendant alteration in the direction of a child's formal education. In the capitals of Europe the number and variety of schools is dizzying, only slightly less so in such cities as Tokyo, São Paulo, Montreal, and Manila. The richness of choice is one of the great attractions of these cities, but the problems of language difference, cost, and educational objective confront the parent with a befuddling number of possibilities.

In developing countries and away from major cities, the alternatives might not be so great. As one educator said, a parent will still have choices, all of them bad. It may not be quite that grim, but the International Schools Service, an organization with long experience in counseling parents going abroad, suggests that education of an American child in another country will often demand unusual solutions. They forthrightly advise that if parents are unwilling to accept unusual, often uncertain, solutions for educating their children, perhaps they should think twice before moving abroad at all.

Very generally, the alternatives for your child's learning in another country will include: (1) the national schools of a country, both public and private; (2) the so-called American schools; (3) for lack of a more precise label, the third-country schools, counterparts of the American schools abroad, be they German, British, or French, often affiliated with religious organizations; (4) teaching the children yourself, or supplementing available education with correspondence instruction; and (5) sending the children away to boarding school: the schools of Switzerland, Holland, and Germany, for example, have long been a favorite of some parents living in Africa and the Middle East; the schools of Japan and Honolulu for those in Asia and the Pacific.

NATIONAL SCHOOLS

These are the equivalent of various U.S. public school systems. In some countries, such as Canada and Australia, the schools are administered by state departments of education much as they are in the United States. Particularly in many developing countries they are run by a ministry of education of the national government. I've also included here the private schools, often church-run, for two reasons. Their curriculum will be essentially the same as the public schools'. And like them, all instruction will be in the language of the country.

The principal difference between public and private schools is usually cost and the quality of teaching. The government-financed public schools are often crowded, undersupplied with materials and textbooks, and the teachers unbelievably overloaded. One teacher I spoke with in Barbados taught six classes a day with between fifty and seventy pupils per class, and assured me she was not an exception. But it is difficult to generalize even about the schools on so comparatively small an island as Barbados; the great variance in quality of public schools is perhaps their greatest characteristic.

In Canada, Australia, South Africa, and England, which calls its government-run schools "state schools" or "council schools" (and conversely, its private schools "public schools"), their quality may be good, with a certain number of students qualifying for universities or further study in technical fields.

In schools on the Continent, and those in developing countries modeled either on the British or French system, students at certain levels suffer periodic rigorous examination, determining firmly and forever who is qualified for the next level of higher education. Generally the national education systems abroad, through the primary and secondary levels, are as rigid as the American ones.

In many cases the advantage of the private over the public schools is based on qualitative factors, smaller classes, more attentive instruction. In South Africa the private schools are preferred because, among other things, they emphasize sports and recreation, which the white South Africans deem important. Sometimes the increased tuition fees and subsequent restrictiveness give attending a private school a certain status appeal. In Sydney or Melbourne the public schools, which are of good quality, are bypassed by many of the middle class in favor of sending their children to church-run private schools, because it is the "done thing." Such private schools in Australia, South Africa, and a number of other places may cost upwards of the equivalent of $700 per year, plus the cost of books and school uniforms, a large portion of a parent's income.

Even considering these factors, the general structure of education in the private schools will be similar to that of the public schools. They will be aiming at the same educational goals, which is the point to remember. It may be that their goal is to prepare a choice few for society's more remunerative professions, or perhaps simply to provide the citizenry in general with the ability to read and write, and the knowledge of enough history and geography to make them adequate citizens.

Given a choice, most American parents abroad search for other alternatives, especially for those children transferring from American-style schooling and somewhere in educational midstream. Often language difference alone prohibits taking advantage of national schools for the first year or two of residence in a foreign country.

AMERICAN SCHOOLS

There are about 250 "American schools" spread around the world, sometimes in unlikely places—Cali, Colombia; Ankara, Turkey; Calcutta, India; Cochabamba, Bolivia.

Most of them are private schools, financed in large part by tuition fees paid by parents or by the companies the parents work for. Sometimes they are run by the companies themselves. Aramco maintains a chain of schools covering the Arabian Peninsula for employees' children, as does United Fruit Company in Central America.

Most American schools have no direct connection with the United States government. The State Department accredits some 136 of the schools as suitable for children of U.S. government employees abroad, and in certain cases the government subsidizes them in part.

What makes these schools "American" is that they have American-style curriculums aimed at the goals of American education, and usually a high proportion of American teachers on the staff. College Board preparation or study for Advance Placement Examinations is usually heavily stressed. Turnover of students is sometimes high, often 30 percent of enrollment, due to the peripatetic nature of business and government assignments abroad.

One sure appeal of these schools is that they are perhaps the most "international" of schools abroad. In a survey of the schools accredited by the State Department, 64,487 children were enrolled from seventy-four different countries. Slightly more than half were Americans; another third were children from the country where the school was located; and the remainder, nationals of other foreign countries.

In the large American schools abroad the quality of instruction is comparable to any similarly sized school in the United States. Sometimes they offer boarding facilities. Many have accreditation, not only by the State Department but also by the regional accrediting associations in the United States, which means that credit for courses taken is accepted in the United States. One educator suggests this as an important point to consider when looking at a school, especially if returning to the United States while the children are still of school age is a possibility.

Tuition fees in the American schools are moderately high, competitive with those of eastern private schools in the United States. The Overseas School of Rome (800 students) has tuition fees for nonboarding students of between $1,300 and $1,600 per year. An average tuition fee for an American school abroad might be about $1,000 per year. The small, attentive (teacher-student ratio one to five) Butler Institute in Guadalajara, Mexico, charges a fee for boarders of $2,500 per year, on a par with the Swiss boarding schools favored by diplomats and high-level businessmen on assignment in Africa and the Middle East.

Another style of American school found abroad is those run by the Department of Defense for the children of American military personnel. These "dependent schools" are usually located on U.S. military bases, and sometimes take the children of nonmilitary citizens on a space-available basis. Fees are usually modest. (See "Finding Out More.")

THIRD-COUNTRY SCHOOLS

These are the French, German, British, or Swiss equivalents of the American schools abroad. Essentially, like the American schools, they are national schools set in another country. Their structure and curriculum will be modeled on that of France, Germany, or Britain, with the language of instruction usually to match. They are widespread, and in total outnumber American schools considerably. They are often found where American schools are not, especially in former colonial areas—former French-speaking Africa, for example.

The important point is that in the variety of choice available in foreign countries lies an inherent danger.

Each system of education—national, American, French, or whatever—has different objectives. An Englishman or a New Zealander is less likely to turn pale at the news from his sixteen-year-old daughter that she is "leaving school," roughly equivalent to an American's graduation from high school. Little feeling exists in either country that a college degree is a necessity for making your way in life.

Similarly, a French or Brazilian father may feel that the money spent on a daughter's higher education might be better invested in a Swiss finishing school or a course in Pitman shorthand than in attending one of their own universities. An Argentine professional man may goad his son into taking a degree in architecture or medicine, knowing full well that both professions are overcrowded in his country; the degree will help assure his son's status as a gentleman, whatever small practicality the study may have.

All nationalities place different value on formal education. In the United States the objective is often some tangible end—a degree, a diploma, a certain number of hours' study as the symbol of proficiency. Without a high-school diploma we are told we are doomed to be messenger boys or farm laborers. Without at least a B.A. degree we lack the "union card" to enter business or many professions. Without a Ph.D. the academic world refuses to accept us.

Our objective is the light at the end of the tunnel, and seldom do we stop to extract the most from the moment; without reaching the end, we bear the stamp of failure in our own minds, as well as in the minds of others. With the end rather than the voyage as the object of our formal schooling, national education in the United States has done well delivering what has been demanded of it, whether, as a growing number of critics are beginning to suggest, we have been demanding the right thing or not.

One consultant in international education commented that many countries' educational systems are fully as effective as our own, given their national feeling about what an education is supposed to mean. "The problems arise when you start out in one system aiming toward a particular goal, and then try to change systems."

Many Americans abroad embrace the influences of another country's culture upon their children while, initially at least, pushing them toward the objectives of an American education. That lingering Americanness shows itself most clearly in a reluctance to enroll children in something other than an American school, for fear of dooming them forever, should they want to attend a university in the United States. Most often, it is an unrealistic worry.

One well-traveled international businessman contends that emigration allows a parent a practical way to shake off the pursuit of an American-style education for his children, by settling in a country with more humane educational aims.

He suggests that every parent thinking about emigration should make an "educational inventory" of each school-age child in his family—an honest assessment of ability, the aims he sees for the child's education, and what it will take to fulfill those aims. Often the physical act of writing out such an inventory and facing the abilities and aims of each child can focus a parent's attention on what educational needs will have to be satisfied by any country considered.

To borrow the title from a recently published book by educator Don Parker, somewhere early in the thinking "where do we go?" a parent must look at his children and face the question "education for what?"

FINDING OUT MORE

Books, Pamphlets, and Guides

Schools Abroad of Interest to Americans. Porter Sargent, Publisher. A directory of some 700 primary and secondary schools open to English-speaking students in 100 countries. Also has a general discussion of different education systems. The last edition is dated 1967. It is still more valuable than anything else around. The publisher says a revised edition is in progress, but as yet can announce no publication date. Price $4.40 postpaid. Order direct from the publisher. Porter Sargent, Publisher, 11 Beacon Street, Boston, Mass. 02108. Massachusetts residents add 3 percent sales tax.

The European Council of International Schools publishes a directory every two years of the better private schools in Europe. The 1972–73 directory has complete information, including costs, on forty-eight elementary and secondary schools. Available for one dollar from the European Council of International Schools, Nidelbadstrasse 49, 8802 Kilchberg, Zurich, Switzerland.

The State Department's Office of Overseas Schools compiles a listing of the State Department-assisted "American schools" overseas, numbering 136 as of April, 1971. The listing is limited to correct address and name of headmaster. It is free from: Office of Overseas Schools, A/OS; Room 901, SA-11; U.S. Department of State; Washington, D.C. 20520. They also have a one-page "fact sheet" on each school, which may be requested separately.

U.S. Department of Health, Education and Welfare offers a number of publications on the educational systems of various countries. Most of them cost a dollar or less. They are written by educators, and are descriptive rather than evaluative—you won't find many opinions here. A current list of what is available is free from: U.S. Department of Health, Education and Welfare; Office of Education; Institute of International Studies; Washington, D.C. 20202. Ask for "Publications in Comparative Education: Current List."

Swiss Federation of Private Schools, 13 Rue le Vaucher, Neuchatel, Switzerland, publishes a free pamphlet titled "Private Schools in Switzerland" with information about its member schools.

The Institute of International Education publishes a list of publications on the educational facilities of a number of countries. Write to: The Institute of International Education; 809 United Nations Plaza; New York, N.Y. 10017; Attn. Information and Reference Services Division. Ask for: "Study Abroad for Americans at the Elementary and Secondary School Levels . . ."

Governmental

You should write to the consular section of the American embassy in the country you're considering. Ask them specifically for any list of schools they might have. The larger consulates abroad have lists—the one sent out by the American embassy in Paris is excellent, for example, as is the one for Rome. Consulates will not recommend schools; you'll have to write to them yourself.

Also write to the embassy of the foreign country in the United States. Ask for information on schooling in their country. The usual problem is that with the countries where education is most difficult to find, information is scarce. Germany, France, and Britain will all send you information about their schools.

For information about the overseas dependent schools run by the Department of Defense, write: Director for Dependents Education; Room 1-A-658; The Pentagon; Washington, D.C. 20301.

Counseling

International Schools Service. 392 Fifth Avenue, New York, N.Y. 10018. (212) 695–8520. A nonprofit organization specializing in setting up schools for industrial concerns abroad, and hiring teachers and administrators for a number of overseas American schools. They also have counselors who for a modest professional fee will advise you on your overseas educational problems. Write a query initially, explaining where you are going and when, sketching your children's educational needs. If they can help, they will advise you what such counseling will cost.

Porter Sargent, 11 Beacon Street, Boston, Mass. 02108. These are the publishers of *Schools Abroad*, but equally consider themselves educational advisers. They function on the same basis as the ISS, charging a professional fee. They do not take fees from the school they recommend; hence they are working for you, not the school. Query letter first.

Correspondence and Self-Education

Calvert School, Tuscany Road, Baltimore, Md. 21210. The oldest, best-known correspondence-school system of primary schools, kindergarten through eighth grade. The Calvert courses are prepared for the use of parents with no teaching experience. The curriculum and the schools are approved by the Department of Education of the state of Maryland. One educator suggests that the Calvert courses can often by very effective, especially if there is a good relation between the teaching parent and the child. The standard fee is $100 for a year grade course, which includes tuition fee, lesson manual, textbooks, workbooks, and supplies, sent postpaid by book post or parcel post. Air freight is extra. The Advisory Teaching Service for the same grade is an extra $50. The service corrects papers, offers the parent-teacher guidance, and so forth. Includes airmail return of your child's graded papers. They have a newly devised Kindergarten Course. Suggest you write for details.

Certain "American schools" in Liberia, Somali Republic, Cameroon, and a few other places offer correspondence instruction to children of people away from urban centers. If this is likely to be your case, mention it in both your letter to the consular section of the American embassy in that country and the State Department's Office of Overseas Schools. They will help you identify such schools, although you should always write directly for up-to-date information.

A large number of universities offer correspondence courses for high-school and college credit. The best single source of information about them is: *A Guide to Independent Study Through Correspondence Instruction.* Available for fifty cents from National University Extension Association; Suite 360; 1 Dupont Circle; Washington, D.C. 20036. Has a bibliography of publications concerning independent study. Of the university-administered programs for high-school study, the University of Nebraska is probably the best-known.

Nancy McCormick Rambusch. *Learning How to Learn: An American Approach to Montessori.* Helicon, 1963. A nice, unimpassioned book written before the current Montessori craze took hold. Has an almost 500-item bibliography of Maria Montessori's works, and writings about them.

Elizabeth Hainstock. *Teaching Montessori in the Home: The School Years*. Random House, 1971. A book of 55 exercises based on actual classroom activities. Designed to supplement schoolwork. Mrs. Hainstock also wrote an earlier book, *Teaching Montessori in the Home: The Pre-School Years*.

WHO WANTS US
(Will Accept Us; Can Stand Us)

Immigration laws and visa regulations don't happen by chance. They reflect a country's economic problems; former colonial ties; and attitudes toward race, culture, even age. They are often subject to immediate, radical change in response to political issues, national attitudes, or change in government.

Let me offer several examples.

The massive immigration schemes of Australia and Canada grew out of both countries' need to fill space with people and to feed hungry, growing economies. Neither country has an "open door" to all comers, although Canada's immigration laws for Americans are perhaps the most welcoming in the world. Both countries, because they need people, have immigration policies liberal enough to allow a wide range of new settlers to qualify.

In contrast, recent laws in Switzerland aim at restricting new foreign settlement in many parts of the country. These laws, and a national debate, resulted from the sudden discovery in the mid-1960's that one person in six living in Switzerland was an alien.

In the United States 6-percent unemployment makes recession a topic of national concern. Yet many developing countries exist year after year with three times as great an unemployment rate, compounded by unskilled rural workers moving to already crowded cities, people preparing for jobs that don't exist, and a "skill drain" of their best technical people. Such countries are not apt to look favorably upon a foreigner interested in further dividing a pie already sliced too thin. Mexico, Tanzania, and many other Latin, Asian, and African countries restrict settlement to those aliens who have critically needed skills or capital.

111

RACE AS A FACTOR

Immigration laws can be an instrument of national policy—toward race, for example.

Australia and New Zealand make an effort to maintain their "homogeneous" predominantly white populations in their recruiting of new settlers. Britain is considering tightening immigration from Commonwealth countries, in part because it cannot quickly enough assimilate the increasing numbers of migrants from East Africa and the Caribbean into its population. One not unpopular Conservative member of Parliament has suggested financing the passage of such newcomers back to their country of origin.

Immigration to the "white" countries of southern Africa is the most racially explicit. Nowhere in the world are there strictly "white" or "black" countries (or yellow or brown). Even in the so-called black African countries there are large numbers of nonblack minorities. About 225,000 French still live in the fifteen formerly French, now independent, African countries. There are small accepted white minorities in every black country, as there are Indians, Chinese, and Muslims.

In South Africa, Rhodesia, and the Portuguese colonies of Angola and Mozambique, the whites are also in the minority. The difference is that the white minority governs these countries, which in the eyes of their black self-governing neighbors is the heart of the problem. The attempt to attract white immigrants to South Africa and Rhodesia is in part an effort to increase the white population faster than is biologically feasible.

In South Africa, the 1970 census showed that while the white population had increased slightly more than 200,000 since the previous census, the Bantu population had gained more than two million. In Rhodesia, the African population outnumbers the European (white) population about twenty to one; in South Africa, about five to one. Both governments are aware of the pressure of numbers; immigration is an attempt to maintain a balance.

Immigration to the Portuguese colonies of Angola and Mozambique not only favors whites but also is currently restricted to Portuguese citizens as well.

Race influences citizenship in the black African countries, but is less a concern for residence than a number of other factors. Crowded countries have no interest in attracting people, be they in Asia, Africa, or Latin America. Of the 136 sovereign nations in the world, only six might be considered actively people-seeking, with perhaps another half-dozen amenable to a number of new settlers.

IMMIGRATION POLICIES AT A GLANCE

People-Seeking Countries. These are countries which have a policy of searching for settlers, even though the numbers are sometimes quite small. They are not to be confused with an "open door" to outsiders. They may have open racial or religious preferences, or *de facto* policies excluding certain types of people. Prior application for settlement is required. Opportunities for finding employment are usually good and varied.

Australia	New Zealand
Canada	Rhodesia
Israel	South Africa

People-Accepting Countries. These countries will accept foreigners for long-term residence, especially investors, corporate and individual. A transitory category. Many of these countries were once people-seeking, and large numbers of immigrants may make up part of their population. Most are evolving into "Allowing, Restrictive" category of countries, although given the right circumstance might revert to the "Seeking" category. Immigration laws may seem flexible enough in print; operationally, these countries accept outsiders very much on their own terms.

Argentina	Costa Rica
Brazil	Ecuador
Chile	Liberia
Colombia (new immigration laws under consideration)	Venezuela

People-Allowing Countries. These are nonimmigrant countries with liberal policies toward permanent residence of aliens. They have no need to seek immigrants; many already have dense or fast-growing populations. Good possibilities for individuals with unique skills or a fixed income. Will have some procedural red tape, but generally not xenophobic. To an extent they have come to terms with, or learned how to handle, foreigners in their midst.

Austria	Germany	Japan	Singapore
Bahamas	Greece	Malaysia	Spain
Barbados	Honduras	Morocco	Sweden
Belgium	Hong Kong	Netherlands	Switzerland
Britain	Ireland	Norway	Thailand
Denmark	Italy	Panama	Trinidad
Fiji	Jamaica	Philippines	Turkey
France*	Portugal*		

*Metropolitan—not including overseas territories

People-Allowing Countries, Restrictive. This includes many developing countries that need foreigners in critical skills and industries, one of which may be tourism. A work contract is usually a requirement for residence permit. Generally they have serious labor problems, large numbers of unskilled and unemployed. Common people are friendly to outsiders as a rule; governments are red-tape-bound, cautious, or suspicious. Opportunities exist for the patient, slow-going foreigner, but success is strictly an individual thing.

Afghanistan	India	Mozambique
Angola	Indonesia	Nepal
Bolivia	Iran	Paraguay
Ceylon	Kenya	Peru
Dahomey	Korea	Senegal
French Polynesia	Lebanon	Sierra Leone
Gabon	Malta	Tanzania
Ghana	Mauritius	Tonga, Kingdom of
Guyana	Mexico	Trust Territory of the Pacific Islands
		Western Samoa
		Zambia

Most former British Caribbean islands (Grenada, St. Lucia, Antigua, St. Kitts, St. Nevis)

SOMETHING TO DO

In the majority of countries, residence of foreigners is a one-by-one process, more closely tied to skill, profession, or trade than anything else. Liberia is the only black African country that will accept immigrants in the true sense of the word. In reality, the number of immigrants Liberia has received in the past decade is small. Negro ancestry, as in most black African countries, is a requirement for Liberian citizenship.

Liberia, like many African countries, is cautious in its encouragement of black American immigrants. A settler's willingness to assimilate and to contribute to the future of the country is desired by all immigrant-receiving nations, even if it is more a national feeling than a part of formal legislation. Liberia's experience is that few black Americans are willing to assimilate or even to take citizenship. African countries seldom encourage black Americans "back to Africa" because they feel that they bring with them a "Western" culture that is more separating than their color is uniting.

The late Tom Mboya, former Kenyan Minister of Economic Planning and Development, said: "The American Negro who comes here has only one thing in common with Kenyans: his color. Beyond that he will be in a totally foreign and strange community—a strange culture, strange habits, and strange attitudes of mind."

Mboya's critical point was that the American blacks who wanted to contribute to Kenya's future were free to do so, but the country needed teachers, engineers, and experienced businessmen, and if black Americans could bring those skills to Africa, there could be great areas of contact between black Africans and black Americans. (I later heard almost the same phrase on the Caribbean island of St. Lucia.) Mboya said that Africa had not rejected American blacks. "Our policy is not to encourage mass [American] Negro immigration. . . . Africa's role is to help them in that struggle, not help them run away from it."

Beyond racial attitudes and preference for certain skills and professions, immigration laws are sometimes modified by *de facto* policies, or harder-to-pin-down cultural biases.

In some countries there are preferences given to age. Canada gives added value to applications for permanent residence from people under thirty-five, but in no way penalizes those older. Both Switzerland and New Zealand, for different reasons, quietly discourage inquiries about permanent residence from pensioners. A number of other European countries decline requests for residence from people seeking treatment under national health programs.

Costa Rica, Malta, Mexico, and Panama, on the other hand, have special categories of resident visas for people with fixed incomes. Ireland, Portugal, Greece, and a number of other countries are amenable to pensioners, especially if they are returning to their country of birth.

Often, adequate funds can mitigate age or skill requirements. An underlying principle in many countries' immigration laws is to keep foreigners from competing with local people for jobs. Demonstrating an independent income soothes this concern, as does having a special know-how not available locally. Brazil and Mexico have special visas for investors; Canada treats the entrepreneur differently in its point system; Britain weights heavily the ability to sustain oneself from outside sources in considering foreigners for residence; Australia and New Zealand look favorably on people wanting to invest in their economies, who might be otherwise deficient in skill or professional training. Money may not talk, but the possession of capital to invest often whispers loudly in the ear of those considering applications for residence.

HAIR

Some countries have an absolute dread of the contaminating influence of American or "Western" culture, at least its most visible manifestations. Hair, for some time now, has been something of a focal point. Many countries, especially in Asia and the Middle East, consider an abundance of hair a symbol of Western decadence. The lush Indonesian island of Bali has banned "hippies." The city-state of Singapore has a record of refusing entrance to Western young people who appear as though they might socially pollute their own younger generation. Sometimes dress and appearance prejudices are rooted in a country's culture. In Thailand and Malaysia, hair is ugly. In Saigon the police have been known to go on rampages of haircutting with bayonets and shears, even among their own local young people. In San José, Costa Rica, people have been requested to take showers and have haircuts before entrance through customs. Those refusing have been sent out on the next plane.

The tolerance of what some people may consider exotic life styles is not widespread. The casual acceptance of the outward manifestations of a particular life style, which might go unnoticed in New York, London, or Amsterdam, may be cultural insults, religious gaffes, or considered outright threats to aspects of life in another culture. Sometimes great furor stems from the most innocent of intents, as the leggy German girl who walked miniskirted into a Milan cathedral found out. Dress or appearance that may in private cause little but admiration may in public cause a foreigner great difficulty. The thing to remember is that immigration officials are among the most public of servants. Whatever attitudes may be harbored by a country's most conservative citizens will be mirrored by immigration officials at airport or ship tenfold.

But whatever the factors and attitudes are that influence immigration laws, the pivotal question implicit in most applications for permanent residence is: "What can you do?"

Even the dozen or so countries seeking immigrants or accepting them have preferences for settlers with certain skills and trades. Canada rates the skill of a prospective immigrant against a computerized list of the country's labor needs at that moment, and assigns points of value accordingly.

New Zealand, Rhodesia, Brazil, Liberia, Costa Rica, and South Africa all have what might be called "preferred-immigrant lists"— that is, a list of skills, trades, and professions desired in general. A number of countries require prior employment before permanent residence is granted.

If there is a single key to residence abroad, it lies in the skill, trade, or profession you hope to practice in another country.

WHAT CAN *YOU* DO
The Employment Environment Abroad

In his book *The American Challenge*, French politician and publisher Jean-Jacques Servan-Schreiber enumerated the reasons why American business so successfully penetrated Europe.

Added to the ability of the giant American firms to amass and focus large amounts of capital (ironically, raised in Europe, he notes), Servan-Schreiber observed that American companies have "an art for organization," a "capacity for innovation" not found in European companies. American companies are flexible, certainly one of the most cherished words in the lexicon of American business. To paraphrase Servan-Schreiber, American companies did well in Europe not so much because of what they could do. They succeeded because they did things others could not.

A country's willingness to let a foreigner settle in its midst is closely related more than anything else to an individual's trade, profession, or skill. There is no certain advice on how a person can obtain a job overseas; if finding a job were easy or sure, there would be more Americans abroad than there are. But the single thread that connects all Americans working in other countries is that each can, or has been able to convince officials he can, do something others cannot. Perhaps it is a tangible skill or trade. Or the ability to speak another language fluently. It may be something less tangible, a peculiar kind of know-how or mental attitude that allows one to succeed when another might fail. Perhaps it is the "finagle factor" in operation, which I discuss at the end of the chapter.

What immediately follows is a look at the environment for doing what others cannot in several professions and skills that Americans going abroad are likely to possess. It is but a glimpse of trends as they exist now, as though we had stopped a length of movie film on a single frame, knowing that once set in motion again, the single frame, however clearly we might have viewed its contents, is immediately and forever lost to the past.

Let's start with that awesome creature, the American businessman.

MR. BUSINESSMAN

As Servan-Schreiber confirms, the reputation of American business abroad is extraordinary, its successes studied not only by European businessmen but also by an increasing number of Asians, Africans, and Latins as well. But as Servan-Schreiber intimated, and a number of foreign businessmen know, it is the sophisticated methods and techniques that have made American business powerful, not necessarily the American businessman in general. Critical-Path Method, computer time-sharing, cash-flow accounting, cost-benefit analysis, and a dozen other specialized techniques have found their way into management and manufacturing in American-owned business abroad, although their implementation into actual operations is usually the work of a few key people.

American business know-how, that pillar of corporate strength, is usually in the hands of a rather small part of any company's management, the majority of slots extended beneath these key figures filled often with talented but less than critically needed functionaries. In filling these slots, there is nothing intrinsically more valuable about an American, who just happens to have chosen a business career.

In quantitative terms, the most sought-after man in international business today is the national of a particular country who has been trained in American business methods. A number of executive-search organizations, which are generally at the cutting edge of employment trends, note two linked factors in the hiring of personnel for American companies abroad. Most American-owned companies are shrinking back the number of Americans in management, often doubling up positions. Most companies are hiring people at all levels locally whenever possible.

A large German-owned personnel-consultant firm active throughout Latin America first articulated a generalization, since repeated often: There are only two types of American businessmen being sought for overseas assignments. Managers at the top. And key financial and technical people. In short, businessmen who can do something others cannot.

Another influence behind the trend to look locally for all but key positions is the nature of the American businessman himself.

First of all, the American businessman abroad is unreasonably expensive. His salary demand is most often higher than that of his national co-workers. And he usually expects—and where hired today still receives—an entire "benefits package," which may include cost-of-living allowance; dollar salary, a portion of which is banked tax-free in the States; schooling fees for the children; and a paid home-leave for the family every two years.

One company in Brazil estimated the transfer cost of an American manager and his family to Brazil to be about $20,000. *Business Week* reports that Du Pont pegs the cost of moving a $12,000-a-year technician and his family to Europe and back on a three-year assignment to be more than $25,000. Amortized over the length of the assignment, with adjustments and bonuses, the $1,000-a-month employee ends up costing $2,500 a month.

Putting aside language, which is no small part of the increasing preference for nationals, the problem of cultural adjustment makes an American more of a gamble, the risk increased with each member of his family. One marketing man I knew maneuvered himself a promotion and transfer from the London office of his American firm to their office in Madrid because the idea of Spain fascinated him and his wife. About six months later a chance opening came in their Paris office, which my friend jumped at. He convinced management that his "know-how" would more than offset the expense of another transfer. After three months of coping with Paris, both he and his wife hated it. He asked to be reassigned to London, was, and three months later resigned to take a better position with a competing company.

The peripatetic nature of Americans in international operations is another factor influencing the search for nationals with American experience. In Japan it is not uncommon for a businessman to work his entire life with one company. The third American manager in two years of a large American publisher in Brazil found it extremely difficult to get the Brazilian book trade to accept him with any seriousness. Finally a Rio bookseller explained why. Latins prefer a long-standing personal relationship as the basis of good business, even more than a company's reputation. "So we do a little business," said the bookseller, "and in a year or two you're gone. You Americans never stay any place. You never become a part."

Another reason behind the trend to search for personnel locally is that there are more competent nationals in the job market than a decade ago. American-style business schools can be found in a growing number of countries. Master degree programs in business administration in American universities enroll an increasing number of students from abroad. One director of a nonprofit organization operating in Venezuela and Brazil now staffed almost entirely by nationals observed simply: "The *latinos* have learned a lot in ten years."

The trend to hire locally is increasingly pressured by foreign governments. Many require *quid pro quo* labor arrangements before allowing American companies to establish operations in the first place, backing up agreements to employ and train nationals in all but the most key positions with strict labor laws. Such labor laws now exist in most developing countries. Mexico, Panama, and Costa Rica require any business enterprise to be 90 percent staffed by nationals. In many cases employers must prove that imported managers and technicians are absolutely essential before a residence permit or visa is issued. A technican must often train one or more national counterparts in his job as he works.

When American companies do decide to fill an overseas position with an American, they begin the search by thoroughly reviewing the transfer possibilities from their own staff. Only after they have exhausted possibilities within corporate walls do most companies turn to classified advertising, or increasingly to executive-search organizations, called most often by companies that have lost staff to them, "head hunters."

The right executive for an overseas post, whether sought within the company or by the "head hunters" must have topnotch professional credentials. He must additionally have a language or cultural adaptability that points toward a smooth adjustment to living and working in a foreign environment. The search to fill positions abroad is seldom hasty in any case. One company comptroller on his way to Paris negotiated the position for fourteen months, a length of time not uncommon. A year of interviews and negotiations would be a good rule of thumb.

Certain American businessmen with unique, specialized skills are becoming a growing part of what geographer Wilbur Zelinsky termed the "mobile elite."

Already a number of scientists and professors divide their year between two or three professional homes. The limnologist on a three-month U.N. assignment to Chad, and the demographer consulting to the Philippine government are already staples of international air travel. Add to them a constant circulation of fashion photographers, actors, orchestra conductors, jazz musicians, missionaries, and international nomads, and one has the "mobile elite"—perhaps no more elite than in years past, but more diverse, and never more able to move about the planet with ease.

The professionals among the "mobile elite" are perhaps the samurai of the late twentieth century. Unhindered by undue concern over nationality and the previously great demands of travel, these intellectual or technical mercenaries are increasingly free to move wherever their own specialized brand of action cannot be found locally, available at a price to government and private firm alike.

Sociologist Judith Fortney, writing in the journal *Population Studies,* pointed out five reasons for the increasing mobility of a wide range of professionals: (1) Their advanced training is usable without adaptation. (2) Professionals tend to know more than one language. (3) Communication among professionals in different countries is good. (4) Demand usually exceeds supply. (5) Cost of transportation is small in relation to salary.

The highly trained, specialized businessman is a fairly recent addition to the "mobile elite," although he may before long be its largest component. If, as Herman Kahn suggests in his book *The Year Two Thousand,* time and space will no longer be a problem in communication, much of the routine of international business management may be monitored from the home office by telex and closed-circuit television. Nationals in charge of daily overseas operations would periodically be "brought in" to the home office for training and briefing. The role of the American businessman in international operations would be that of troubleshooter shuttled when and where needed by Concorde or SST, to return to Cambridge, Atlanta, or Santa Monica a week, ten days, or two months later.

To an extent, this has already begun to happen. Long-term transfer of large numbers of American staff abroad is increasingly rare for any single company.

One of the most valuable guides for the businessman searching for a position abroad is the *Executive Employment Guide,* compiled by: American Management Association; Management Information Service; 135 West 50th Street; New York, N.Y. 10020. This is a list of executive-search organizations throughout the United States that are AMA members, with addresses. Valuable section on procedures for making contact, and free.

One of the most borrowed-from series of publications by many of the guides that claim they can help you find a job overseas is *American Firms, Subsidiaries and Affiliates in* [*name of country*]. Published by, and available from: Bureau of International Commerce; U.S. Department of Commerce; Washington, D.C. 20230. A series of directories country by country (excluding Britain, Canada, Germany, and Italy) of American-owned companies, with addresses. Price one dollar per country postpaid. Compiled with the idea that people interested in working abroad can write directly to the company or its Stateside office.

A good first source of information about working abroad, though dated, is *Employment Abroad—Facts and Fallacies.* Price twenty-five cents. Also deals with other sources of information. Available from: International Department; Chamber of Commerce of the United States; 1615 H Street N.W.; Washington, D.C. 20006.

THE PROFESSIONS

For Americans in the more traditional professions—law, medicine, architecture, dentistry—a permanent move to another country may be fraught with complications.

Convincing immigration officials that you can do something others cannot is extremely difficult. Part of the reason is that around each of these professions in other countries are the same institutional paraphernalia found in the United States—qualifying examinations, professional boards, state licenses, and so forth—often made more difficult by residence requirements and the demand for literacy in the language of the country.

In many countries the professions are already crowded. Pressure, formally or informally, is put upon government officials to restrict competition by foreigners. In Latin America the classically oriented curricula graduate great numbers of doctors, lawyers, and engineers, often with little place for them to go in society except back into the universities to help turn out new generations of professionals with no place to go.

"Reciprocity" deals the professional man or woman a severe blow.

The rule of reciprocity is one of the guiding principles of modern diplomacy. It means in essence: I will allow you to do exactly what you allow me to do, and less if I can get away with it. Certainly no more. The restrictions on the practice of foreign professionals in the United States is mirrored, because of reciprocity agreements, or more often the lack of them, between the United States and each foreign country. If doctors from X country are forbidden to practice in the United States without residence requirements and stiff examinations in English, then American doctors in X country can be assured of treatment in kind.

American qualified doctors are virtually forbidden from practicing in Mexico, Argentina, and Portugal. New Zealand has recently eased its licensing requirements for American-trained doctors, but they still must pass an examination and serve what amounts to a year's internship in a hospital.

Law is perhaps the most difficult profession to practice abroad. Often the practice of law by foreigners is forbidden by treaty. In other cases a minimum requirement is usually citizenship, which requires years of residence, fluency in the language of the country, and examinations dealing with the particular system of law. Israel has a number of American-trained lawyers, and I know of one case where a former corporation lawyer has been admitted to the bar in Australia.

With the exception of the Latin-American countries, a broad range of engineers have an easier time of it. In Canada and Australia they may work by becoming a member of the appropriate engineering institute in the state where they intend to reside. Most often the requirements are credentials from an American university and at least two years' practical experience.

One engineer suggests that most American-trained engineers must take a broader outlook toward their field when they move abroad. A specialist in semiconductors is often expected to know a great deal about the general field of electrical engineering. Many countries require engineers of a kind fast fading from the American scene—civil engineers with road-building experience, power-plant engineers. Israel, South Africa, and India have a wide variety of needs for engineers in all phases of the aircraft industry.

The most wanted engineers are those trained in computers. Almost all the "preferred lists" of favored occupations mention computer engineers and the long list of computer technologists.

In all professions, professional organizations and journals are the best source of information about opportunities and requirements for working in a foreign country.

THE MOBILE PROFESSIONS

Teaching. There are somewhat more than 5,000 Americans teaching abroad. In Britain alone there are an estimated 700 American teachers and researchers. Some are members of the "mobile elite," teaching or carrying out scholarly research for limited periods of time.

The majority are elementary- and secondary-school teachers, not a small number of which are virtual expatriates.

Any teacher, at whatever level, wanting to teach abroad should at the outset arm himself with a copy of *Teaching Abroad,* a twenty-two-page bulletin with names of agencies, organizations, and informational services aimed directly at the teacher who wants to live overseas. It is revised yearly and is available free from: Institute of International Education; 809 United Nations Plaza; New York, N.Y. 10017.

University-level teachers and scholars have two additional pluses that, at least in the short run, add to the appeal of teaching in another country.

First, many countries have a special class of visa for people engaged in scholarly activities. Where issued they usually carry fewer requirements, rather easy renewal, and surprisingly less scrutiny into the nature of the teaching than if you proposed to enter the country as an investor. Governments and government officials are often awed or mystified by scholars. The term "professor" preceding a person's name in many countries brings the same kind of respect generally reserved for bishops, great surgeons, and perhaps rich distant relatives. Abroad, scholars often carry a level of prestige no longer fashionable in this country.

The second major advantage of being an American scholar abroad is that frequently dual taxation treaties exclude the taxing of professors in the country in which they are temporarily teaching. In other words, a professor who spent two years teaching in Sweden might very well avoid Swedish tax on his income, and because he has been outside of the United States for more than eighteen months, would avoid a portion of U.S. income tax as well. This is a point to explore, mainly because income-tax treaties are made separately between the United States and each country, and the provisions for each treaty are likely to vary.

The one drawback for university professors, with Canada the exception, is that permanent positions are rare. I do know of a case, however, where a teacher of geography has managed to teach in Denmark "temporarily," going on his seventh year.

Most university professors arrange to teach abroad through personal contacts or their professional organizations. Outside of these, the longest-standing, best-known way to obtain a position abroad is through the university-lecturing and advanced-research grants (several hundred a year) made under the Fulbright-Hays Act. A doctorate is a minimum requirement. For information, write: Conference Board of Associated Research Councils; Committee on International Exchange of Persons; 2101 Constitution Avenue N.W.; Washington, D.C. 20418.

There are a number of organizations that hire American secondary- and elementary-school teachers for assignments abroad. The sources of information about positions abroad for these teachers are probably the best of any profession. Let me comment on the environment for teaching (1) in the national schools of a country, (2) in one of the American schools around the world, and (3) for a number of other organizations that are interested in teachers.

Teaching in the national school system of a country is either warmly welcomed or prohibited by law. The state of New South Wales in Australia every year sends a team of teacher-recruiters to the United States to help replace the number of Australian teachers drained off by Canada. Mexico and Argentina prohibit nonnational teachers in their public schools, even for the teaching of English as a foreign language. The idea of foreigners teaching in national schools is frequently a loaded issue politically, entangled with nationalism and the belief that foreign teachers, particularly Americans, will somehow impart to the ready minds of youth the corrupting aspects of Western culture. In any case, few Americans could live on the salaries paid teachers in developing countries, the most common complaint of many national teachers as well.

In many British commonwealth countries it is possible for American teachers to find employment, but not without meeting modest requirements. Most Americans prefer teaching in one of the American schools abroad.

Their standards are usually as high as any good school district in the States, and with the competition so keen, they can afford to be. Many will pick up teachers abroad at the last minute, but all try to work on the basis of contracts arranged beforehand. Many American schools overseas use the International Schools Service, a nonprofit New York-based organization, to screen prospective applicants, sometimes to fill posts directly, or to arrange meetings between overseas school administrators and prospective teachers.

The International Schools Service cites as minimum requirements at least a bachelor's degree plus two years of successful teaching experience. Many teachers hired abroad have higher degrees. Family size is considered closely because of the spartan accommodations many overseas schools provide. One ISS official said that at the moment the most difficult teacher to find was the single male elementary-school teacher with experience and a willingness to rough it. Teachers with strong math or science backgrounds have also been in demand for some time, with the social studies and English at the opposite ends of the scale. The ISS registers about 800 teachers a year, and from that number manages to fill about 250 positions in American schools abroad. For information, write directly to: International Schools Service; 392 Fifth Avenue; New York, N.Y. 10018.

Teaching in the Department of Defense schools situated on military bases around the world requires direct application on the Standard Form 57, complete with references, all mailed early with the expectance of a long wait. For information, write directly to: Department of Defense; Overseas Dependent Schools; Office of the Assistant Secretary for Defense; Manpower and Reserve Affairs; Washington, D.C. 20301.

An additional way to go abroad as a teacher is via the Peace Corps. Five years ago they wanted mainly primary and secondary teachers, and teachers of English as a second language. At present they have shifted to an emphasis on teacher training in the developing countries, and they use volunteers with degrees in math and science, not necessarily with teaching experience, who can teach their field to others. In 1971 almost 40 percent of the total number of Peace Corps volunteers were doing some kind of teaching. For information, write: The Peace Corps; Office of Volunteer Placement; Washington D.C. 20525.

(Note: At the time of writing, the Peace Corps, Teacher Corps, and VISTA were being amalgamated into a new organization called Action. In all likelihood the Office of Volunteer Placement will recruit for them all. The Peace Corps also maintains field offices in major cities.)

In addition to the Peace Corps, the U.S. Information Agency seeks small numbers of English teachers for binational centers. For information, write: Chief; Personnel Division; U.S. Information Agency; Washington, D.C. 20547.

Small numbers of teachers are also hired to teach in American territories. The territories are widespread, many seemingly in paradise, but in reality the attrition rate of teachers is quite high. Wherever possible, teachers are hired on the spot. A surprisingly large number of these positions are filled by ex-Peace Corps volunteers who got to know the area first-hand and when their assignments were over were able to obtain teaching positions.

For Guam, write: Director of Labor and Personnel; Government of Guam; Agana, Guam.

For the Trust Territory of the Pacific Islands, write: Personnel Officer; Government of the Trust Territory of the Pacific Islands; Saipan, Mariana Islands.

For American Samoa, write: Director of Education; Department of Education; Pago Pago, American Samoa.

For the Virgin Islands, write: Assistant Commissioner of Education; Department of Education; St. Thomas, Virgin Islands.

For the Canal Zone, write: Personnel Director; Panama Canal Company; Box 20112; Balboa Heights, Canal Zone.

Two books for secondary and elementary-school teachers looking for jobs abroad:

Opportunities Abroad for Teachers. U.S. Government Printing Office. Price twenty cents. Cite Catalog No. HE 5.214:14047. Contains information on teacher-exchange programs authorized by the Fulbright-Hays Act.

The Complete Guide to International Teaching. Gordon E. Speed. A concise booklet that gives advice on how to do it, and more importantly, many addresses of organizations and schools abroad that you can write to directly. At a price of five dollars, postpaid, the booklet is expensive but there is nothing else like it. Order directly from: G. E. Speed, Publishers; 16 Netherall Gardens; London N. W. 3; United Kingdom; or from his stateside distribution center; 1207 Seminole Road, Atlantic Beach, Florida 32233.

Nursing.   I once shared a compartment on a train from Cannes to Calais with three nurses on their way back to England after working in France. I've run into Australian nurses in Fiji, a Scotch nurse in Colombia, and American nurses with the Peace Corps in the Caribbean. Nursing is one of the most mobile professions. Part of the reason American nurses may find it easy to obtain jobs and residence in Britain, Jamaica, and a number of other countries is precisely because large numbers of national nurses have migrated elsewhere.

To an extent, reciprocity and language restrictions affect nurses, as they do doctors. But a qualified, experienced nurse can still pick from a wide range of choices—working for AID in Vietnam; an assignment with the United Nations World Health Organization; or eased immigration into countries with chronic shortages of nurses, including Australia, Canada, Switzerland, and South Africa. For more detailed information about employment abroad, nurses should write: American Nurses Association; Professional Credentials and Personnel Service; 10 Columbus Circle; New York, N.Y. 10019.

The ANA no longer administers an exchange program. It publishes a bulletin, *General Information About Nursing Employment Abroad*, which has more than two dozen addresses of private and government organizations that are able to place nurses abroad.

SKILLED TRADES

A man who can work with his hands probably won't go hungry anywhere in the world. He won't earn $5.50 an hour either, or work a standard forty-hour week, or be looked at fondly by his co-workers if he goes looking for overtime.

Almost all the people-seeking countries need a wide range of skilled workers; the skilled trades rank high on the "preferred" immigrant lists. In most cases, when applying for residence or immigration, skilled workers are expected to show proof of apprenticeship or journeyman status, and if you have diplomas from technical or service schools, they should be presented.

As it also turns out, most of the people-seeking countries have strong labor unions, as do Britain, France, and Argentina. The working man abroad generally works longer hours for less pay than his counterpart in the United States, not only in real terms but in buying power as well.

The biggest shock for skilled Americans who emigrate to Australia or New Zealand is the difficulty of "earning a buck." Even though your skill may be in demand in another country, special care should be taken to find out what people earn. Most people-seeking countries have information on wage scales and union requirements available from their consulates in the United States.

The single exception to the rule of lower wage scales for American skilled workers in foreign countries is those working for an American contractor who has a project abroad. There are a number of "professional" overseas construction men—heavy-machinery operators, project supervisors, journeymen in a variety of construction and building trades. And working overseas is in their blood. The pay is good, the pace easier, and every couple of years a change of scenery. Most of the construction projects outside of the United States are in developing countries, with Vietnam at the top of the list since about 1954. But they are also in Indonesia, the Middle East, and to a lesser extent South America. Europe offers few opportunities, simply because most American skilled workers can do nothing local European workers cannot. There is also little demand for unskilled construction workers anywhere, since most contractors have to agree beforehand to hire as much local labor as possible.

For more information on the possibilities with contractors, see *Engineering News Record,* a weekly magazine for the construction industry published by McGraw-Hill Publishing Company.

The Construction Men's Association is a thirty-year-old nonprofit organization run by former construction men who have worked overseas. They have an elaborate underground for finding out who is doing what abroad in construction, and what skills are needed. They are not an employment agency, but deal in information. To become a member you must have at least five years' experience as a journeyman or in your particular administrative profession, be passed by their membership committee, and pay modest yearly dues. For this you receive their monthly newsletter, *What's Cooking,* information about jobs overseas, advice, and fringe benefits, which include inexpensive accident insurance. There are currently 16,000 members. Write directly to: Mr. James Dillon, President; The Construction Men's Association; 17 Avenue of the Americas; New York, N.Y. 10013.

WORKING FOR UNCLE SAM

On the surface, a government job looks like the surest way to move abroad. Almost every agency of government has some overseas slots. The biggest U.S.-government employers in foreign countries are the State Department and its two semiautonomous agencies, the United States Information Agency and the Agency for International Development. Added to these is a long list of others, including the Department of Defense, the Foreign Agriculture Service of the Department of Agriculture, the Treasury Department (assigned the job of narcotics policing), the Internal Revenue Service, the Department of Labor, and the Atomic Energy Commission.

The main trend in hiring of government employees for jobs abroad is this: the total number of openings are few and lessening.

Since about 1968 all agencies of the U.S. government have been going through an "operations reduction," to use the governmental phrase.

On the President's White House staff is a small, well-staffed organization named the Office of Management and Budget. Outside government circles, or perhaps outside Washington itself, few people have ever heard of the Office of Management and Budget, yet it is one of the most powerful in the present administration. Among its other regulatory functions is the power to establish ceilings on the number of employees each department and agency of the government may employ. For most government agencies functioning overseas those ceilings have been forced consistently lower over the past few years, and most departments of government have let their staffs shrink by attrition.

Slightly fewer than 40,000 civilian Americans now work abroad for the U.S. government, some 6,000 persons fewer than in 1969. Government employees account for less than 4 percent of the total number of Americans living overseas.

The State Department. American embassies abroad are the responsibility of the State Department. They do not hire Americans on the spot. Clerical people in nonsensitive positions are usually foreign nationals, which as of mid-1971 made up about half of the total State Department employees.

The Foreign Service staff are assigned from Washington, and new Foreign Service officers who make up embassy and consular staff must pass competitive examinations. In the fiscal year ending June, 1970, the State Department's Foreign Service had about 10,000 inquiries from people interested in becoming Foreign Service officers. Fewer than 250 new employees were assigned to posts abroad, of which only 97 were Foreign Service officers. Candidates for the Foreign Service Officer Corps must be American citizens of at least seven and a half years' standing and between twenty-one and thirty years of age. For more information, write: Department of State; Recruitment and Examining Division; Office of Personnel; Washington, D.C. 20520.

AID. The Agency for International Development, once the heavyweight of government agencies abroad, is in a greater personnel bind than the Foreign Service. AID has been the administrator of those billions of dollars spent in assistance to foreign governments. Shortly after coming into office, President Nixon asked the former head of the Bank of America, Rudolph A. Petersen, to look at the whole foreign-aid organization and recommend ways it might be more effective. The resulting much-quoted "Petersen Report" made a number of suggestions, among them that AID be dismantled and replaced by several new agencies with more defined purposes.

Foreign aid is due for a drastic restructuring that will probably take place no later than 1972 or 1973. Between 1968 and 1970 AID cut its overseas technical staff by 25 percent. At present most AID people assigned abroad are transfer assignments from one overseas AID mission to another, or from Washington overseas. AID looks beyond its own establishment for personnel only when absolutely necessary. For information, write: Office of Personnel and Manpower; Agency for International Development; Washington, D.C. 20523.

Other Government Agencies Abroad. Most personnel that work for government agencies abroad must have competitive Civil Service status. That means they have taken the Civil Service examination appropriate to the position and have whatever additional qualifications might be required by the job.

The prime rule for filling any position in any government agency is transfer from within. That is, slide people already working in the agency into positions abroad. In rare situations when no one on the staff is qualified for the position, the second guiding principle of government employment is to look for personnel in another government agency. The "Jack-in-the Box" syndrome is the greatest characteristic of government employment. A program administrator who finds his position eliminated in the Department of the Interior is likely to pop up in the Environmental Protection Agency. A lawyer eased out of a staff position in Health, Education and Welfare is likely to turn up three months later in the Department of Justice.

The director of a major government agency once told me that he personally had turned down a candidate for a specific overseas assignment in Central America, only to be introduced to the same man two months later; the man had been hired by one of the director's subordinates to fill a post in the Middle East. This tremendous lateral movement of government employees from one government agency or department to another is welcome protection for those already employed by the government, but discouraging for those who are not.

Only if a qualified candidate for an overseas position cannot be found anywhere in government (a highly unlikely situation) is the Civil Service register searched. The register is a list of people who have successfully passed the Civil Service qualifying exam; essentially they are people standing in line waiting for positions to open.

Under the system of Civil Service, seldom is it possible to apply for a specific job opening in a specific country and receive an offer. You must qualify generally by passing examinations, which allows your name to be added to the proper hat from which a candidate will be plucked. The Department of Defense, for example, has a computerized register called AOERP (Automated Overseas Employment Referral Program) which comes forth with names of people already qualified and recommended, as positions overseas open up.

In rare cases the Department of the Army has openings for librarians and recreation specialists which may be filled by people without Civil Service status. The minimum requirement is a college degree and the required skill. But even those positions are few. For information, write: Special Service Section; Department of Army Recruitment Center; Washington, D.C. 20315.

For most government agencies the idea must be to get the foot in the door first, then maneuver the whole body abroad.

The government publishes several pamphlets with information about working for government agencies, both in the United States and abroad. The following are revised yearly and available from: Superintendent of Documents; U.S. Government Printing Office; Washington, D.C. 20402. Send check or money order, not cash.

Federal Jobs Overseas. Price ten cents. *Federal Career Directory: A Guide for College Students.* Price $1.25. Both are published by the Civil Service Commission.

Foreign Service Secretaries: Assignment Worldwide with the U.S. Department of State. Price fifteen cents.

THE UNITED NATIONS

The idea of working abroad for the U.N. is one of those cherished dreams a number of people working in government carry around with them, one that very few make a reality. Because the U.N. is an international organization, Americans have no inside track on obtaining employment. The number of U.N. staff assigned overseas is growing slightly. Competition for positions is as stiff as for top slots in business.

About 80 percent of the United Nations budget is spent on its development programs in foreign countries. These development programs are requested initially by the foreign governments themselves, and might be in any one of a wide range of developmental areas from malaria control, to environmental research, to population studies.

A country's request for United Nations aid is funneled through one of the U.N. offices in ninety-two countries to a branch of the U.N. named the United Nations Development Program. The UNDP, as U.N. staffers call it, is the key financier and administrator of all United Nations aid. Development programs that it approves are then in turn assigned to the U.N. agency best qualified to carry out the program, such as UNESCO, the World Health Organization (WHO), the International Labor Organization (ILO), or the Food and Agriculture Organization (FAO). In a number of situations the program is assigned to the United Nations Secretariat itself, to its Office of Technical Coordination.

The actual office in the Secretariat that finds talent for the OTC is a group called the Technical Assistance Recruiting Service. In the course of a year they may send about 1,000 specialists from more than seventy countries abroad on technical assignments that vary from a few weeks to a year. Seldom are more than about 20 percent of the total Americans. A technical specialty is a necessity, as is both job experience and an understanding of life overseas. Many of the people found by the Technical Assistance Recruiting Service are nominated by foreign governments. All at one point are approved by the government in the country where they will work. The screening process for these technical advisers is thorough and may be lengthy, the average time from the beginning of screening to actual assignment being about ten months.

Information on all aspects of employment with the United Nations can be obtained from: Secretariat Recruitment Service; Office of Personnel; United Nations; New York, N.Y. 10017.

For a complete list of names and addresses of the separate United Nations agencies, as well as additional information about working for the United States government, obtain the periodical *Intercom*, Number 2, March/April 1970. The entire issue was dedicated to the topic "Careers in World Affairs." Price $1.50, postpaid. Available from: The Center for War/Peace Studies; 218 East 18th Street; New York, N.Y. 10003.

VOLUNTARY SERVICE

One government worker in his mid-fifties mentioned with open envy the increasing number of opportunities for voluntary service abroad. "Young people today have it made," he said. "The range of opportunities is fantastic. When I was twenty years old you had *one* place to serve if you wanted to try to do something for somebody. Fighting with the Abraham Lincoln brigade in the Spanish Civil War."

The traditional precept of voluntary service has been that we as people who are the "haves" in this world might well spend a portion of our lives helping the "have-nots." The two best-known organizations of volunteers, the Peace Corps and VISTA, are now amalgamated into a supervoluntary organization called Action, which will attempt to pursue the voluntary spirit in America on a grander scale than ever before. But there are hundreds of lesser-publicized, nongovernmental, and church-affiliated voluntary organizations that have been involved in service in the United States and abroad for decades. The Commission on Voluntary Service and Action estimates that during 1971 there were some 26,000 openings in several hundred different voluntary projects, the majority requiring volunteers from eighteen to thirty years of age.

The growth in voluntary service cannot be separated from the growing social awareness of Americans as a whole, particularly the generations born in the 1940's and 1950's. Many have put off the pursuit of formal careers until they have had a chance to experience a wider glimpse of life than college allows. Others search for an alternative way of living. If America can manage to reorder its national priorities after the end of the Vietnam conflict, volunteerism may well come even more into its own in the 1970's.

For precisely this reason the voluntary-service organizations have gone through something of a soul-searching. They have had some hard experience in the past decade and have begun to ask themselves important questions about what volunteers should and should not try to do. Some wonder if American young people ought to be serving abroad at all, whether the money might not be better spent developing volunteer programs run by a particular country's nationals. Some question whether volunteers should play a more serious role in technical development or whether they should deal primarily with changing hearts and minds. What is "development," after all, is a question often heard. The construction of a rural irrigation system or creating an environment that will allow responsive social change? One Latin-American president has his own answer to that: "Hungry bellies don't think."

The answers may not be as yet forthcoming. But the voluntary-service organizations have started to ask themselves hard questions, and volunteerism has begun a transition. What it will become by the end of the 1970's no one is quite sure. At the moment, however, there are at least two trends in the nature of volunteer assignment abroad.

Being able to do what others cannot is coming to mean more for a volunteer too. The large majority of volunteer assignments now require a volunteer to possess a tangible skill, profession, or trade.

Many volunteer organizations have begun to move away from the idea of volunteerism for its intrinsic values, toward becoming technical-assistance organizations that make use of volunteers as manpower. The newly created United Nations Volunteer program works in precisely this way, using volunteers on development projects under the watchful eye of a technical expert. There is some criticism that this isn't what volunteerism is for. At the moment, however, skills count.

Additionally, almost all volunteer organizations, whether church-sponsored, secular, or government, agree that there is another trend in volunteerism today not likely to reverse itself.

Paternalism is dead.

They have realized that a young volunteer who arrives in a foreign country armed only with an ill-defined willingness to help other people is not enough. Many highly idealistic volunteers have been shocked by the experience of finding that those he came to help were uncaring and unappreciative of his goodwill. A volunteer is a stranger. He is not patted on the back for living in impoverished dwellings and eating tortillas or taro. He might even be thought of as odd for doing so, since most volunteers can obviously afford better. Who, after all, would live poor if he didn't have to? When his two years of service end, many a volunteer has left unthanked, realizing that he has accomplished nothing lasting at all, despite the undiluted purity of his original intentions.

Most volunteer organizations have learned that the most dangerous vanity an American going abroad can have is "I'm here to show you what it is all about." At the heart of much of the change in volunteerism is the concurrent change in the relationship between the volunteer, who is there to serve, and those whom he serves. It can no longer be the father lecturing his son. In these times it must be a meeting of equals who may or may not have something to teach and learn from each other.

The head of one church-financed volunteer organization advises anyone considering voluntary service to look deeply at his own motive. If it turns out to be a vague desire to impart our values and perhaps scant knowledge to a materially poorer (but perhaps culturally richer) people, then be aware that the desire will go unfulfilled.

Or if it is a pining to enjoy "a meaningful cross-cultural experience," as one wistful young woman spoke of it (meaning a free, paid vacation of limited duration and measured commitment), then be warned. The worthwhile assignments abroad are hard work. And the effect they have on complacent values is hard to control.

But if skill counts for more, and vague idealism less, why become a volunteer at all? Why not sell the skill in the marketplace?

The answer is that if money *is* your prime concern, you should. Volunteers rarely earn more than a modest subsistence income. In some instances the volunteer must pay for transportation and other miscellaneous costs. But most volunteer assignments share a quality hard to obtain in any other manner. They force you into direct contact with another country's ordinary people.

The program administrator may sit behind his desk dealing with politicians and buffered by paperwork. A businessman in a foreign country moves from Hilton to chrome-and-glass office, which are the same in Houston or New Delhi. But the volunteer is at the leading edge. Social change has been defined as what happens when one person breaks through to one other person. By that definition the volunteer at least has a chance to be where something real is happening.

It is this day-to-day contact with another country's nationals that brings the greatest benefits, even if they do come slowly, and are paid for in sweat and frustration. "I'm not sure what they learned from me," goes the typical volunteer refrain, "but I sure learned a lot from them."

The effect on Americans of total involvement with another culture is often profound. Studies sponsored by the U.S. government on Peace Corps and VISTA volunteers confirmed what most volunteers knew already. The volunteer experience is mind-bending. As a result, life goals may change, occupations prepared for in college tossed aside, energies and priorities redirected. With some, the necessity of redefining poverty and human existence in terms they never dreamed of causes an irreversible politicization. A new awareness of oneself, an objective look at the United States, and the discovery of the complexity of humanity accompany service as a volunteer. It is rarefied air, and it is not for everyone.

The following are a few of the major voluntary organizations that assign volunteers overseas. The Peace Corps is larger and better financed than the remainder, in total placing several thousand new volunteers abroad each year. For information on the Peace Corps, see the "Teaching" section of this chapter.

For the other organizations, write directly for information. Generally, placement abroad may take several months, and tends to be selective, although with many organizations there always seems to be a constant scramble to fit unique skills into last-minute openings.

United Nations Volunteers. The first volunteers under the auspices of the United Nations went into the field in late 1971. Volunteers will be used in development programs in a variety of economic and social fields, supervised by technical experts. Volunteers must be over twenty-one, and willing to serve two years. "Selection for these assignments will be based on the candidate's competency in technical and professional skills, on his ability to communicate knowledge effectively to the nationals of the host country, and on his personal qualities, including his desire to be of service. . . ." Additionally, volunteers must be sponsored in their nomination by a national or an international organization, either official or nongovernmental, and in most cases it is up to the prospective volunteer to find an organization to sponsor him. For more information, write: United Nations Volunteers; Secretariat; United Nations; New York, N.Y. 10017; or: United Nations Volunteers; United Nations Development Program; Palais des Nations; Geneva, Switzerland.

Two organizations presently acting as clearing houses for United Nations volunteer applications and who can supply names and addresses of organizations that may sponsor applicants are: International Secretariat for Voluntary Service; 12 Chemin de Surville; Geneva-Petit Lancy 1213, Switzerland; and: Coordinating Committee for International Voluntary Service; 1 Rue Miollis; Paris 15eme, France.

The second organization, the Coordinating Committee for International Voluntary Service, also acts as a central clearing house of information for some 300 nongovernmental voluntary-service organizations in more than 100 countries, including Eastern Europe and the developing countries. They publish the only complete directory of these organizations, as well as a monthly *Voluntary Service Bulletin* and a mimeographed newsletter, *Clearing House News.* They do not place volunteers, but serve as a source of information about voluntary assignments.

International Voluntary Services, Incorporated. 1555 Connecticut Avenue N.W., Washington, D.C. 20036. A private organization that does take government contracts, it is currently operating programs in fourteen countries, including Vietnam. Assignments are for two years, most paying $80 per month plus expenses. Volunteers are taught languages where needed.

The International Executive Service Corps. Director of Executive Selection, 545 Madison Avenue, New York, N.Y. 10022. An exception to the preference for youth in voluntary organizations. Most volunteers are recently retired, experienced executives. Requests to IESC for volunteers come from locally owned firms in foreign countries, and since 1969 they have aided 2,000 organizations in forty-five different countries. Most assignments are for a few months. Volunteers are paid expenses only, and expenses for wife if she goes along. See also Julietta Arthur's book *Retire to Action: A Guide to Volunteer Service.* Abingdon Press, 1969.

American Friends Service Committee. 160 North 15th Street, Philadelphia, Pa. 19102. One of the longest-standing humanitarian organizations working in the United States and overseas. They have good success at placing conscientious objectors in alternate service. Many short-term summer programs exist that require volunteers to pay modest expenses. Also one program for long-term volunteers in Guatemala.

United Church of Christ. Specialized Ministries, R.D.#2, Pottstown, Pa. 19464. They have a one-year volunteer program, with some overseas assignments for older volunteers. Also shorter programs in Europe. They will try to place conscientious objectors.

United Presbyterian Church in the U.S.A. Division of Voluntary Service, Board of National Missions-Commission on Ecumenical Mission and Relations, Room 1133, 475 Riverside Drive, New York, N.Y. 10027. In 1970 they had some 185 volunteers serving in twenty-seven countries in a wide variety of skill categories. They offer summer, one-year, and two-year assignments. Volunteers usually pay transportation costs, but housing is paid for. Any concerned Christian is acceptable.

Mennonite Central Committee. 21 South 12th Street, Akron, Pa. 17501. One of the largest and most active religious-sponsored voluntary organizations working abroad. Currently they have about 600 volunteers in thirty countries. Mennonites are preferred, but there are some exceptions.

The Commission on Voluntary Service and Action. 475 Riverside Drive, Room 830, New York, N.Y. 10027. They do not recruit volunteers, but are a good first source of information about the myriad volunteer programs and what it means to serve as a volunteer. They publish a yearly directory, *Invest Yourself,* which is essential for anyone interested in voluntary service but who doesn't know where to begin. Price one dollar postpaid. They also have a number of smaller publications and reprints available. Ask for their list, "Publications Available from CVSA."

THE SMALL INVESTOR

George Bernard Shaw once advised people to be careful what they wanted in this world because they were very likely to get it.

In many foreign countries Americans with modest amounts of capital, even the proceeds from selling a home or automobile, can indulge in the dream of a lifetime. Land, a small farm, an independent business enterprise. A tranquil poultry farm in rural Australia can be bought for perhaps $20,000. An American in Costa Rica invested $8,000 in a new automobile, installed a taxi meter, hired a driver, and then sat back while the taxi and the driver paid for themselves, enjoying a healthy profit.

Americans do have a knack. Put them somewhere, anywhere, and they will find things done poorly or inefficiently that can be done better. Or they will stumble upon something they could easily do that isn't being done at all. The ability to recognize chance is almost a national characteristic.

In Brazil one of the most retold stories of American innovation is the success of Bob Falkenburg. He started a string of American-style hamburger and ice-cream parlors with stand-up counters and quick service. Before Falkenburg's operation, the Brazilians had nothing like it. The low prices and lack of formality helped make the idea an instant success, especially among the young, and a considerable fortune for Mr. Falkenburg.

An ex-G.I. with a Tahitian wife made a sinilar transfer of ideas in a busy center on a Pacific island. With a modest investment he set up an American-style hot-dog stand next to the city's busiest bar and nightclub. His business day started at four in the afternoon and ended after he'd served the last of the none-too-sober patrons from the bar, anxious for a bite before they tottered home.

A laundromat in Hobart, a distributorship of paper goods and ball-point pens in Panama City, a one-man jobber of American textbooks in Nairobi—all enterprises started by individual Americans who found their ideas and experience transferable to another country.

American life and society are so full of innovation and novelty that to the open eyes of many Americans other parts of the world seem a vacuum waiting for ideas to rush in. Put an American in Australia,

Argentina, Kenya, or the Canadian prairies, and invariably he'll be struck not by what is there, but by what is not.

Which brings us to the first problem of the small investor, that most vulnerable of Americans who go abroad. The question is seldom: "Will I find a way to invest my money?" In most places in the world the answer will be a definite *yes*. Ideas will beckon from every side, will sing in your ear, often with the voice of a Lorelei. The first question ought really to be: "Do I want to tie myself down by investing in that particular idea?"

Many times I've heard this from Americans: "I'm an idea man. I like to take something and get it started, then let someone else see it through. Daily operations bore me. I get itchy to try something new."

Approached with that attitude, investment in anything abroad will be a high risk venture. Making a "fast buck" in another country is becoming extremely hard to do, if only because decades of foreign exploitation have made many countries wary of foreigners who come with that attitude. In practice, most Americans are more poorly equipped to exploit speculative situations in a foreign country than most nationals.

The main principle for the small investor is to choose only investments that he can honestly live with over a long pull. Andrew Carnegie once observed that the joy is in the work. Unless an American truly enjoys (and understands) poultry farming, or raising bananas, and appreciates the country he has chosen for investment, his money rests on a shaky foundation.

One American in his early thirties with ten years' hard experience in restaurants went to Sydney with what looked like a novel idea for Australia, hoping to make quick, easy money. He quickly and efficiently set up an operation similar to the kind he had started many times before. A small steak house with a limited menu, and a large cocktail bar which from experience he knew would bring in a larger margin of profit than the food operation. Two years later he was back in the States complaining that Australians were indifferent restaurant goers, poor tippers, and would rather take their drinks stag in a pub than with the missus in nice surroundings.

I told the story to a long-time Australian restaurant owner, who listened with a knowing smile. "If he thought it was bad then," he said, "he should have been in Australia ten years ago. Most Australians didn't know what the inside of a restaurant looked like. Ten years from now they'll be no different from Americans."

A willingness to look at investment from the long-term point of view is the first quality the successful investor abroad must have. The second quality is the ability to last, which is not quite the same thing. The first implies an attitude: the investor is there to stay, barring revolution, calamity, and the always expected risk of having made a bad investment. The second implies the ability to deal with forces outside of the investor's control, which are usually directly related to another major problem the small investor is likely to face abroad—having enough capital.

The most realistic advice I've heard on the subject of investing in another country was from a Brazilian financier. "If you have a $10,000 idea," he said, "you better have $30,000 behind it."

Probably more small investors get their fingers burned, even with sound investments, because they are undercapitalized than for any other single reason. In different business environments money is often eaten up in unexpected ways: inflation; labor rates and fringe benefits under governmental control; unreliable suppliers; unusual tax structures; unbudgeted costs, which may include bribery (*bakshish,* the *mordida,* and a dozen other equivalents, a quite normal business practice in some countries); high interest rates on short-term loans; and labor difficult to convince that finishing a job today is really more important than continuing it tomorrow. Unthought-of, unfamiliar expenses can drive costs of even the smallest business venture beyond all expectations.

Some of the saddest Americans abroad are those who have had their ventures fail in mid-course because they ran out of money. The idea may have been faulty or brilliant, but they never had the satisfaction of knowing. In a boatyard in Honolulu I once saw a mammoth, half-completed oceangoing catamaran that had been designed to sail in a grand manner from Honolulu to Tahiti with a dozen or so wealthy adventurous passengers, making the round trip in about five weeks. The hull was rotting, construction having stopped when the money ran out. The ship never sailed, the idea remained untested.

One businessman in his late thirties whose fortunes have been up and down several times tells of the first time he went broke with a good idea.

Born in Lima of Scotch and American parents, he knew the west coast of South America well and spoke fluent, idiomatic Spanish. On a visit to coastal Ecuador he recognized a problem, and better yet, realized he had a solution that could make him quick money.

Each of the banana plantations in the region shipped its bananas to the coast in its own trucks and separately booked space aboard freighters. In essence, each duplicated the facilities of his neighbors. The businessman calculated that by forming a cooperative, which he was willing to finance, and consolidating the bananas of many plantations as though they were a single shipment, they could make optimum use of personnel and trucks and cut shipping costs by buying a large block of space on a single ship.

As it turned out, his greatest task was convincing the plantation owners to trust each other enough to form a cooperative, but he finally succeeded. The cooperative formed, he built a warehouse to use as a collection point. His financial resources already running thin, the businessman made his first and fatal mistake. He contracted with a lesser-known shipping firm for transportation of the bananas. All went smoothly until, with the bananas waiting at dockside, the ship failed to arrive. By the time other arrangements were made, the bananas had ripened and spoiled. The cooperative went broke, and the plantation owners parted, more distrustful than ever.

Undaunted by this first failure, the businessman tried to convince the plantation owners to try again. But even while most of them admitted the idea of a cooperative was sound, none of them would consider a second try. In retrospect, he said he had been shortsighted on two counts. He had underestimated the necessity of making the cooperative successful right from the beginning. Once burned, the people's pride would not allow them to risk being thought foolish by trying a second time. More important, his attempt to take advantage of the right idea at the proper moment had made him enter the project undercapitalized, which had necessitated using the cheaper but unreliable shipper. In his business dealings since then he has developed a particular talent for turning up cash to back his enterprises.

Avoiding get-rich-quick investments and being backed by enough funds to cushion the unexpected are the two most basic rules for the small investor going abroad to remember. Trade advisers, bankers, and investors themselves offer a consensus of additional points worth heeding.

(1) Never invest in anything sight unseen. Real estate especially. That virgin tropical coast may indeed be untouched by man's footprint. It may also be several hundred miles from roads, water, and electricity.

(2) People who speak English aren't inherently more trustworthy. Said one long-time American resident in Costa Rica: "I don't know what happens to people when they get here. Shrewd, competent businessmen at home somehow lose their bearings, their sense of judg-

ment, maybe because all the signposts are different. The first guy that comes along speaking English and sounding like a right guy could sell them shares in a lead mine or a piece of swamp if he chose."

(3) Never transfer capital without expert advice.

(4) Don't kid yourself. Is the investment you are considering a sound investment over the long haul? Are you still going to be interested after the novelty of the first year has worn off? If the voice in the back of your mind begins to whisper *no,* listen to it.

There are two preliminary sources of information open to the small investor interested in investing abroad. Many countries have trade offices in the United States that will happily supply information. I've listed their addresses in sections on each country in "Part Two" of the book. These trade offices may have several shortcomings. They are usually staffed not by businessmen or investors but by bureaucrats and economists. They tend to have little first-hand knowledge about specific opportunities in their country. And they'll have a strong bias toward making the country look stable and attractive.

A second source is the U.S. Department of Commerce field offices in about forty cities around the United States (see Appendix for addresses). Many requests for investment information sent by U.S. citizens to embassies around the world are replied to by a standard form letter advising the prospective investor to contact one of the field offices. Most of the offices have libraries with considerable commercial and investment information arranged by country. The Department of Commerce also publishes *Overseas Business Reports* and a number of trade bulletins, valuable for an initial overview of the investment and business climate in another country.

THE FINAGLE FACTOR

Being able to do what others cannot is most easily demonstrable by displaying one's skill, profession, or trade. Or by backing such a claim with money to invest. But the ability to do what others cannot often transcends the obvious. One Italian counsular officer made a circling gesture with one hand and shrugged. "Who can tell what will be wanted? Perhaps in one country a shoemaker, in another an opera singer." The remark reminded me that at that time Costa Rica was searching abroad for musicians for their national orchestra.

Which unusual talents, outside of the standard professions mentioned here, might allow a person to settle abroad is anyone's guess. Every talent or skill has its place and its time. In 1966 Mac Cato and

Dick O'Brien, two young graphic designers, went to London with a few thousand dollars, their own talents, and the conviction that the design revolution apparent in Italy and Scandinavia was just beginning in England. Their success is an example of the same thought Pasteur offered about scientific discovery: chance favors the prepared mind. The two Americans hit the right place at the right time, armed with the needed talent. Four years later Cato O'Brien Associates employed fifty people and occupied most of a five-story office building in Bayswater.

Even the most cautious countries have needs that can be filled by Americans, even if the burden of proving the ability to do something others cannot is upon them.

Two governments particularly cautious toward outsiders, especially Americans, are French Polynesia and the east African country of Tanzania. Yet on the island of Mooréa, an ex-lawyer from Los Angeles named Hugh Kelley, an ex-stockbroker, Jay Carlisle, and a third Californian, Don McCallum, all in their early thirties, bought a small vanilla plantation in the 1960's. Working slowly and unobtrusively, they later built a small tourist hotel that caught the boom in jet travel to the Pacific at the right time. Though still not given permanent-residence status by the French, they have managed to convince officials that they are doing something others cannot; and what they do benefits everyone.

In Tanzania I know of another American who has been able to capitalize on the national desire to stimulate tourism and the country's lack of understanding of what is involved in keeping foreign tourists happy. He exists in a slightly uneasy symbiosis with Tanzanian officials while earning himself a tidy living from a growing number of enterprises, of value not only to his bank account but to the Tanzanian economy as well.

There are few places in the world today that allow a person to take without giving. But there are few places, too, no matter how restrictive their residence and immigration laws might be, that aren't susceptible to the "finagle factor"—the right combination of skill, persuasiveness, and capital.

Sometimes persuasiveness is the larger part of the formula. One twenty-year-old political-science major at Harvard discovered he had an equal affection for machinery and radical politics. He began to take courses in auto repair at the General Motors Institute. By the end of his senior year he had developed skill at truck and auto maintenance, and tried to think of someplace he could put the knowledge to use.

He decided upon Africa, and wrote a personal letter to the governments of some forty African countries describing his background and his willingness to work, if they could guarantee him a job upon arrival. It went against the grain of much advice in this book, and if asked, I would have said it was probably wasted postage. It was. In all but a single case. The Minister of Transportation in the small African country Botswana said come ahead.

But the recent grad didn't stop there. He went in search of someone to help with his fare. He focused on men's service clubs, and finally convinced a chapter of Rotary to sponsor his adventure. They even put up money to ship his motorcycle as well.

The "finagle factor" might be looked at as the opposite of Catch-22. Whereas the latter may always turn up to confound you, the "finagle factor" allows the possibility of success when all things measurable point toward failure. The ability to capitalize on the "finagle factor" has allowed a number of Americans to live and work in other countries, against all odds.

FINDING OUT MORE

Job Opportunities Abroad. This is a bibliography of books, pamphlets, and organizations of interest to the person starting out to find a job abroad. Free. Write: Institute of International Education; Information and Reference Division; 809 United Nations Plaza; New York, N.Y. 10017.

American Chambers of Commerce Abroad. The United States Chamber of Commerce (not government-sponsored) has forty-five offices and branches in foreign countries. These are organizations run mainly by foreign nationals which have as members individuals and companies somehow connected with U.S. business and investments overseas. *They are not employment agencies, nor will they help you find a job overseas.* But many publish newsletters in English with up-to-date information on investment and employment trends, and some circulate employment bulletins among their members in particular countries. For businessmen and investors they can be extremely useful for making initial contacts. For more information, obtain their pamphlet *American Chambers of Commerce Abroad*, price seventy-five cents. Send check or money order to: International Group; Chamber of Commerce of the United States; Washington, D.C. 20006.

For People Under Thirty

Employment Abroad. Revised yearly. Aimed mainly at sources of summer work for young people abroad. Good bibliography. Price fifty cents, from: Council on International Educational Exchange; 777 United Nations Plaza; New York, N.Y. 10017.

The CIEE also has a number of bulletins on study abroad, as well as free "Fact Sheets" on study and work in Japan, Latin America, the Soviet Union, and Eastern Europe.

The Directory of Overseas Summer Jobs. Editor, Charles J. James. Revised yearly. A British publication with probably the most comprehensive list, country by country, of jobs in Europe. Price $4.95. Distributed in the United States by: National Directory Service; 266 Ludlow Avenue; Cincinnati, Ohio 45220.

THE PILOT TRIP

The most successful moves abroad are those made by Americans who know their chosen country first-hand. No amount of research and reading can accurately give you the "spirit of place," as poet Lawrence Durrell called it, and at the heart of it, that is the most important thing.

Of the Americans who have settled permanently in Canada, a large number had made numerous prior visits. About three-fourths of the American Jews who have gone to Israel since 1967 had visited the country at least once. Even among top-level international business and technical people, few are willing to accept "blind assignments." If they don't know a country, they want to see what it's like. Often the most experienced Americans overseas are the most insistent on a pilot trip. They have an appreciation of the complexity of what it takes to settle happily in another country.

If you are thinking of a move to a country you don't know first-hand, the advisability of a pilot trip may be the single most weighty piece of advice in this book. It is recommended by the majority of consular and immigration officials; not surprisingly, it is the most frequent suggestion made by Americans already resident in foreign countries.

An American in his late twenties who preceded his move to Buenos Aires by a good deal of globetrotting offered a comment that is typical:

> My one piece of advice to anyone thinking about moving abroad is take time off and spend some of that precious money you've saved on a visit to the place you've finally chosen to go. Spend a couple of months if you can, the longer the better. Talk to the people in the international community who are there to stay. Then find the disenchanted ones who are leaving at the first opportunity. Research the trip first so your time will count. Then make up your mind. Some people are just dreaming and there is no better way to find out if you are one of them.

Several months of steeping in a place would definitely round your perceptions and do away with any "fantasized" pull factors that might linger. Would that we had the time or money. Consider the idea of a three-week pilot trip, as a minimum. With planning and enough energy, you can reach a number of the objectives in this amount of time that any pilot trip should aim at achieving.

First, let me say that the period of three weeks isn't arbitrary. Many people have three-week vacations, or have two weeks paid, with the feasibility of another without pay. The investment of one vacation period is modest if you are seriously considering a move.

Another reason is air fare. It is likely to be the greatest single expenditure of the trip. Most airlines offer a fairly standard 14- to 28-day excursion fare, with considerable savings over the usual air fare for the same route. Some airlines offer 21-day excursions over selected routes, with greater savings on 29- to 45-day excursions if you can afford the time.

For example, at this writing, the basic economy-class air fare set by the International Air Transport Association (IATA), of which most airlines are members, between Los Angeles and Auckland is $984 plus tax round trip. The 14- to 28-day excursion is $700. From New York to Sydney and return is $1,388 standard, $1,000.40 plus tax on the excursions. I've chosen those two in particular to illustrate the extremes of cost we're talking about in air fares. Considerably more money could be saved if a group of people interested in migrating to the same place were to charter an entire airplane. The only organization that operates this way as a matter of procedure is the Association of Americans and Canadians for Aliyah, which makes frequent pilot trips to Israel with its members and has found the pilot-trip idea extremely worthwhile. We'll look at some of the other costs in a moment.

Another good reason for three weeks is that most people less than superhuman can't keep working at top speed beyond this limit. Many major companies now limit trips by their domestically based international people to two or three weeks abroad, if the trip is meant for serious business. I've talked to government employees at the tail end of six- to eight-week junkets away from home who, blurry-eyed, admitted that in the last weeks they were faking it. Few people can stay at peak form for more than a few weeks without a slump. On your own money you can't afford that.

WHAT TO DO

There are three main areas of concern on a pilot trip: employment, housing, and schooling.

Consider these points, summarized from previous chapters:

(1) Few employers will offer a job sight unseen. And many countries forbid you to find work in the country and then change your tourist status to that of resident while still present. This means finding the job and then leaving again to apply for residence. If you do receive a firm job offer on the pilot trip, get something in writing.

(2) Remember, the current trend, even by American companies operating overseas, is to find talent locally.

(3) Schools should never be chosen on the basis of hearsay, or worse yet, from promotional brochures. Often the American embassy in a country will provide you with information about schools (see also chapter on "Your Child's Learning") but will never make recommendations. The decision is yours. Often the location of the school in relation to your residence is a deciding factor.

(4) Like schools, apartments should never be rented without first-hand appraisal. For reasons mentioned in the previous chapters, renting an apartment in a foreign country is no less fraught with hazard than in the United States. Do not rent or buy property on the pilot trip. This should be done only after employment is obtained and residence granted. Scout neighborhoods and look at apartments to test the market. Talk with realtors and learn the ropes on rental agreements. Find those you can later trust. Primarily look for short-term accommodations where you can live six to twelve weeks while looking for permanent accommodation. Many people get backed into hotels at prohibitively expensive rates, having to eat all meals out. Whatever culture shock may strike Americans abroad, it is small by comparison to the nervous strain of having to live with spouse and small children for several weeks in a single hotel room.

PLANNING

The key to a successful pilot trip is to have your agenda arranged beforehand. Know what you will do, the places you intend to visit, the essential people you must see. Invariably gaps in the agenda fill in as you begin to "snowball" your original appointments into follow-up talks with other people.

Don't wait until you arrive to make appointments. Few people are as casual at making (and breaking) appointments as we are. Often people find it rude or annoying to discuss business over the phone, although that aspect of American business practice is beginning to make inroads in many places. In your initial letter to people asking for appointments, always include the question: "Is there anyone else I should see?"

And don't forget the official sources. Visit the American embassy and talk to the consul; visit the American Chamber of Commerce if you are in business or an investor. Check private and social clubs if you think you might be interested, school principals, an accounting firm, perhaps even a lawyer if you intend to bring fair amounts of capital into the country. If you are intending later to bring household goods into the country, you must talk with a reliable customs broker. Many of your heavier household items will end up being left at home, when you delve into shipping costs and customs duties. The central idea is to talk to as many people as possible, exposing yourself to a wide variety of advice and opinion, which can be accepted or disregarded later.

Take the time to read a few bits of history and geography of the country. It will add dimension to things you see that would otherwise have gone unnoticed.

Avoid major holidays. Every country has them, most more than we do. The Easter and Christmas seasons in Latin countries are poor times to do anything; other countries have long summer "high seasons," during which almost all commercial activity grinds to a halt. Nothing can take the wind out of a pilot trip like sitting for four days in your hotel room waiting for a holiday weekend to pass, unless perhaps you've been fortunate enough to land in the midst of Carnival, held the weekend before Ash Wednesday in many Latin countries. That might be an introduction to a place on its own.

HOW MUCH WILL IT COST?

A three-week pilot trip to Canada by automobile might cost a few hundred dollars. One to South Africa or Australia in the range of $1,500 per person. A lot of money. But considering what is at stake, is the expenditure really so great?

I know of one situation where a couple intended to move to a South American country, taking with them the proceeds from selling their house, plus savings, about $40,000. He had a job arranged, and they had several months before the move. During that period the anxieties built up to unimaginable proportions, since neither had ever been to the country. The anxieties were concerned with schooling, how difficult will it be to find a house, "what the place will really be like," and most important, are we doing the right thing? Not one worry they had couldn't have been solved on a pilot trip, an expenditure of about 5 percent of the total intended cash investment. The thought never occurred to them. Yet there isn't a gambler in the world who wouldn't toss in 5 percent of the pot to look at a whole handful of cards.

The best way to approach the expenditure of a pilot trip is to include the idea in your thinking from the beginning. Consider it as a business expense, necessary, but for which you will receive no immediate return. An odd thing happens to people willing to invest without expecting a quick return; they invariably save money in the long run. In addition to transportation costs, include a minimum of $25 to $35 per day per person for housing, food, and miscellaneous expenses. In less expensive countries you may not spend it, but you'll come close. You might live in many countries on five dollars a day, but you can't travel on it, and call you're own tune.

Budget your pilot trip, spend wisely, then forget about the cost. If the trip is successful, the expenditure will never be missed; if the trip convinces you that a move is unwise, it will be money thankfully spent.

PART
TWO

PART
TWO

AUSTRALIA

Area: 2,968,000 square miles (just under continental United States). Population: 12,700,000. Capital: Canberra (135,000). Other cities: Sydney (2,-780,000); Melbourne (2,425,000). All figures June, 1970. Language: English.

Not quite twenty-five years ago Australia embarked on a grand plan to populate its vast continent with new settlers.

World War II had shocked Australians into realizing just how vulnerable their country was. Japan had avowedly entered the war because it needed more space for its growing population, and while Australia's men fought in North Africa, Australians at home watched while the Japanese rolled south, occupied the Australian portion of New Guinea, bombed the city of Darwin, and shelled Sydney from submarines. The clash of Japanese and American naval forces at the battle of the Coral Sea, and the subsequent invasion of Guadalcanal, in all likelihood prevented Japanese invasion.

Following the war, under the banner "Populate or Perish," Australia set about attracting more settlers.

Most Americans have little idea of the extent of the Australian scheme. The Australians will tell you their effort has resulted in the largest controlled migration of people to a new country in the history of the world.

Since the end of World War II nearly three million migrants have settled in Australia. One person in five is a postwar settler or the child of one. In the official year ending June, 1970, the number of new settlers for that one year passed 180,000 for the first time. A population of 25 million by the year 2000 is often mentioned as a goal, which, added to natural increase, would mean about a quarter of a million new settlers a year between now and the end of the century. The slogan "Populate or Perish" has disappeared these days, replaced by more moderate justifications for needing people—"to diversify the

Australian economy," "to maintain full employment," and "to keep up the standard of living"—although the feeling remains, often unspoken, that somehow Australia's security as a nation has something to do with a larger population.

The new Australians are mostly European, with migrants from Britain predominating. But there are also Yugoslavs, Greeks, Italians, Dutch, Germans, and large numbers of Eastern European refugees, particularly Poles. About 80 percent are under thirty-five years of age at the time of immigration.

In the overall picture, Americans are so small a portion of the new settlers as to be often listed in the category "Other." Since World War II about 60,000 Americans have gone to Australia with the idea of settling.

At first the idea of Americans coming to Australia to settle permanently surprised and perplexed Australian officials. The American migration has been largely unsolicited. Australia advertises heavily in Britain, with sun-soaked advertisements, and has migration agreements or arrangements with almost every European nation. The American migration is self-generated and quite recent. Before 1960 the number of Americans settling in Australia was well below 1,000 a year. Since then it has steadily crept upward, until in 1970 more than 7,000 Americans arrived in Australia with the intention of staying.

This figure has not displeased the Australians, for several reasons. Large numbers of the European migrants, especially the Eastern and southern Europeans, come semiskilled or without a skill. Over half the Americans (men or heads of families) are qualified administrative or professional people, with another 17 percent skilled in a trade. Besides that, Australians for the most part like Americans. Many Australians over forty believe that if it hadn't been for the Americans, Australia would have been overrun by the Japanese in World War II.

Americans are culturally similar to Australians, in many cases closer in temperament and in their dislike of pretense than the English who settle in Australia. Western Americans especially find the Australian approach to life and the enjoyment of the outdoors much akin to their own, and they laugh at the same sort of rough humor. Immigration officials have said that they would like to see settlers from the United States reach a much higher level than at present.

The perplexity is that Americans don't seem to stick.

Australia has probably the best record of any country at keeping the settlers it attracts—something between 84 and 91 percent of the total. Americans have a much poorer record than average. One estimate is that two in three fail to last out much past two years. The Australian government estimates one in four. The total number of Americans resident in Australia, both temporary and permanent, was about 25,000 in mid-1971.

There haven't been any formal studies as yet to determine exactly why some Americans leave, although one is currently in progress. But some of the suspicions tell us as much about the Americans that migrate as about Australia.

One Australian official believes that Americans come with too many unreal expectations about Australia, the most common being about the cost of living. Australian sociologists have studied the whole problem of why migrants leave, and though not considering Americans exclusively, include other reasons such as homesickness (usually more on the part of women than men) and bad employment prospects. But the sociologists also point out that pure economic factors alone were seldom the reason for leaving.

The Australian studies of all migrants show that the first three to four years are critical.

Migration specialist Professor William Bernard of Brooklyn College suspects that Americans in Australia often have an earlier critical threshold. Americans tend to reach their first crisis point during the first eight months or so, which, as mentioned in the chapter on "The Culture Leap," is not uniquely true of Americans in Australia.

And for a reason not entirely clear, otherwise careful Americans have a number of unreasonable illusions about Australia. When people talk about a new life elsewhere, Australia invariably is one of the first countries mentioned. There is something almost mystical about the idea of a Great Southern Continent, almost empty, waiting for people to take advantage of it. The "wide-open-spaces" myth, along with two others—"they know how to handle the blacks" and "easy money to be made"—seem to predominate.

"WIDE-OPEN SPACES"

With a land area almost equal to that of the continental United States, but with fewer Australians on it than cars in California, it is hard to make a case that Australia is anything but underpopulated. By simplest definition, underpopulation means that the land can support more people than it has, and by this definition, Australia is indeed underpopulated.

But there are subtleties to the formula. Support at what level—

subsistence? And in what manner—stacks of high-rise apartments to conserve useful land? Some critics of immigration have already said Australia has enough people (as they have since the population first reached eight million people).

And despite the undoubted size of the Australian continent, all of the land isn't equally productive. The northern extremes are tropical, the weather influenced by the monsoonal systems of Asia. There are no great mountain ranges, hence no great river systems. Much of Australia's interior is a hot, arid Patagonia, or, closer to home, climatically and physically similar to central Nevada, and even emptier. Given the present level of technology, such land is uninhabitable.

To those Americans who imagine Australia as a land of craggy-faced sheep drovers wandering idyllically over the Outback, the fact that Australia is perhaps the most suburban country in the world may bring a shock.

Nine-tenths of the population is concentrated in the extreme east, southeast, and southwest of the country, clustered around Sydney and the five other state capitals. Only about 16 percent of the people live in what might be called rural settings. Less than 9 percent are farmers, a proportion of the population about twice as great as our own.

The Australian ideal apparently is to live in your own home in a suburb of a big city, an ideal that about 70 percent of Australians have made a reality. Incidentally, Australians are more avid TV watchers than Americans. A study of an average suburb revealed that 98 percent of the residents go out at night only on Saturdays. Eighty-five percent watch TV daily, for all or a part of the evening, with TV sets on for an average of thirty hours a week, more than four hours a day.

Land is available in Australia, and on the whole is cheaper than the same comparable land would be in the United States. That still might not be cheap. For example, a normal house lot, something between 50 and 70 feet across and 100 to 150 feet deep, might cost as follows: Within five miles of Sydney, good lots exceed $11,200, in harbor suburbs $22,500. From five to ten miles outside of Sydney, from $6,150 to $13,450. In Perth, there is very little land within five miles of the city; prices are up to about $22,500. Within five miles of Melbourne, prices range from $11,200 to $33,400. In the suburbs of most cities the best values are generally to be had from ten to fifteen miles from the city center, although in some cities these areas are not completely serviced.

One American family in Australia advises Americans to have a minimum of $20,000 with them for a down payment on a house and for lasting through the settling-in period. In Australia, house renting is rare.

The generalization holds true for agricultural land—cheaper than comparable land would be in the United States, but not necessarily at give-away prices. In prime agricultural areas such as the Murray river valley, land is available freehold starting at about $560 per acre in multiple-acre blocks. Great tracts of land are available leasehold, or partially developed from commercial land developers for what appear to be low prices on paper. Even in Australia, however, if the land is dirt cheap there is a reason for it.

There are a couple of general points to remember about agricultural land in Australia.

First, the Australian government has no settlement schemes for the establishment of migrants on farming properties. To obtain land for farming, the immigrant has open to him only the same course available to the Australian citizen. He can buy land outright (freehold), lease land, or share-farm.

Second, each state government has control over the land administration within that state's borders, and has sovereign rights over the Crown (public) lands in that state. Some states have minor restrictions on the eligibility of aliens to obtain farmland. For example, to obtain Crown land in the state of New South Wales, a non-British migrant has to have a year of residence and file a declaration of intention to obtain Australian citizenship. In Queensland a non-British migrant has to obtain a permit from the Attorney General. There are currently no restrictions on the eligibility of migrants to buy or lease land in Victoria, South Australia, Western Australia, and Tasmania. In actual fact, the competition for Crown land is so stiff that when it is opened up, balloting is usually required to see who gets the opportunity to buy or lease it.

In any case, land may be a small part of the expenditure for a successful ranch or farm. It is overall development costs which make farming expensive. Because of the high capital expenditure needed to bring areas into profitable production, farming in Australia tends to be big business these days. The Australian government suggests that only experienced farmers, well-financed, stand much of a chance on the land.

The government of New South Wales once did a study of the *minimum* capital investments needed to carry a single investor until the returns in an enterprise exceeded the running expenses. The estimate allowed for land, buildings, residence, machinery and equipment in used condition, stock, and expenses. At least 50 to 70 percent of these figures would be needed in ready cash, in which case the rest could probably be borrowed from commercial sources. All figures in U.S. dollars.

Cotton	$90,000
Rice Growing	$84,000
Beef Raising	$68,000
Merino Wool Growing	$67,000
Prime Lamb Raising	$67,000
Citrus	$46,000
Dairying	$40–43,000
Poultry Farming: Broilers	$22,000
Poultry Farming: Eggs	$20,000
Bananas	$17,000

Several points of advice have been suggested by the New South Wales Department of Agriculture for anyone considering buying agricultural property in Australia.

(1) If the main concern is to enjoy a particular kind of climate, choose a district for its climate, then practice the kind of agriculture that has proved itself profitable in that locality. If you want a particular kind of agriculture, go where it is firmly established.

(2) Remember, size of property is related to purpose. You don't need 20,000 acres to keep bees. Soil, topography, layout, subdivision, water supply, roads, markets, and social amenities must be considered. Check local ordinances regarding land use and zoning.

(3) Don't start off in a new country with the handicap of a poor farm. Inherent quality of the land is probably the main factor in a farm's earning power. Next is the need to make a start with good, disease-free stock.

(4) Inspect before you buy. Evidence of what a property is currently producing, history of the land (how often has it changed hands). Remember that even relatively poor properties may appear highly productive during a good season.

(5) Persons coming to Australia to settle on the land should avoid making any arrangements to purchase property sight unseen. (Another point for the pilot trip.) Acquire land with great caution.

For the experienced farmer, such points of advice are perhaps old hat. The best single point of advice for the nonfarmer who thinks he'd like to try it in Australia was given by an Australian economic-development adviser: "It's simple. Find a rural area and work on a farm for a while. You get a better understanding of what's meant by 'Australian conditions.' It's a big empty country, and a lot of it for good reason."

See "Finding Out More" for information specifically on farming.

"THEY KNOW HOW TO HANDLE THE BLACKS"

There are few racial tensions in Australia, and the government very frankly intends to do what it must to keep it that way. A formal policy of the Australian government is directed toward maintaining a predominantly homogeneous population, which means predominantly white. But immigration officials contend there is no such thing as a "White Australia Policy," nor, surprisingly enough, has there ever been one.

Early on there was a generally approved set of restrictive practices against the Chinese, who had flooded in during the Gold Rush of the 1850's, and "Kanakas" (Pacific islanders) brought in to work the sugar plantations along the northeast coast. The feeling at the time was that these races were just too different culturally to assimilate with the almost exclusively British (often convict-descended) rough-hewn settlers of the country. There was an even greater fear that inexpensive workers would dominate the Australian labor scene. The restrictive policies were never primarily to keep Australia white; they were to keep out labor that would compete with the Australian workingman, who generally went about things without undue stress. In time, many of the Chinese and Pacific islanders were sent home; even the Chinese who remained into their third or fourth generation were less accepted than British-descended settlers fresh off the boat.

Several years ago the growing feeling that Australia's restrictive policies were unreasonable reached a climax. In 1966 immigration policies were revised to admit a wider range of "non-Europeans." The term "non-European" in fact means nonwhite; to the Australian, in practice it means Oriental. If there are eyes worried about the threat of other races, they have always looked toward Asia.

But even that is changing, especially with the younger generations. Some 23,000 "non-Europeans" hold Australian citizenship, about half of them naturalized and about half by birth. Included among those naturalized are 752 Japanese, something almost any Australian twenty years ago would never have believed possible. Even though many Australians clung to a suspicion of Japan much longer than most of her former enemies (and some Australians still do), the old animosities are breaking down. Almost 4,000 Japanese are residing in Australia, and in the 1960's Japan became Australia's chief trading partner.

The current policy does not exclude "non-Europeans." For many years there has been provision for the entry of non-Europeans as immediate family members of Australian residents. In 1966 the Australian government decided that they would consider application for residence from non-Europeans who had "the capacity to integrate readily into the community" and who had qualifications that were in demand and of positive value to Australia.

From January 1, 1966, to the end of 1970, 4,631 non-Europeans were admitted as relatives of Australian residents, and an additional 3,216 entered as migrants on the basis of their qualifications. The majority of the latter were professionally qualified—medical practitioners, engineers, teachers, university lecturers, nurses, and accountants. Admittance of "non-Europeans" is authorized for those who possess a specialized technical skill; high achievement in the arts; "to practice in a profession in which they may readily be absorbed"; for experience and qualification of value in trade or business; plus a long list of compassionate considerations aimed at keeping families and relatives from being separated. These guidelines are public and may be obtained from the Department of Immigration. It was emphasized to me by one immigration officer that in the final analysis a black American would be judged on his ability to contribute to Australia, and on his character.

If there are subtle anxieties in Australia itself, it is not over the difference between "non-European" and "European" migrants, but over migrants in total. Immigration is not-so-gradually changing the cultural life of the nation. As novelist Arthur Koestler pointed out, many of the older, traditionally beer-swilling, mate-befriending suburbanites aren't quite sure what to make of the increasing number of dark-eyed gentlemen in strangely cut suits that are becoming more and more a part of a cultural mosaic. Some critics claim that migration is too expensive for what it is worth, a cost of $74 million (Australian) a year. Other critics look at the problems, the tendency of the new settlers to cling together in national groups (which most sociologists feel is beneficial), or the whole problem of "assimilation," or the fact that some Australians ignore the new migrants altogether by pretending, as Koestler mentioned, that they do not exist.

Presently under the sponsorship of Minister of Immigration Dr. A. J. Forbes, Australia is making a number of careful studies on the long-range need for immigrants between now and the end of the century. Australia, like Canada and a handful of other countries, will want new settlers for some time to come. How many is another question. The tendency might well be toward fewer and more highly qualified.

For the year 1971–72 Australia reduced its goal for new immigrants from the previous year's 180,000 to 140,000, a level equal to that of the mid-1960's. Authorities felt for the first time that the increasing number of new arrivals was beginning to compromise standards, as well as straining the ability of the Australian economy and society to absorb them.

Any lessening in the desired total will probably less affect interested Americans—who usually come with some skill or talent—than unskilled, non-English-speaking Europeans.

Whatever other changes may take place in Australia's immigration policy, the "homogeneity" plank will doubtless remain in the platform, liberalized though it may be. Six years ago a black American, a Japanese, or a Malaysian would have found it near impossible to take up permanent residence in Australia. It is no longer impossible. It depends largely upon qualifications, character, and the energy an individual is willing to expend in an effort to share Australia's destiny.

"EASY MONEY TO BE MADE"

Fortunes have been made in Australia, as they have in almost every country, rich and poor alike. In Australia the great fortunes have been made in mining—zinc, lead, and perhaps in the near future iron and oil—and to a lesser extent in agriculture, grazing, and the manipulation of real estate. These have been high-capital ventures, in the jargon of the money dealers "high-risk/high-gain" enterprises that have usually been corporate undertakings of considerable size.

In fact, probably the greatest initial shock to most Americans who migrate to Australia is how little everyone makes, and how little it seems to bother people. Salaries and wages are considerably less than they would be for the same occupation in the United States. And what is more, since the prices of consumer goods are fairly high, the buying power of each dollar earned is less in real terms than it is in the United States.

According to statistics released in early 1971, only one in ten of the wage earners in Australia earns more than $7,840 per year; only 3 percent earn more than $11,200 per year. The average wage for a man is about $68 per week (all figures in U.S. dollars).

Most Australians don't appreciate a "get-rich-quick" philosophy. They are content to enjoy their superb climate and outdoor life, relying on the government to make sure everyone has a "fair go," an equal shot at what society has to offer. This egalitarian view of life bothers Americans who come to Australia hoping to multiply little but their own energy into a fortune. Energy, even ambition, is not enough in Australia, and not even particularly admired characteristics in the folkways of the Australians.

The new settlers that fare best in Australia are the ones who intend to do something very like the work they left behind. Few places in the world, Australia included, are very kind to the person with a little cash in his pocket and a vague idea about "going into business" or "waiting for the right opportunity." One Australian trade official said: "Ten thousand dollars is nothing in Australia these days." Then added his unofficial opinion. "There are only two kinds of Americans that will stick in Australia. The kind that has money to invest and knows how to do it, an entrepreneur, if you like. He can still make a killing. The other kind of American is the average guy that goes to Australia looking for something that can't be measured in dollars and cents."

An echo of the same thoughts comes from Bill Craig, a former Californian and an ex-lawyer for Douglas Aircraft Company who went to Australia in July, 1968. Bill suggests that Australia can offer a satisfying life if: (1) you have sufficient capital ($50,000–$100,000) and *know-how* (not vague ideas) to start or buy a business or farm, and to live for several years until it turns the corner; or (2) you obtain acceptable employment *before* emigrating; and (3) you and your family have a genuine spirit of adventure and willingness to accommodate yourselves to new circumstances and ways.

He and his wife, Sandra, and their five children live in Hobart, Tasmania. In July, 1971, Bill became an Australian citizen, which is prerequisite to admission to the Australian bar. In the meantime, Bill and Sandra supported the family in a variety of ways, including partnership in a self-service laundry. The Craigs are in Australia to stay, and understand the pros and cons of living in Australia for Americans.

The average Australian does not have as high a material living standard as his American counterpart. His wages are about 50 percent of what he would receive in the United States for comparable work. His house tends to be small or less comfortable. His car is smaller, and often there is only one. His wife uses a clothesline instead of a dryer. He has few electrical appliances about the house. His children make more use of public transportation. The family tends to make do longer with clothing or other items, and they eat out less in restaurants.

But in some ways Australians are better off than Americans. Unpretentious by U.S. standards, but good schools and facilities for golf, tennis, and yachting are available at a cost within the means of anyone of moderate circumstances. Cultural activities tend to be subsidized and are by comparison less costly. Public transport is good and inexpensive. Ocean beaches and uncluttered countryside are more accessible to all. So is a rented or family-owned cottage at the seashore or in the mountains. . . .

Immigrating to Australia requires considerably more adjustment than would moving from California, say, to Vermont. I wouldn't recommend it without serious study.

Australian opportunities are not so superior to like opportunities in the United States as to warrant moving on economic grounds alone.

Then why do it at all? The answer, I suppose, is simply "man does not live by bread alone." Australia, and particularly Tasmania, has been kind to us.

PROCEDURES

Australia requires visas for all persons going to Australia. A *visitor's visa* is good for an initial stay of six months for business or pleasure, and usually permits the holder multiple entries into Australia over a period of four years. Stay may be renewed in Australia for up to an additional six months. *Visitor's visas* are not valid for actually taking a job in Australia.

Australia offers one unique class of visa, worth noting. A *working-visitor visa* can be obtained by any single American, twenty-five years of age or younger, of demonstrable good character. The intention behind the visa is to allow young people to go to Australia and have a look.

Visas are also issued for *temporary residence,* for example to the employees of American companies being transferred to Australia on assignment.

Americans planning to settle permanently in Australia should apply for a *permanent-residence visa.*

There are no quotas for Americans applying for permanent residence in Australia. The principal source of information on obtaining permanent residence is one of the three Australian consulates in the United States (see "Finding Out More" for addresses). It is unnecessary to obtain a lawyer or any other migration counselor in an attempt to have your application treated with special favor.

Write the consul nearest you. Tell him you are interested in immigrating to Australia, and you would like information. Such requests are no surprise; in 1970, Australian consulates in the United States handled 120,000 such requests.

You will receive a form letter, a bright orange "Application for Entry for Residence" (form M47), and eight booklets of information.

These booklets are revised often, and so-called "inside-information" publications advertised in magazines about Australia are usually this material rehashed (and out of date). The booklets are free, and contain the latest official information available. The booklets are

Your Journey to Australia. Detailed visa and customs regulations, what you should bring, what you should not. A discussion of Australia's assisted-passage plan, which allows up to $375 allowance toward the cost of transportation for adults over nineteen. Persons under nineteen travel free. Discusses restrictions on receiving assisted passage (the upper age limit is fifty, for example). Generally the plan is more liberal than New Zealand's or Rhodesia's, allowing you to travel either by boat or plane at a time of your choosing, as long as you travel to Australia directly.

Health and Social Services in Australia. Describes Australia's comprehenisve social-services scheme, which Americans are entitled to from the moment they arrive as permanent residents. The booklet discusses maternity benefits, worker's compensation, and pension schemes. Lists typical medical costs.

Education in Australia. Functions basically on the British system, with generally free public education and modest private school fees. Most young people wanting to attend university must take a series of exams at age seventeen or eighteen, pass them, or end up a "school leaver." The consulates also put together a leaflet, "Facilities for Higher Education in Australia," not part of the standard information packet. If you have children aiming toward university, ask for it. Also available from the Australian News and Information Bureau, 636 Fifth Avenue, New York, N.Y. 10020.

Wages, Prices, and Taxes in Australia. If you studied only one of the booklets, this would be it. Americans seem to have trouble comprehending the lower salaries in professions, without compensating lower prices for a wide range of goods. The booklet has a table of average salaries for most skills and professions. Income tax is usually withheld from salaries, similar to our own system. There are no state or local income taxes, and except for tax on dividends, income earned abroad is not taxed as long as it is subject to taxation in the country where it is earned. There are no tax breaks for new settlers. You're treated as an Australian from the first day. The income-tax rate is a sliding scale on all income over about $470. A married man with two children would pay about $2,580 on a taxable income equivalent to $10,000. On $22,400 the tax rate would rise, and he'd have to pay $9,606 in taxes. (All figures in U.S. dollars.) Personal income taxes average higher than either Canada or the United States, but slightly less than New Zealand.

Employment in Australia. This booklet is particularly important for skilled workers. It skims a bit lightly over the trade unions, which are as powerful and strike-prone as any in the world. Australia prides itself on the success of its high employment practices. Current unemployment rate is about one percent of the work force. For more information on employment, see section "Working in Australia."

Housing in Australia. A nice section on the Australian home, which should sound familiar to American suburbanites, although to most Australians our split-level or sprawling ranch houses look almost palatial by comparison.

Opportunities on the Land in Australia. The fattest of the booklets. A brief survey of each of Australia's six states, then a crop-by-crop discussion, including beef, dairying, wool production, and poultry.

The state of New South Wales also publishes an excellent bulletin called *Getting Started in Farming in New South Wales.* Many details on finance and land prices, the information often applicable to all Australia. Older editions had a nice map of the state, which is the most developed in Australia. If the consulate doesn't have a copy, write to the New South Wales Center; 680 Fifth Avenue; Room 1306; New York, N.Y. 10019. The Australian and New Zealand Bank also publishes a booklet, *Farming in Australia: Importance in the Economy,* but it is inferior to either of the above. At the time of writing, farming and its associated industries in Australia were in a slump due to a couple of years of overproduction, low world prices for wool and wheat, and a drought. But as farmers will tell you, things eventually change.

Australia. A fairly typical government handbook, with brief general discussions of Australia's history, the structure of the government, the economy, and so forth. The other books are more important.

If in your parcel of booklets *Australia—Questions and Answers* wasn't included, write to the Australian News and Information

Bureau; 636 Fifth Avenue; New York N.Y. 10019. This is a brief pamphlet prepared by the news bureau, answering twenty-one of the most-asked questions about Australia.

There are two other booklets and leaflets, not part of the general package of information they send out, that are worth seeing. Ask for them at the consulate in person, or in your initial letter.

House Purchase in Australia. A booklet prepared by the Australia and New Zealand Banking Group, and revised frequently. Has a good section on house financing. If not available, write directly to: The Migration Officer; Australia and New Zealand Banking Group Limited; 55 Gracechurch Street; London EC3B 3DL, England.

Australia's Immigration Policy. Not really their whole policy at all, but an explanation of "non-European" immigration.

APPLYING

The "Application for Entry for Residence" contains three pages of questions (twenty-nine headings, all told). There is a cautionary note on the front page of the application advising you not to quit your job or sell your house before approval of the application. The application asks details of yourself and your family, your work experience and qualifications, your plans in Australia (where you intend to settle, whether you plan to ask for subsidized passage), and the approximate value of the funds you plan to take with you. Your skill, or intended way of making a living, is the most important.

You must return the application with three photographs of you and your family, singly or together, but no other documents need be sent at that time.

Following that, there is a good possibility you will be asked to an interview, especially if you are requesting assisted passage. You can request an interview yourself if you have additional questions. There are nine full-time counselors employed in the Australian consulates. They make frequent trips to cities within their region.

These interviews or consultations last up to an hour, and serve several purposes. One is to make sure there are no unresolved questions hinted at by your application. They will be particularly sensitive to marital status and provision for dependent children. You will have to show proof of divorce, if that is your case, for example.

At the interview they will tell you what your skill is worth, and will be frank if they feel immigration to Australia is not in anyone's interest. The acceptance of immigrants is an extremely subjective process.

But the flexibility works both ways. Australia really does want people. They have a critical need for a wide range of skills, and compete for them with a number of other countries—civil engineers, people in the building or metal-working trades, teachers, accountants, and geologists. Australia will take TV actors or research librarians if they believe there is a reasonable chance for them to make a go of it. Even if your skill isn't in demand, they will take you if you can convince them you have something going for you. If you're not right, they will tell you.

The entire period for information-application-interview procedure usually spans three to four months. In special circumstances it can be accelerated to about six weeks.

WORKING IN AUSTRALIA

Australia is one of less than a half-dozen countries that do not require a firm promise of employment to obtain permanent residence.

But Americans who have been through the job-hunting mill in Australia strongly suggest having a definite job arranged before packing bag and baggage for the move "down under."

One difficulty shared with almost every other country is that employers are reluctant to commit thmselves without a personal interview of a job applicant.

Under the law, Americans are usually employable on the same basis as Australian citizens, except for permanent appointment to the public service, which is generally limited to Australian citizens or people of British nationality. The citizenship requirement also applies to some professions, principally law.

Another difficulty many Americans find is that their experience and their formal education (professions excepted) don't carry as much weight in Australia as in the United States. One American businessman, whose job with an American farm-machinery manufacturer in Perth ended suddenly when they decided to cease operations entirely in Western Australia, said this:

> Not getting credit for your experience elsewhere is the great frustration facing all newcomers from England, Holland, Germany, anywhere. A lot of them have to take jobs far below their capabilities and look around constantly for something better. It's their biggest gripe, and because of it, many don't stick out their first year.

Generally, however, Australia is more liberal than neighboring New Zealand in recognizing United States professional credentials and qualifications. As in the United States, the requirements governing recognition of professional credentials vary from state to state, and the process may grow somewhat complex. In the nonregistrable professions, such as engineering and accounting, membership in a professional organization is usually a prerequisite for employment. Skilled workers are usually required to join local trade unions.

It is advisable for professional people and those with higher educational qualifications to obtain an assessment of their qualifications, along with an evaluation of their employment opportunities from one of the Australian consulates general *before* departure. This can be done at the same time the application for migration is being handled. The consulate general will arrange with the professional-migration section of the Australian Department of Immigration to have your qualifications assessed by the appropriate registration board or professional association, and will have inquiries made about employment opportunities.

As an alternative, you may write directly to the board or association in Australia yourself. The consulate will provide addresses. It is essential in either case to supply evidence of your degrees, experience, and training. Good-quality photocopies will be accepted.

The Australian consulates are busily adding to their list of brochures about opportunities in specific professions. Currently available are separate bulletins for engineers, teachers, the computer fields, accountants, and librarians, with others to follow.

On arrival, all new residents have the free facilities of the Commonwealth Employment Service (the government employment service) to help find a job. There are offices in major centers throughout the country. They also maintain a Professional Employment Office in each capital city to assist those with professional qualifications or executive experience.

For those who have a trade, or are semiskilled or unskilled, an assessment of job prospects can be obtained by writing to: The Secretary; Department of Labour and National Service; P.O. Box 2817AA; Melbourne, Vic. 3001; Australia. When writing, include details of age, marital status, family, educational qualifications, occupational training and experience, type of employment sought, and any preferences regarding location. They will assess your chances at the moment, and claim that each letter is treated individually and answered as soon as possible.

The Australians make extensive use of newspapers for advertising job vacancies, with the Saturday editions the most important. If you wish to obtain copies or place ads, the principal morning papers are: *The Australian* (a national daily), 46 Cooper Street, Sydney, N.S.W. 2000; *The Sydney Morning Herald*, G.P.O.Box 506, Sydney, N.S.W. 2001; *The Age*, G.P.O. Box 257C, Melbourne, Vic. 3001; *The Courier-Mail*, G.P.O. Box 130B, Brisbane, Queensland 4001; *The Advertiser*, G.P.O. Box 392, Adelaide, S.A. 5001; *The West Australian*, G.P.O. Box D162, Perth, W.A. 6001; *The Mercury*, G.P.O. Box 650B, Hobart, Tas. 7001; *The Canberra Times*, 18 Mort Street, Canberra, A.C.T. 2600.

Teachers should ask the Australian consulate for the leaflet *Employment in Australian Schools of Teachers from Abroad*. Secondary-school teachers are constantly raided from Australia, by Canada mainly, and there has been a chronic shortage—particularly of teachers of science and mathematics. Public education is the responsibility of each of the seven states. The New South Wales Center (680 Fifth Avenue; Room 1306; New York, N.Y. 10019) also recruits teachers specifically for their state, the capital of which is Sydney. Their usual method is to bring in several teacher recruiters for a four- or five-month period; there is talk of having one full-time teacher recruiter stationed in the United States. Query them by mail, with a description of your qualifications.

FINDING OUT MORE

American Firms, Subsidiaries and Affiliates in Australia. U.S. Department of Commerce; Commercial Intelligence Division; Washington, D.C. 20230. One dollar, prepaid, by check or money order.

Establishing a Business in Australia. Overseas Business Report. U.S. Government Printing Office; Washington, D.C. 20420. Fifteen cents.

Information Guide for Doing Business in Australia. Price Waterhouse and Company; 60 Broad Street; New York, N.Y. 10005. Write on letterhead.

Tax and Trade Guide for Australia. Arthur Andersen and Company; 1345 Avenue of the Americas; New York, N.Y. 10019. Free. Write on letterhead.

Australia, New Zealand and the South Pacific. A Handbook. Edited by Charles Osborne, with fifty contributors. Praeger, 1970. All the facts one could want. Four-fifths of the book is on Australia. Extensive lists of further reading suggestions, by section.

Australian Migrants' Handbook. A guide to new settlers. Warwick Boyce Publishing Pty. Ltd.; 283 Clarence Street; Sydney N.S.W. 2000; Australia. A newsstand item, aimed mainly at the European migrant. From first words, "A man who can't get some money in his pocket in this country isn't half trying," to last words, "No reservation need be observed in Australia in asking for assistance in locating lavatories or rest rooms," a source of primary information, opinion, and scuttlebutt. Definitely not an official publication, but worth it. Write to the publisher directly. Send, in some form that is internationally negotiable, $1.00 (U.S.) plus postage—an additional $1.82 for air mail, twenty cents for sea mail (takes about six to eight weeks).

Donald Horne. *The Next Australia.* Angus and Robertson, 1970. An insider's book by an outspoken newspaperman. This began as a revision of an earlier book, *The Lucky Country: Australia in the Sixties,* in which Horne peeled a bit of the enamel from some of Australian society's more cherished beliefs about itself, and came to the conclusion that Australia among other things was one of the most static societies on earth. He found he couldn't simply rewrite the old book, since too much had changed. The new one is an examination of how the Australians have become what they are, and how they might cope with their future. Horne believes that the 1970's will be Australia's greatest decade of change, with more ways of turning, good and bad, than he had imagined when he wrote the earlier book. A book to read after you know a bit about the country.

Unfortunately, *The Next Australia* and another illuminating book, George Mikes's *Boomerang,* Andre Deutsch, 1968, are not as yet published in the United States. If you have an acquaintance in Australia write him and ask him to send you copies. They're worth the trouble.

Art Linkletter. *Linkletter Down Under.* Prentice-Hall, 1968. Chronicles TV personality Art Linkletter's first disastrous investments (rice paddies in a place named Humpty Doo) to his eventual "showplace" at Esperance in Western Australia. Light, but informative. Australian cartoonist Paul Rigby's illustrations help.

Organizations

American Chamber of Commerce in Australia. 17 Castlereagh Street; Sydney, N.S.W. 2000; Australia. The American Chamber (AM-

CHAMS, they like to call themselves) is not able to offer any assistance to prospective settlers. Once in Australia they may be of some assistance if you are a businessman needing advice, particularly in finding export markets. Other offices in Brisbane, Melbourne, and Adelaide.

Australian-American Association. Lower Fort Street; Sydney, N.S.W. 2000; Australia. A voluntary cultural association "for the better understanding, mutual appreciation and friendly co-operation of two great pacific democracies." Their letterhead has a seal with an eagle and a kangaroo shaking hands, so to speak. They plan regular informal evenings to help new American settlers meet Australians.

The American Society. 10 Heely Street; Paddington; Sydney N.S.W. 2021; Australia. The best-known organization of its kind in Australia (also with branches in major U.S. cities). Mainly a charitable organization for the well-placed. Luncheons, fashion shows, rummage sales, and a Fourth of July ball. Eight hundred Americans in Australia belong. Inexpensive membership.

Commonwealth Banking Corporation, one of Australia's biggest banks, has a Migrant Information Service for "friendly assistance with any problem you may encounter after arrival in Australia." The service is free; of course, they would like your banking. Inquiries through: The Director; Migrant Information Service; Commonwealth Banking Corporation; Corner Martin Place and Pitt Street; Sydney, N.S.W. 2000; Australia.

The American Families Association of Queensland. 15 Kapunda Street; Toowong, Queensland 4066; Australia. So far, the only really long-lasting association of American families in Australia. Toowong is a suburb of Brisbane, the capital of the state of Queensland. Will provide a six-page bulletin of advice to prospective American families moving to their state; it is the most straight-from-the-shoulder you are likely to get. Memberships vary with your age. Write for details.

New South Wales Center. 680 Fifth Avenue; Room 1306; New York, N.Y. 10019. Mainly a center for industrial information. They provide information and counseling for companies already established in New South Wales, and companies thinking about it. They have a wide range of information available, in addition to actually recruiting teachers. They are not a source of investment information on stocks and shares. Two of the best publications available through them are: *New South Wales, A Handbook for Investors.* This is a survey of the industrial potential of the state, with tables and maps. 183 pages. *Businessman's Guide to Australia* is published by Australia and New

Zealand Bank Limited, but available here. Lots of boiled-down information, addresses, simple maps. Pocket-sized.

Australian consulates. Write to the one closest to you for immigration information: Australian Consulate General, 636 Fifth Avenue, New York, N.Y. 10020; Australian Consulate General, 1 Post Street, Croker Plaza, San Francisco, Calif. 94101; Embassy of Australia, Immigration Department, 1601 Massachusetts Avenue N.W., Washington, D.C. 20036.

American embassy; Warra Lumla; Canberra; Australia.

CANADA

Area: 3,850,000 square miles. Population: 21, 069,000 (1969 est.). Capital: Ottawa (290,741). Languages: English and French.

Australia's appeal in part is that it is distant and unknown. Canada's appeal is closeness and familiarity. To many Americans, Canada seems almost an extension of the United States itself. In a geographic sense, at least, it is so. Two of Canada's great physiographic regions, the Rockies and the Great Plains, are extensions of the same features that dominate the central United States.

Our economies are entwined (but not inseparable). More U.S. money is invested in Canada than in all of Europe. But Canada is a rich country with or without the United States, possessing nickel, water power, oil, vast farming lands, and industry.

Viewed governmentally, Canada often appears strong-headedly resistant to U.S. pressure. Canada was the second Western nation to recognize Communist China, with whom Canada trades, as it continues to do with Cuba. Canadian immigration officials put no formal stigma upon American draft-resisters applying for *landed-immigrant status,* the single category allowing permanent residence in Canada. A twenty-four-year-old American now living in Vancouver adds: "Don't be sold the story that Canadians are just like Americans. Young people from the U.S. especially. They'll have no trouble dropping into the subculture if that's what they want, but you have to go slower with other people. Most Canadians are more conservative than Americans."

But the closeness of Canada and the United States physically and culturally cannot be denied.

The closeness is heightened by reason of three-fourths of Canada's population living within a hundred miles of the long common border, within hours' drive of two of the three most densely populated parts of the United States.

There has always been a measure of border immigration in both directions. The closeness of Detroit to Windsor, Seattle to Vancouver, or Toronto to New York and Boston has meant that a number of Americans and Canadians know each other's country first-hand; for a small percentage, a move of a hundred miles or so has appeared to be not such a great move at all.

But the migration to Canada of large numbers of Americans has been a recent phenomenon. Like the immigration to Australia, the number of Americans going to Canada remained fairly constant during the 1950's, taking an upturn in the 1960's with a sharp increase during 1967. During 1970, more than 24,000 Americans became landed immigrants, about 10,000 of whom were actual wage earners, the rest dependents.

About half that total of Americans came from six states—Washington, California, New York, Illinois, Massachusetts, and Michigan. More American citizens now live in Canada than in Australia, Mexico, England, Israel, and France combined—240,500 by U.S. State Department figures. Still, this impressive number is less than 10 percent of the total number of new settlers that have entered Canada since the end of World War II, almost three million people coming from all over the world.

Canada still has a total population smaller than the state of California. That is one of the greatest appeals of Canada for Americans. A feeling of space.

The new migration to Canada from the United States is a young migration. In 1959, twenty- to twenty-nine-year-olds made up only about 20 percent of the total. By 1969, they made up 45 percent. Actually, the later figure corresponds with the age distribution of all migrants to Canada.

There is a misleading assumption on the part of some people that Canada has appealed strictly to young dissenters. Canada has taken a liberal attitude toward draft-resisters and deserters partly because of policy, partly due to necessity.

Under Canadian law, neither draft resistance nor unilateral resignation from the United States armed service is an extraditable offense, nor is either officially penalized in an application for landed-immigrant status. The government is extremely tolerant, as are Canadians in general. But it depends on the individual.

The unfortunate aspect of the matter is that most dissenters never attempt to qualify for landed-immigrant status. The Refugee Service of the World Council of Churches puts the estimate of American dissenters illegally living in Canada at between 25 and 75 thousand. Another eyewitness source says it is closer to 25 or 30 thousand, with perhaps another 10 thousand wives, children, and girl friends. These people do not show as part of the American migration to Canada. Most have gone to Canada as tourists and melded in, something Canadian officials are aware is only too easy for Americans to do. It is an uneasy life, not only because living without status in any foreign country is uncomfortably chancy, but because enforced exile is something most Americans don't live easily with.

But for the majority of Americans going to Canada, the appeal is closeness, space, and apparently finding a certain tranquillity missing in American life at the moment. The large majority have made previous trips to Canada, often repeated trips prior to application for landed-immigrant status. Such trips are highly recommended by Canadian immigration officials.

In an attempt to make immigration a simpler, more objective process, Canadian immigration policies underwent reform in 1967. The pressure to liberalize the immigration laws came from within Canada itself. Earlier policies left the burden of decision squarely in the hands of a single immigration officer. Critics felt that this lack of objective criteria hurt minorities, mainly southern Europeans, and blacks along with them. About 4 percent of the total number of landed immigrants prior to that time were classified "nonwhite," a category broad enough to include such diverse nationalities as Pakistanis, Samoans, and Trinidadians.

The reformed system is based on qualification by "assessment units"—points, in other words—most assigned on objective criteria. The system is discussed in detail later on. It weights occupation and skill heavily, but also language, education, and age. There remains room for subjective judgments, but the thing to remember is that Canada wants and needs talented hard-working people and is trying to get them. Immigration is controlled not by a justice department, as in the United States, but by a Department of Manpower and Immigration.

Canada can scarcely be thought of primarily as a haven for those on the run from American laws. But the country often moves quite independently of American laws and regulations. Offenses against U.S. Selective Service laws, for example, are neither extraditable offenses in Canada nor of much concern to immigration people. There is some feeling that individual immigration officers, especially those at the borders, are not particularly sympathetic to the idea of American deserters taking nest in Canada. But under Canadian law such breaches of U.S. law have little influence on acquiring landed-immigrant status.

But there are four general classes of people who are prohibited from immigrating to Canada. *Political subversives,* which does not include Communists (the party is legal in Canada) or student activists. The law is aimed at those whom immigration officials have reason to suspect might advocate subversion or engage in sabotage or in any other activities detrimental to Canada. *Drug pushers.* Even suspicion is enough to keep anyone out, or immediately deport those already in. At present, no distinction is made between marihuana and hard drugs. *Criminal offenders* convicted of crimes of "moral turpitude," which is roughly equivalent to U.S. felony convictions. There are some cases where people with former criminal records may be permitted to enter Canada. Ask Canadian consular officials.

The fourth prohibited class is a miscellaneous category that includes prostitutes, homosexuals, persons who are mentally or physically defective, alcoholics, and anyone who might appear to an immigration officer likely to become a public charge. Canada is not unique in such prohibitions. A similar restriction applies to immigrants coming to United States, and exists in all the "people-seeking" countries, whether written as law or a *de facto* policy.

PROCEDURES

Anyone can apply for immigration to Canada from any country in the world. There are no quotas, nor is there a limit set on the total number of immigrants allowed admittance.

There are three categories of immigrants:

(1) Independent Applicants. This is the most common category for Americans who apply. You must be eighteen years of age or over, and meet certain selection criteria. Having a job offer does not ensure acceptance, but it helps. Having a job lined up is not compulsory for admission as a landed immigrant. A demand for your profession or trade is considered an important factor, however.

(2) Nominated Applicants. You can be nominated by a relative in Canada if he is a citizen or a landed immigrant. Nominated relatives must be sons or daughters aged twenty-one or over, parents or grandparents under sixty, nephews, nieces, uncles, aunts, and grandchildren. Cousins don't count. Nominated applicants are required to meet reduced criteria, based mainly on skill.

(3) Sponsored Applicants. This is a nonworking category used mainly for dependents of landed immigrants or citizens already in Canada. They do not have to meet any selection criteria other than having good health and character. Sponsored applicants are limited to wife; husband; fiancée; unmarried sons or daughters under twenty-one; parents or grandparents aged sixty or over (or younger if they are widowed or unable to work); and orphaned brothers, sisters, nephews, nieces, or grandchildren under eighteen.

You can apply independently for landed-immigrant status in Canada itself, at the Canadian border, or at a Canadian consulate in the United States, which will require at some stage your sending your application directly to Ottawa.

In each case, the assessment process is essentially the same, except that if applying within Canada, you are not given assessment units for having a job offer. If applying within Canada, you'll need all of your documents with you. If you are turned down for other than statutory reasons—your profession or skill not currently needed, for example —you may apply again later.

Currently a number of people apply for landed-immigrant status at the border. The Toronto Anti-Draft Movement recommends it as the best way if you have been properly counseled, know what to expect, and are prepared for it. The application-and-interview procedure is still the same. The entire procedure for border application is under review, however, and there is some feeling that it may be discontinued or modified.

Canadian immigration officials recommend application by mail, either preceded by a visit to the consulate for information or followed by an interview with an immigration Officer.

All advice points in one direction: visit Canada first, *before* you apply for landed-immigrant status. The borders won't close while you are thinking about migrating. Probably the most successful Americans going to Canada already know it well. You will be looked upon as even more desirable by immigration officials. Better yet, you can look for a job while on your visit, as long as you don't actually try to work.

The application form, "Application for Permanent Residence in Canada," is available (1) from the Department of Immigration, Ottawa 2, Canada; (2) in person from any Canadian consulate in the United States (see "Finding Out More" for cities with consulates); or (3) by mail from those same consulates.

If you request information by mail from a Canadian consulate, you will receive, in addition to three copies of the application form, the following: a very courteous letter that begins "Dear Friend"; a set of instructions for filling out the application; a single-sheet bulletin titled *Initial Information* ("Canada welcomes people of good character and in good health . . ."); a summary of customs regulations for settlers; three "fact sheets," one each on "Geography and Climate" and "Social Benefits," and another, different, "Initial Information," which contains the warning that all services of the Department of Manpower and Immigration are free—there is therefore no need to deal with or pay money to an outside agency for special consideration beyond the merits of your qualifications. In other words, you can't pay anyone to do anything to help you get into Canada that you can't do for yourself.

The application process can be looked at as having three parts: (1) filling in the application itself, and acquiring the proper supporting documents; (2) its assessment, based on units and the interview; (3) the occupational outlook as far as your skill and chosen region in Canada are concerned at the time of application.

Assessment of your qualifications, as stated in your application, is the most important. But it is nothing to shy away from. Most Americans with either a strong educational background or some professional competence can qualify fairly easily. The whole idea behind the "assessment-unit" system was to allow for your outstanding attributes to be considered, in whatever field they might be.

There are nine separate categories of assessment, each with an allotted number of assessment units. Usually a total of 50 to 100 points is required for admittance as a landed immigrant.

The categories are as follows:

(1) Education and Training. Up to 20 units, awarded on the basis of one unit for each whole, successful year of formal education or occupational training. A high-school education would be worth 12 points, a two-year junior-college degree 14.

(2) Personal Assessment. Up to 15 units, based on the immigration officer's assessment of the applicant's adaptability, motivation, initiative, and so forth. This is the only "subjective" category. The units are given at the time of personal interview, either at the border or in a consulate in the United States.

(3) Occupational Demand. Up to 15 units if your skill is in strong demand. The Department of Manpower and Immigration has 130 economists and a big computer whose job it is to analyze needs and data from all over Canada. The result: a series of "Occupational and

Area Demand Guides," revised every three months. Skills and trades are reordered as needed. Used also in category (9).

(4) Occupational Skill. Up to 10 units for the professional, ranging down to one unit for unskilled labor. If admitted in a certain skill category, you are not required to actually work in that occupation once in Canada.

(5) Age. Ten units for applicants under thirty-five. One unit deducted for each year over thirty-five, down to the limit of zero.

(6) Arranged Employment. Ten units if you have already arranged a job in Canada. One of the best reasons for the preliminary visit.

(7) Knowledge of French and English. Up to 10 units, depending on degree of fluency in French and English. If you can read and write English, you'll get at least five here. You may have to demonstrate your language facility.

(8) Relative. Up to 5 points for a relative in Canada able to offer you help in becoming established, even though unprepared or unable to help you enter as a sponsored or nominated applicant.

(9) Employment Opportunities in Area of Destination. Up to 5 points if the applicant intends to settle in an area with a high labor demand. See category (3) above. If you are self-employed or an entrepreneur, there is a special category in place of skill. Kind of business and money to invest are important here. Up to 25 points.

Even with this system of assessment, you are not strictly a victim of numbers and the computer. If there are good reasons, the immigration officer can approve your application even though you have fewer points than 50. Likewise, if your application does not truly reflect your poor chances of making a go of it in Canada, the immigration officer can refuse your application, despite a high number of points. This seldom happens.

The application form is designed to provide information to measure against the nine categories of assessment.

Be sure to print carefully or use a typewriter when you fill it out. This is not an effort to be pedantic. An extraordinary number of applications received by the Canadians are illegible.

Beyond that, be honest, since you'll have to prove anything you claim, but try to display yourself as steady and responsible. All questions must be answered. At some point you will be asked to show the following proofs: (1) A birth certificate or certified copy. (2) Proof of marital status—marriage, divorce, separation, death certificate if widowed; original or certified copies. (3) Proof of schooling and training —high-school diploma, college degrees, proof of completion of formal apprenticeships, transcripts, union cards, government diplomas. (4) Proof of good character. (5) Proof of financial assets—things you plan to take with you, bank statements, insurance policies, list of stocks and bonds. (6) Vehicle ownership. (7) Other documents—draft card; passports; if not a U.S. citizen, an Alien Registration Card.

The Selection Interview.   This will be given by an immigration officer in a Canadian consulate in the United States, or, if you decided to apply at the border, in a customs office.

If you have applied by mail directly to Ottawa, you will hear from an immigration officer in the United States six weeks to two months later, unless you are found not acceptable, in which case they will notify you by mail. If an immigration officer calls for an appointment, this does not mean you have been accepted. You should not quit your job or rashly conclude your personal affairs. The cost of transportation between your home and the interview is your responsibility.

The main purpose of the interview is to attempt to determine how well you will settle into Canada. The interviewing officer will have a copy of your application and its assessment, and will probably go through it asking you questions. One question most likely to be asked is: "Are you prepared to do other kinds of work in Canada, initially at least, outside of your profession or trade?" You can be direct with these people. They are curious, want to find out if you'll work, but are not hostile out of principle. The immigration officer will assign up to 15 units on this personal assessment of you. Another question he will probably ask is: "Why do you want to migrate to Canada?". The best advice is to be positive about Canada rather than negative about the United States.

If the selection phase of the interview goes well, there is a secondary purpose to the interview—a counseling phase. The immigration officer will discuss the various services the government provides for new migrants. He will probably mention the subsistence scheme, aimed at supporting you if everything goes wrong or if you were to be injured or taken ill, thus preventing you from working. He will advise you about registration with professional associations, if you haven't done it already. (See section on "Working in Canada.") Here is your chance to ask questions—about schooling or about language-learning facilities if you are intending to settle in French-speaking Canada.

The entire selection interview will probably take from one to two hours.

Following the interview, you and your family will have to take a medical exam. Children under eleven are usually exempt from x-ray and lab tests. All family members must be examined before the first is allowed entrance to Canada with landed-immigrant status. The immigration officer will advise you exactly what must be covered by the physical, but the expense is yours.

The final qualification requires money too. Before you are admitted to Canada you must satisfy immigration officials that you have enough to support yourself and your family initially. This is critical if you are applying for status at the border. This is another plus for having a job lined up beforehand; the financial requirements and burden will be less. Immigration officials are always reluctant to recommend amounts of money, and tend to recommend high. One independent expert suggests $300 minimum for a single person. With a family, expenses seem to increase in geometric proportion to the numbers. But the X-factor is the new city. There is no relation between the cost of living for a settled household and the start-up or shock costs of arrival. If you are without a job, you'll want to have enough cash to keep from dealing from a panic position; dealing from a position of power is the best way to go job-hunting in Canada, too. Figure $1,000 as an absolute minimum, with family, without job.

WORKING IN CANADA

Technically, having your skill or talent accredited is easier than in any other country. Work regulations and accrediting of your credentials come under the jurisdiction of the province in which you intend to work and live.

The Occupational Research section of the Department of Manpower and Immigration publishes a series of bulletins called "Canadian Occupations." They are available from the Canadian consulate. One for your skill or trade should be acquired before application, even before your first visit to Canada.

The bulletins are produced for a number of occupations, major and minor, and are revised frequently. Each bulletin contains information on how a particular occupation is prepared for in Canada; what the registration, certification, or licensing requirements are for migrants; the separate requirements for each of Canada's provinces; how your qualifications will be assessed (and any fees for assessment and licenses); and most important, the names and addresses of relevant organizations you can write to for information.

If you are accepted as a landed immigrant without a job, 300

Manpower offices are available to help you find work, *once you are in Canada.* Remember, you are not required to work in a particular occupation or in a particular region, once you have landed-immigrant status.

As a landed immigrant you have a number of the same rights and obligations as a Canadian citizen—working, owning property, transacting business. But you cannot vote, and you are not required to serve in Canada's armed forces. Landed-immigrant status does not affect your American citizenship. After five years as a landed immigrant you are considered domiciled, and are eligible for Canadian citizenship. It is unnecessary to become a Canadian citizen to continue residing in Canada. Becoming a Canadian citizen would require renunciation of your American citizenship.

FINDING OUT MORE

Manual for Draft-Age Immigrants to Canada. Byron Wall, editor. Toronto Anti-Draft Program. Fifth edition, 1970. This is the best book, bar none, for Canadian immigration procedures. Revised frequently. Available from the above for two dollars. P.O. Box 41, Station K; Toronto 315, Ontario; Canada.

Tax and Trade Guide for Canada. Arthur Andersen and Company; 1345 Avenue of the Americas; New York, N.Y. 10019. Free. Write on letterhead.

Information Guide to Doing Business in Canada. Price Waterhouse and Company; 60 Broad Street; New York, N.Y. 10005. Free. Write on letterhead.

Taxation in Canada. Bank of Montreal. A forty-four-page booklet revised yearly. Available from the head office in Montreal or from Canadian immigration authorities.

Canadian Consulates in the following cities: Los Angeles*; San Francisco*; Washington, D.C.; Chicago*; New Orleans; Boston; Detroit; New York City*; Cleveland; Philadelphia; San Juan; Dallas; Seattle. Asterisk (*) denotes immigration officer in residence. New offices are due to be added.

Canadian Embassy; 1746 Massachusetts Avenue N.W.; Washington, D.C. 20009.

American Embassy; 100 Wellington Street; Ottawa 4, Ontario Canada.

ISRAEL

Area: 8,000 square miles (about equal to the state of New Jersey). Population: 3,000,000 (1971). Capital: Jerusalem (266,300). Language: Hebrew.

If you think Israel needs you, nothing doing, you're a fool, stay away. But do you need Israel? That's the question.

—HAROLD ISAACS, *American Jews in Israel*

Every so often history has a way of reminding Jews how much they need Israel. For an earlier generation it was Europe's holocaust, followed by the independence of Israel, realization of the Zionists' dream of a place to go.

Between independence in 1948 and 1966 a million and a half Jews made *aliyah*—the coming up to—Israel. Many were refugees from Eastern Europe or from Yemen, Egypt, Iraq, and other parts of Asia and Africa. The majority became Israeli citizens under the 1950 Law of Return, which makes Jews without citizenship Israelis upon crossing the border, with few restrictions. During this period American Jews supported Israel morally and with contributions, but few actually made the *aliyah*.

The ones who did were mainly the younger idealists who had been raised on the idea of Zionism by parents and the older pensioners. The total number of American and Canadian Jews going as *oleh* (migrants) never exceeded 1,700 in any one year.

For a new generation of Jews the Israeli-Arab war in 1967 (Jews refer to it consistently as the Six-Day War) turned out to be their reminder. The war has been catalytic. Since then Israel has received a wave of new immigration, primarily nonrefugee, of which Jews from North America are a larger part than ever before.

In the year following the Israeli-Arab war, the number of migrants from Canada and North America jumped to 4,300. In 1969 the figure rose again to 6,500, and in 1970 to more than 9,000. Officials look

185

toward a regular migration of North American Jews to make up about 20 percent of the yearly goal of about 40,000. They are hoping to tap the large reservoir of American Jewry that has never felt the need of Israel to the extent of considering it as a place they too might choose to live permanently.

Up to a point it has already begun to happen. The American Jews going to Israel are different from the earlier *oleh*. A photograph of any group departing would show a fairly typical group of middle-class Americans, maybe a few more smiles than most, and perhaps a larger proportion of young children. In 1970, nearly 30 percent of the men were professionals—teachers, engineers, doctors, social workers. Most were under forty-five with families, although one-third of the total were aged nineteen to thirty. There were few rich among them, although there is an increasing number of wealthy American Jews who have built apartments in Tel Aviv or Jerusalem and now spend the winter months there rather than in Miami.

To some extent the push factors in America—crime, racial problems, the increasing difficulty of having a cohesive family life—have focused many Jews' thoughts on Israel. But when American Jews talk about why they are going to Israel, they overwhelmingly reflect Israel's pull. They go "to seek a Jewish identity" or for the "opportunity to shape our destiny as Jews." Some feel the need "to find a more Jewish life" or the need "to live in a Jewish country." For many, Israel might properly be called less a place than a state of mind. As one Israeli official said, if Jews weren't committed to the idea of Israel, there was no other reason to go. "It is a tired piece of geography with miserable summers. This isn't Europe. This is the Middle East."

The liabilities of living in Israel are prodigious, but for the newer immigrants they seldom outweigh the country's attractions. One fairly typical comment on the existing mixture of pluses and minuses came from a man in his mid-forties, currently living in Jerusalem with his wife and two sons, one Israeli-born. As a teen-ager he had dropped out of high school in Canada to fight for Israeli independence, later going to graduate school and teaching in the United States. He is currently undecided whether to stay in Israel because of the difficulty of "hacking it financially," one of the greatest problems for Americans who go to Israel without some independent income. He writes:

> I'm the last one to claim this country is perfect or ideal. There's much to criticize. They drive terribly here, people tend to be rude and short-tempered, and red tape is everywhere. The taxes are the highest in the

world. The cost of living is ridiculous, There's a lack of what Americans consider luxury, and unless you've got money to burn, it goes on and on. But you stop short when you've said all that and begin to think. You've no fear of being mugged or murdered on the street. And there's a feeling here you don't find elsewhere. As a Jew you're finally in a country of Jews, and you are at home. And best of all, this is a wonderful country for children. Everything here is oriented toward the younger generation, toward building a future. Take it all into consideration and then add on the historical and religious value of the country, and you're sort of overwhelmed by it all.

A woman agreed it was the idea of Israel that was important, but then rolled her eyes and shrugged. "But how can you generalize about our motives? Jews can't even agree on what a Jew is."

In his perceptive book *The Israelis,* Israeli journalist Amos Elon noted that cultural and social dissensions over just such questions as "What is a Jew?" at one time threatened Israel's stability. The conflict between religious and secular Israelis, between "dark-skinned" Oriental immigrants and "white" European immigrants, between the older ideologically oriented generations and the more pragmatic *sabras* (Israeli-born), all threatened, as Elon put it, to abrade the delicate tissues of a new society.

Much of that was prevented by Arab hostility. Writes Elon:

Arab antagonism has helped to foster the sense of shared social purpose, unity and cohesion that continues to prevail among a people notorious for their quarrelsomeness. There are times in the lives of communities when an enemy renders a service that even a friend cannot match. . . . In this respect, Arab antagonism has been a great help to Israel.

The Israeli-Arab war has done more than unify the Israelis. It is in large part responsible for the increased immigration of American Jews to Israel. By constantly focusing their attention on the homeland, many American Jews have made a personal rediscovery of what the country means to them.

Another reason for increased immigration has been the realization by Israeli officials that while a new demand may have been created for the product, the old machinery for recruiting migrants and helping them adjust to Israel hadn't worked very well for Americans. Better management has played its part.

The first step was a revitalization of the recruiting arm of the World Zionist Organization, the Israel Aliyah Center. Actually there are fourteen centers throughout the United States and Canada, charged with the mission of helping interested North American Jews move to Israel.

The Israel Aliyah Center in New York City occupies the eighth floor of a building owned by its sponsoring organization, on Park Avenue between 59th and 60th streets. The northwest-corner office is occupied by former Israeli Army Colonel Nachum Golan, who, as of spring 1972, directs the recruiting operations for the centers in North America.

The easy metaphor would be that Colonel Golan directs the operations with military precision. Indeed, there are certain accessories of the military—a map of the United States on one wall of his office showing the Israel Aliyah Centers and their districts, along with grease-pencil numbers on each state of the Jewish population as estimated by the *American Jewish Yearbook.* None of the offices or fittings are posh.

But the center itself has neither the feel of the military, nor even of government, although the organization is most certainly an official Israeli presence. Nice-looking secretaries seem extraordinarily busy. A physical closeness of the desks gives the impression that space is important. Waiting in one of the center's usually crowded reception lounges, one senses what the Latins would call *movimento.* There is something at stake, either money or high purpose. If the center were an advertising agency, which it most resembles—minus the posh offices— it would be both. But here there is only purpose, an interest in spreading the word. An indication of the belief in the power of the organization to do that came from Colonel Golan. In an interview he was asked how instrumental the center had been in the growth of the *aliyah* from North America. "It is not a question of how we were instrumental," he replied. "For we are *the* instrument."

Of the 9,000 Canadians and Americans who settled in Israel in 1970, 7,568 were processed through one of the center's offices.

Actually, the Israel Aliyah Center organization has three purposes: (1) promotion of the idea of American Jews returning to Israel; (2) processing of the seriously interested; and implicit in that, (3) screening those American Jews who might be unsuitable or who perhaps have unreal expectations about what they may find in Israel. The center has no authority to deal with non-Jews who might be interested in Israel.

In an office of near equal size to Colonel Golan's is a public-relations man busy with a quarterly newsletter, between his main jobs of dealing with radio and television media and writing up the success stories of new immigrants in Israel. The Colonel himself devotes a great deal of travel to the promotion of *aliyah* to Israel, talking with the press, community, and business leaders and keeping the team of more than twenty counselors in the fourteen offices around the country on their toes.

These counselors are the heart of the operation. The burden of processing and screening falls upon them. They are all Israeli professional men, in the United States on contracts that seldom exceed two or three years. They arrive with a sense of mission and the full knowledge that their assignment is limited, not a bureaucratic nest. Accordingly, it adds a certain zest to their work. Their job is to provide information and advice face-to-face with Jews considering *aliyah*.

Counselors get to know their clients quite well, and the processing of each one may require considerable correspondence with Israel on matters of employment, accommodation, transportation, schooling, and the like. Counselors have the added power of being able to authorize a wide range of benefits and in special cases loans for those who have skills and trades particularly attractive. Very often the processing of a family on its way to Israel may stretch over six to nine months, and in comparison with, say, migrants going to Australia or New Zealand, those going to Israel seem more willing to give themselves enough lead time.

A letter from one of the counselors to the Israeli consulate is a virtual requirement for obtaining a residence visa. By their charter the Israel Aliyah Center deals only with immigration, no tourism, and in that only with Jews.

The Israeli government has made adjustments on the other end too.

Prior to the Israeli-Arab war the Israeli government was geared mainly to handle refugees. Americans didn't get enough help. They showed up as individuals, more separate from the Israeli population by their Americanness than alike because of their Jewishness. As late as 1968, fewer than one-third of the Jews in Israel were born in Europe or North America. (The number of American-born Israelis is still proportionally small, numbering in total about 40,000.) An almost equal percentage were Jews from Africa and Asia. Another 44 percent of the population were born in Israel. When an American Jew talked with an Israeli official about living at a certain standard, it had a different context than the needs of a Yemeni or Iraqi Jew. Americans suffered culture shock, were frustrated with Hebrew, and became lonely when Israel's horrendous bureaucracy ignored them.

Prior to the Supreme Court decision *Afroyim* v. *Rusk* (see chapter on "Rules of the Game") they had an additional liability. They were forced to make a decision between Israeli citizenship and U.S. citizenship very quickly. Most opted out of Israeli citizenship, and with it, full participation in the life and problems of the country. Most Americans ended up quasi-Israelis if they ended up Israelis at all. A high proportion did not; they stayed for a while and then returned. Harold Isaacs, in his 1966 book *American Jews in Israel,* estimates that five in six Americans prior to the Israeli-Arab war eventually returned to the United States. The Jewish agency estimated one-half.

Since 1967 much has changed. *Afroyim* v. *Rusk* has eased the citizenship problem from one side. In 1969 the Israeli government made a special provision for Americans who had previously opted out of Israeli citizenship, until then a one-time choice, to acquire it. Now most American Jews in Israel hold dual citizenship, two passports, without penalty or problems from either government.

And there are indications that the Israeli government is becoming more attuned to the problems of American Jews going to Israel. The revitalizing of the Israel Aliyah Center is only one such indication. In Israel, new legislation gives a number of rights and benefits to the newcomer. Professional people immigrating to Israel may house themselves and their families in newly built Absorption Centers at modest cost, and there receive a five-month intensive course in Hebrew at one of the *ulpanim,* or language schools. Younger people are encouraged to attend city *ulpanim,* or learn the language on one of Israel's many *kibbutzim.*

The attrition rate of American Jews who go to Israel has dropped considerably as the cumulative effect of these measures has begun to be felt. About 90 percent of the Americans who have gone to Israel since 1967 are still there.

Another contributing reason is that American Jews have made effective use of another facet of what it takes to make and sustain a move to another culture—collective action. Americans pride themselves on their individualism, on their ability to go it alone. In moves to other countries, most Americans prepare independently, go independently, and frequently move just as independently into disappointment, frustration, and failure. Even American Jews have a strong strain of individualism that makes the sudden communal life in a small country like Israel a strain at times. Americans in general seem reluctant to combine unless it can be demonstrated that by collective action they will somehow concretely and quickly profit. The Association of Americans and Canadians for Aliyah has made the discovery that there is profit of a sort in their brand of collective action. Or more precisely, collective preparation.

The Association of Americans and Canadians for Aliyah is made up of people who have committed themselves to the *aliyah* within three years of joining. It is finannced privately and by the modest dues of its members in thirty-five groups in the United States and Canada.

One purpose of the AACA is to focus on the practical problems of Americans getting ready for *aliyah*. Most chapters meet monthly to discuss job-hunting, finding an apartment, where and what to buy, the kind and quality of obstetrical care—in short, the problems that really prey on people's minds prior to a move away from home, especially the women of the family. The quarterly newsletter *The Aliyon* includes articles on such topics as tenant laws in Israel and the pros and cons of buying an automobile, with a good deal of attention given to the experiences of the new *olim* and the success and horror stories of their particular moves to Israel.

Another mission of the AACA is to interpret Israel (and the Israeli government's words) for Americans. Because they are a privately financed organization, they find it easier to be objective. Their counseling efforts often collide with the information and advice of the Israel Aliyah Center, although there is a good working relationship between the two organizations.

Their advice is sometimes frank to the point of bluntness. They will not hesitate to counsel people with little prospect of earning a living in Israel to stay in the United States. They frequently advise students and college dropouts to develop their skills before going to Israel; the country has few resources except what its people have to offer, and skills are the key. Since the Israel Aliyah Center will deal only with Jews, the AACA finds itself in the role of having to discourage many idealists and religiously motivated non-Jews from seriously considering immigration to Israel.

The AACA has made the most effective use of the pilot-trip idea of any organization of Americans considering emigration. Often these trial trips are for the purpose of finding a job, but also to look at schooling and housing, which is a greater problem in Israel than in any other major people-seeking country. As elsewhere, Israeli employers prefer personal interviews, and the AACA, realizing that many Americans can't make a pilot trip to Israel, have been encouraging employers to make recruiting trips to the United States. But one AACA executive shook her head, wondering how anyone, even a Jew going to Israel, would consider a move to a new country without seeing it first. A few do, but not many. A large proportion of Americans who do go to Israel have been there before.

The AACA has a sister organization in Israel, the Association of Americans and Canadians in Israel. In addition to publishing a number of booklets that deal directly with the immediate problems that American Jews face in moving to Israel (see "Finding Out More"), they try to ease the initial shock. Representatives meet the new *olim* during their first few days in the country and attempt to show them the elements of social survival in their new setting.

Successful migration to another country still rests squarely upon the tenacity of an individual or a family. But an organization that wants to help, and does so candidly and with a sense of humor, can ease the burden immensely. In that respect, these organizations have no equal.

FINDING OUT MORE

There is one official source for finding out about *aliyah,* the Israel Aliyah Center, Inc., whose national office is at 515 Park Avenue; New York, N.Y. 10022. There are regional offices in Boston; Chicago; Washington, D.C.; Cleveland; Philadelphia; Los Angeles; San Francisco; Forest Hills, N.Y.; Atlanta; and St. Louis.

The Israel Aliyah Center also publishes a free newsletter. The spring, 1971, issue was an excellent treatment of employment possibilities, including a long list of organizations. Write: Editor, *News and Views;* 515 Park Avenue; New York, N.Y. 10022.

The Association of Americans and Canadians for Aliyah; 515 Park Avenue; New York, N.Y. 10022. The AACA publishes two books that are available to nonmembers: *Inside High,* a handbook for high-school students in Israel; and *Woman of Valor,* which discusses the unique problems of the American housewife in a culturally different setting. Each costs fifty cents.

The Association of Americans and Canadians in Israel; 53A Hayarkon Street; Tel Aviv, Israel. The AACI publishes the following booklets, available on request: *Tourist and Pilot Trip Information, The Tenant and the Law, Israel and U.S. Citizenship,* and *Handbook of Helpful Hints.*

The American Embassy; 71 Hayarkon Street; Tel Aviv, Israel.

NEW ZEALAND

Area: 103,736 square miles. Population: 2,856,000 (Dec., 1970, est.) Capital: Wellington (urban area 175,500; April, 1969, est.) Largest city: Auckland (urban area 588,400; April, 1969, est.). Language: English.

Truly contented people usually find little compulsion to talk about their happiness, and so it is, I suspect, with the Americans who have found in New Zealand the sort of life they have always dreamed of. Said one young American living near the city of Christchurch, wallowing each fall in mounds of ripening apples: "I don't want to tell you too much about New Zealand. If people knew how nice it was, they'd sell out and swim down here if they had to."

New Zelanders themselves, especially those living temporarily elsewhere, all talk of home with a begrudging smugness, as though they were the possessors of a secret they weren't sure they wanted to share with anyone else.

They may very well be. James Michener once called New Zealand the most beautiful country on earth, adding that most New Zealanders would find it difficult to believe that there could be a better land anywhere. The country is smaller than most Americans realize, a land area about equal to Colorado, with a population total about the same as Brooklyn, New York.

But the geographic diversity of New Zealand is immense, perhaps more varied than any area of comparable size in the world. Californians are often fond of bragging that within a few hours' drive one can have seacoast or desert, surfing or skiing, city life or country tranquillity. New Zealanders can make the same boast, and make it without excuses for the grinding traffic, the droves of people, the smog, and the general rush that attends enjoying the contrasts in California.

At the northernmost tip of North Island is Ninety Mile Beach, set amid a tropical lushness. If something less than ninety miles long (it measures in fact some sixty miles), it remains one of the most spectacular stretches of seafront in the world. In the waters nearby are marlin, swordfish, and some of the best sport fishing for sharks found anywhere. More world-famous, among fishermen anyway, are the New Zealand rainbow trout, caught in the rushing streams near Lake Taupo, almost in the exact center of the North Island, a wildly volcanic landscape dominated by mounts Egmont, Ruapehu, Ngauruhoe, and Tongariro, with the exception of Mount Egmont all still active volcanoes. On the North Island too are Auckland, New Zealand's largest and most cosmopolitan city, and Wellington, the capital.

The North Island is the more developed of the two islands, more industrialized, and some observers say the less beautiful, although it is probably a subject best avoided among New Zealanders of the North Island.

The South Island is more agricultural, orcharding mainly, with sprawling sheep ranches that account for one of New Zealand's most valuable exports, wool. The New Zealand-bred merino is an aristocratic-looking sheep valued more for its coat than as mutton. The South Island is less densely populated, although strictly speaking New Zealand can't be considered a rural country at all. Some 60 percent of the population live in cities and towns. The South Islanders are considered more conservative, Christchurch said to be the most placid (and stuffy) of New Zealand's major cities.

Of the two islands, the South Island is the more mountainous, with a dozen peaks over 10,000 feet, a spinelike chain of mountains known as the Southern Alps. The glaciered peak of Mount Cook reaches some 12,000 feet in elevation, and the fiorded eastern coast of South Island is more reminiscent of Norway or British Columbia than an island in the Pacific.

Considering the diversity within New Zealand alone, it is easy to see why the quickest way to get under the skin of a New Zealander is to include him in the same breath with Australians (the Australians don't like it, either). Among the English speakers of the world, Americans are perhaps the only ones who can't tell their accents apart, and that is the least of their differences.

New Zealand is some 1,200 miles west of Australia. They are both members of the British Commonwealth, members of the tripartite ANZUS defense pact with the United States, share an interest and influence in the entire southwestern Pacific, and have a trade pact. These are mainly the doing of the politicians. Both New Zealanders and Australians are more likely to have visited England or the United

States than have ventured a trip to each other's country. New Zealand still relies on Britian as its chief trading partner and cultural kindred spirit. New Zealand exports less to Australia than to Japan.

The difference in the countries has caused a good deal of exchange migration between the two, but not of Australians and New Zealanders. Migrants from Britain have made up the bulk of immigrants to both countries. Some who have found Australia too raw, or hot, or "uncivilized" have found New Zealand's conservative ways reminiscent of home.

Because of New Zealand's predominantly British heritage, travel writers often describe the country as "England of old." In a number of easily visible ways the comparison is valid—eating habits, the erratic closing hours of pubs and restaurants, and an English Midlands look to the cities. In attitudes and values New Zealand strongly reflects British antecedents, and the New Zealanders like it that way. But the "England-of-old" label goes only so far. Eight percent of the population, almost a quarter of a million people, are Maoris, the country's indigenous Polynesian population; they are a picturesque and fully integrated part of New Zealand society. New Zealand has traditionally strong ties with the neighboring islands of western Polynesia, and for many Western Samoans, Tongans, and Cook Islanders, Auckland is considered the Big City.

Despite the obvious and considerable appeal of the country, New Zealand has had its share of difficulty holding on to new settlers, British and American. There has been a modest emigration of born and bred New Zealanders as well.

Between 1948 and the beginning of 1967 New Zealand received almost a half-million immigrants, a considerably smaller figure than were accepted by either Canada or Australia. During the same period more than 200,000 people living in New Zealand left for other parts. This sort of coming and going is not peculiar to New Zealand. The movement of people over the planet is probably greater than anyone but demographers and immigration officials realize. A certain percentage of all new settlers to a place, no matter their country of origin, fail to find what they are looking for and return home. Americans may be the most restless of the lot.

According to the *New Zealand Official Yearbook,* the number of Americans who settle in New Zealand and eventually change their minds is greater than average, about four in seven. It is difficult to say why. It appears that many of the attractive things about New Zealand eventually repel a small minority.

Undoubtedly one attraction of New Zealand is the country's geographical isolation. Not only is it more than 1,000 miles from Australia, but some 1,400 miles from its other large continental neighbor, Antarctica. Writer Neil Morgan observed that New Zealand was so remote that the islands seemed to rise from a wilderness of sea. The New Zealanders struck him as kindly people seemingly content "riding out the storm in a secluded corner of the world." The vision of a quiet, untroubled country uninvolved in the hurly-burly of power politics and East-West confrontation appeals to many.

For other Americans, isolation seems to go against an ingrained feeling of wanting to be where the action is. I've talked with Americans living in Argentina and Australia who told me that living in the Southern Hemisphere, so far from everything, gave them a disturbing feeling of being detached from the main concerns of the world. They felt "out of it." Just how factually based such a feeling is, what with radio, jet plane, and supersonic missile, is hard to determine. But geographic isolation, even peace and tranquillity, for some people is a weighty burden. The dividing line between peace and boredom is hairline thin.

Others grow discontented with the "cradle-to-grave" security of the country, as it was referred to by one New Zealander, and the lack of competitiveness in New Zealand society. Again, it is these two aspects of life in New Zealand that appeal to many. The country has been called the workingman's paradise, mainly because of the high employment practices and the comprehensive system of social insurance, which includes not only health and medical benefits but protection for the aged, the unemployed, free public education for all up to the age of nineteen, and a number of other benefits.

Such benefits are paid for in large part by one of the highest personal income-tax rates in the world. A New Zealander who earns the equivalent of $6,500 a year must give half of it to the government. Critics say that the high taxes, combined with the protectiveness of the government, have created a lack of incentive to compete, which strikes many a New Zealander as the proper way to enjoy life, but it works nonetheless against the individual with a craving to climb to the top of whatever heap he happens to find challenging. In New Zealand, apparently, there is no top or bottom; it is all middle, and some personalities find that difficult to abide by.

But the important fact is that a growing number of Americans are settling in New Zealand. During most of the 1960's a total of 30,000 to 40,000 migrants entered New Zealand each year (except for a brief recession-caused slump in 1969), the majority coming from Great Britain.

For most of the 1960's the number of Americans never exceeded 800 in any single year. In 1969, while other immigrants decreased, the number of new American settlers in New Zealand exceeded 1,000 for the first time. In the fiscal year ending March 31, 1971, a record 2,161 Americans arrived to make New Zealand home, more than double the figure of two years before.

Still the total points to anything but a massive American presence in New Zealand. At the moment about 4,000 Americans live in the country, a number equal to those in Denmark, Taiwan, or Korea. Considerably more Americans live in Singapore than in New Zealand.

One of the reasons is that New Zealand's immigration policy is more carefully selective than Australia's or Canada's, and the total number accepted is much less. New Zealand takes about as many new immigrants a year as South Africa.

Despite distance and cost, a pilot trip to New Zealand as a tourist is strongly advised; a number of Americans who finally decide to apply for permanent settlement have been there before. In New Zealand it is particularly difficult to find work at long distance, and unlike Australia, which allows immigration without firm employment, the New Zealanders consider a prior offer of employment practically a prerequisite for issuance of a permit to settle in the country. There are exceptions, but not many.

PROCEDURES

Travelers may go to New Zealand for up to thirty days on a visitor's permit, easily arranged by a travel agent. It requires a passport and a ticket onward or return.

For all visits over thirty days, you'll need a visa of one kind or another, which must be applied for at one of the New Zealand consulates general in this country, prior to travel.

A *tourist visa* is valid for stays of up to three months per visit and can be issued for multiple three-month visits over a forty-eight-month period. In addition to an application you'll probably be asked to show that you have funds to sustain your visit, and a ticket on to a country for which you have a visa, or return home.

There is also a *working-holiday visa* intended for businessmen, and good for up to a year. Here you need to fill out an application, show proof from a bank that you have enough money to live on, and possess a valid passport.

As a tourist you cannot work in New Zealand, nor can you apply for a *permanent visa* or change your visa status while in New Zealand. If you go to New Zealand as a tourist and find a job, you will have to return to your country of origin (the United States), then go through the procedure for applying for a *permanent-residence visa;* all people who go to New Zealand with the intention of settling permanently require a *permanent residence visa.*

Your first step is to contact the nearest New Zealand consulate general (see "Finding Out More" for addresses). Applying for a permanent-residence visa is something you'll have to do yourself, since this is outside the capability of a travel agent.

The consulates general act on behalf of the Immigration Division of the New Zealand Department of Labor. Authorization to enter New Zealand to settle permanently resides in Wellington, not the consulate general. The consulate's principal job is to advise you, provide you with information, and forward your application to Wellington with the proper documents.

Whenever possible the consulates general will offer you information about where to write for employment, and will make an effort to help. But they cannot find you a job; they do not act as employment agencies.

Your initial letter should be in enough detail to give the consulate general an idea of your background, training, skill, and experience. The New Zealand immigration people deal with considerably fewer inquiries than Canada or Australia, and they tend to send you only materials that directly concern you and your particular case, rather than a general packet of information.

There are no immigration quotas for Americans settling in New Zealand. Each applicant is judged individually, with skill, trade, or profession probably the most heavily weighted consideration. The New Zealanders tend to be rather selective.

The entire application process may take up to three months.

FINDING WORK

Central to acquiring permission to enter New Zealand as a permanent resident is obtaining work prior to application. There is no pat process for finding a job in New Zealand.

The role of the consulate general will be to advise generally on the kinds of employment opportunities available in the country at the moment. In addition, the consulate publishes a bulletin, "Information on Employment," which is revised frequently, and one of the better of its type. One of its best features is the list of various ministries and associations in New Zealand to which you can write directly, to find out what your skill, profession, or trade is worth at the moment.

New Zealand, like all countries, has fluctuations in the labor market, and this year's "critical profession" may be next season's dinosaur. The country is trying to industrialize its economy, and does need many kinds of skills.

At the time of this writing the following trades were considered "in demand"—which makes no guarantee that they will be in demand next week, or next year: civil, mechanical, and electrical engineers and technicians; mechanical and tool-design craftsmen; automotive mechanics and engineers; machine-tool operators; welders, boilermakers, sheet-metal workers, ferrous and nonferrous molders; librarians; and nurses and veterinary surgeons.

Even in the fields in demand, Americans often must have their Stateside qualifications validated, or receive licenses to practice in New Zealand. Members of the American Institute of Chartered Accountants, for example, must take an examination for admission to the New Zealand Society of Accountants. Practically all American engineers are required to take the professional interview of the New Zealand Institute of Engineers before being able to register as a member of the Institute. This usually has a prior requirement of a degree from a reputable U.S. university and at least three years' postgraduate experience.

Because there is no reciprocity agreement between the United States and New Zealand, American qualified dentists must "sit" and pass a rigorous series of examinations in New Zealand before being allowed to practice.

The rules regarding American-trained doctors have recently been eased. By passing the examination of the Educational Council for Foreign-Trained Medical Graduates, given in the United States, American-trained doctors, whatever their length of experience, may be admitted provisionally. They must practice a year in a hospital— what amounts to an internship—after which full qualification may be granted.

Most New Zealand employers will not hire Americans solely through correspondence. Many consider a personal interview an absolute necessity. Since, in most cases, a prior firm job commitment is required before permission to settle permanently in New Zealand is granted, the problem has the ring of something from *Catch-22.*

This, of course, is another point in favor of a pilot trip, although such a trip should probably be taken only after making initial contacts by mail, and after prior consultation with the New Zealand consulate general. Some people make initial contacts through newspaper ads. All the New Zealand consulates general have small reference libraries complete with newspapers and periodicals.

The general feeling is that if you have a needed skill and are persistent, you can make at least initial contact with an interested employer in New Zealand. That advice might sound like something from Horatio Alger, but the central fact is that New Zealand's labor market needs certain key skills, but generally isn't as diversified as the United States. Finding a job *outside* the United States is generally as difficult as finding a better one *inside* the United States.

If you do find work, it will probably pay less than the same work would in the United States.

This brings the American around again to the problem of how he measures "standard of living." If it is strictly by the size of the pay packet, New Zealand can't measure up to the United States, nor can any place else in the world. "Low wages" remain one of the major reasons Americans living in another culture decide they can't make a go of it. Especially in New Zealand, salaries and wages have little relation to the United States.

In the tax year 1967–68 (April to March), for example, out of a total 1,316,650 income tax returns filed, only 87,720 persons had total incomes over $4,000 (N.Z.). One U.S. dollar equals $1.12 N.Z dollars. Just under half the total wage earners earned less than $2,000 (N.Z.) per year, and there were less than 6,000 people in the entire country with total incomes over $10,000 (N.Z.) per year. Average salaries of $50 (N.Z.) to $70 (N.Z.) per week for skilled workers are considered good.

One must always consider, however, that unemployment in New Zealand is so low as to be negligible. During the first six months of 1970 there were never more than 2,000 persons in the labor market out of work in the entire country.

New Zealand additionally has free education up to the age of nineteen. The government is extremely proud of its comprehensive social-security system, which covers all residents and includes benefits for medical and dental service, unemployment, sickness, family benefits for each dependent child, and special pensions for invalids, widows, and those more than sixty years of age.

For people with critically valuable skills, New Zealand has recently instituted a new subsidized-passage scheme. Not everyone qualifying for permanent residence in New Zealand necessarily qualifies for subsidized passage. The requirements are strict. The prospective employer in New Zealand must actually undertake to sponsor his new employee in his move to New Zealand. This goes beyond the promise of a job; it implies that an individual or corporate body in New Zealand is willing to stand behind the new migrant with a firm commitment.

The assistance is virtually free air travel from Los Angeles to New Zealand. (Travel to Los Angeles is the responsibility of the individual.) The recipient is required to make a $25 contribution toward the air fare if single, $50 if married.

In addition, the New Zealand consulate general in Los Angeles maintains a matching service for those people with recognized essential skills, whereby they try to put together requests from an employer in New Zealand and the job-seeker who hopes to obtain a subsidized passage. Again, the actual arrangements for employment are your responsibility.

FINDING OUT MORE

James Michener. *Return to Paradise.* Random House, 1950. A series of essays and short stories about the Pacific, Australia, and New Zealand. The one on New Zealand holds up well despite being written more than twenty years ago.

New Zealand Official Year Book. Department of Statistics, Wellington. Most official yearbooks are deadly. This one is an exception. Published yearly.

The following three publications are available from the New Zealand consulate general:

New Zealand Facts and Figures. A mini version of the yearbook, prepared by the New Zealand Information Service. Discusses a number of aspects of New Zealand life.

Education in New Zealand. A succinct six-page summary. New Zealand's educational system is modeled on the British system. Schooling is compulsory up to fifteen years of age, and free from age five on up to nineteen. School quality is good. Additional information can be had in a different publication of the same title—*Education in*

New Zealand; Studies in Comparative Education. U.S. Department of Health, Education and Welfare. Available from the U.S. Government Printing Office, thirty-five cents. Also a complete section on education in the *Official Yearbook.*

Income Tax, Estate and Gift Duties. A model pamphlet of its type. Open format, just enough detail, written for the person without an accounting background. New Zealand income taxes are high. On a taxable income of $4,000 (N.Z.) per year, the rate is 37 percent. On $6,000 (N.Z.) per year, it is 49 percent.

American Firms, Subsidiaries and Affiliates in New Zealand. U.S. Department of Commerce, Commercial Intelligence Division, Washington, D.C. One dollar prepaid by check or money order.

Information Guide for Doing Business in New Zealand. Price Waterhouse and Company; 60 Broad Street; New York, N.Y. 10005 Free. Write on letterhead.

Establishing a Business in New Zealand. Overseas Business Report. U.S. Department of Commerce. Fifteen cents from the U.S. Government Printing Office, Washington, D.C.

A list of newspapers suggested by the New Zealand Department of Labor for those wishing to place a classified ad for seeking employment. Write directly to "The Proprietors": *New Zealand Herald,* Auckland; *Auckland Star,* Auckland; *Dominion,* Wellington; *Evening Post,* Wellington; *Christchurch Press,* Christchurch; *Star Sun,* Christchurch; *Otago Daily Times,* Dunedin; *Evening Star,* Dunedin.

Embassy of New Zealand; 19 Observatory Circle N.W.; Washington, D.C. 20008.

New Zealand is represented by consulates general in Los Angeles, San Francisco, and New York City.

American Embassy; Government Life Insurance Building; Customs House Quay; Wellington N.W.; New Zealand.

RHODESIA

Area: 150,333 square miles (about the size of Montana). Population: 5,-090,000 (of which 235,000 are white). Capital: Salisbury (400,000). Languages: English and tribal.

Prior to the Israeli-Arab war and the continued conflict in the Middle East, the most publicized conflict of the day was Rhodesia's estrangement from Britain, and its declaration of independence in 1965. Even in casual conversation most Rhodesians frequently refer to UDI, the initials standing for "unilateral declaration of independence."

UDI had been brewing since the breaking up of the former Federation of Rhodesia and Nyasaland, which finally became fact in 1963. Northern Rhodesia was given independence and became Zambia. Nyasaland became Malawi. Southern Rhodesia continued a self-governing colonial relationship with Britain, pending future independence. Britain set out five principles that had to be met before Rhodesia's independence would be granted. The most important was "unimpeded progress toward majority rule."

Like South Africa, Rhodesia is a country ruled by a white minority. After the independence of Zambia and Malawi, Britain, at the urging of the United Nations, demanded that Rhodesia move more quickly to advance the Africans politically and bring them into active government of the country. Rhodesian Prime Minister Ian Smith replied that the white minority acted not out of any apartheid sentiment, but because they knew what was best for all the people of Rhodesia. Smith reacted eventually to Britain's uncompromising pressure by proclaiming UDI.

The proclamation was far from the end of the debate. Britain brought a number of trade sanctions to bear on Rhodesia, including a trade embargo. Rhodesia reeled initially, then began to take hold, becoming in the long run more self-sufficient than it had ever been before, and seeking new trade partners. Anxious discussions between the Wilson government and Rhodesia's Prime Minister Smith gave way to hurried meetings aboard British cruisers anchored off Gibraltar, and increased pressure by the United Nations upon Britain to put down Rhodesia's rebellion and the Smith government, which it termed illegal.

Despite economic and political pressure to reconcile itself with Britain, the issues proved insoluble. In March, 1970, Rhodesia made up its mind to go it alone and proclaimed itself a republic, to the diplomatic anger of a number of countries and a furor in the United Nations.

Within a month the United States and eight other countries cut diplomatic relations with Rhodesia, which remain severed still. The Security Council of the U.N. nearly censured Britain for *not* using force to end the rebellion of Rhodesia. In the midst of the uproar, Rhodesia created a new constitution and a controversial land act, and held elections which confirmed the power of the white-dominated Rhodesian Front party.

Rhodesian government officials nonetheless object to the tendency of Americans to lump their country with South Africa, although the two countries are connected by a number of economic and historical ties. They quickly point out that the relationship between white and black in Rhodesia is governed by no formal policy of apartheid, or separate development. Africans have equal protection under the law. There are no restrictive laws against marriage or mixing, nor are there the "pass laws" common in South Africa. Better hotels in Salisbury and the industrial center of Bulawayo admit both Europeans (whites) and Africans. Africans live and work in the cities and in a number of professions and skills that in South Africa are reserved for practice by whites, except in the Bantu states. True, a large majority of Africans in Rhodesia still live at a subsistence level in rural Tribal Trust lands, once called "native reserves," and there are a number of African townships. The Africans have a limited role in government because Smith's government believes they are not ready to be given a larger voice.

The critics, who include the United Nations Security Council, a number of white missionaries working in Rhodesia among the Africans, and a small number of black Rhodesian politicans, claim otherwise. They feel that, step by small step, Rhodesia is sliding toward a white-dominated, separatist society. More specifically, black Rhodesian journalist Justin Nyoka claims the question of land reapportionment will probably lead to an eventual head-on clash. Land, says

Nyoka, has always been a central point of the conflict.

Under the Land Tenure Act, certain land is reserved for European ownership, other lands set aside for the Africans. Many African nationalists claim, among other things, that the better land is being reserved for the whites, while many whites counter that the productivity of African land remains untapped because of the Africans' persistence in using traditional farming practices, which takes time and money to change. With regard to land, the claims and counterclaims have no end, all with partial truth, based on geography and history and on the economic needs of Rhodesia, and sharpened by the language of twentieth-century African politics. On one side is a small minority of articulate blacks arguing the cause of their black brothers, supported by much foreign opinion. And consistently on the other side is a white-dominated government that claims to know what it is doing and that it is best for Rhodesia.

The manifestations of conflict exist below the surface of daily life in Rhodesia.

After the initial shock of sanctions to the economic and social life of the country, felt by black and white alike, Rhodesia has recently begun to thrive again. Before UDI, Rhodesia's greatest exports were high-quality tobacco and chrome, tobacco making up two-thirds of Rhodesia's exports to Britain. Today Britain plays little role in Rhodesia's economy. Ironically, Rhodesia's chrome holdings were developed and are still owned by Americans. In November 1971, after several years of adhering to the U.N. imposed sanctions, the U.S. government quietly gave permission for American companies to resume purchasing Rhodesian chrome. During the sanctions period the U.S. bought chrome from the Soviet Union at scalpers' prices.

Still Rhodesia's independence remains diplomatically unrecognized. It is a landlocked country with few political or economic allies: the Portuguese colony Mozambique to the east, through which it maintains access to the sea; South Africa to the south, with whom its economic ties are growing; and to a lesser extent Malawi, a growing trading partner and one of the first black African countries to trade voluntarily with the two white-dominated countries to the south.

Author's note: As this book went to press British Foreign Secretary Sir Alec Douglas-Home visited Rhodesia in a last effort to patch the rift between the two countries. A week later headlines in the British press bannered "He's Done It," meaning the Foreign Secretary finally convinced Ian Smith to knuckle under to British demands. Most observers felt, however, that Britain gave more concessions than it got, the agreement in total closer to Ian Smith's contentions all along. Regarding "unimpeded progress toward majority rule," one professor of constitutional law at Queen's College pointed out that if everyone stuck to his bargain, the Africans would reach political parity with the whites in 64 years, the year 2026. As is often the case the real short term effect of the "settlement" as the press called it, is found on the financial page. The thaw of frozen assets, resumption of trade and tourism, all will be well under way again by mid-1972. The "settlement" isn't expected to deter Rhodesia's search for new "European" immigrants.

Like South Africa, Rhodesia has embarked on a revitalized effort to attract new European immigrants, both to provide skills for an expanding economy and to augment a white population that while increasing in absolute numbers shrinks to a smaller proportion of the total yearly. Despite the running feud between Rhodesia and the British government, ranging from the trade embargo, which hurts less every year, to the stubborn insistence of the British press in calling it "Southern" Rhodesia, immigrants of British origin predominate. There are also growing numbers of Canadians, New Zealanders, Australians, and Americans, with a smattering of immigrants from thirty-five other countries. Additionally there is a good deal of exchange migration between Rhodesia and South Africa.

The Rhodesian government is reluctant to disclose the exact number of migrants from each country, claiming their secrecy is vaguely related to the sanctions against them. The total number of new immigrants averages now about 1,000 per month.

In 1970 Rhodesia received 12,345 new settlers, the largest number in twelve years. They also suffered an emigration of 6,018 people, many South Africans on their way home. Of the major immigrant-receiving nations, Rhodesia has the poorest record of permanent settlement. Inexplicably, the number of Americans living in Rhodesia was dropped from the 1970 State Department statistics of Americans resident overseas. In 1969 the figure was 1,100. Rhodesia refuses to disclose its own figure of Americans living in Rhodesia "because of sanctions."

There is reason to believe that the number of Americans living in Rhodesia has increased slightly over the past two years. Despite all the formal outrage, there is a small, loyal underground of Rhodesian supporters in the United States. They range from Friends of Rhodesia groups, to the Liberty Lobby, to a number of industrial and ranching concerns which find Rhodesia's appeal primarily economic.

Rhodesia seems to appeal also to the streak in some Americans to side with an underdog just out of principle, or to admire persons who seem to know their own minds, even if not agreeing with them. With most of Africa and the rest of the world lined up against Rhodesia, at least in the political arena, the country surely qualifies as an underdog. And Prime Minister Ian Smith and his cabinet are both vocal and resolutely firm on what they believe to be the best course for the country, even if it is counter to outside opinion.

In an era when most developing countries are pushing for an increased pace of economic growth, for example, Prime Minister Smith in a political address observed that the country's economy was expanding too rapidly, leaping ahead without first building firm foundations. "Something has got to be done to reduce this fantastic tempo of development," Smith said, adding later in the same speech: "Many people have said to me that the main thing to our credit in Rhodesia is that we have managed to preserve our balance, managed to preserve our sanity. Let's keep it that way."

Rhodesia's President Clifford Dupont reinforced the idea of Rhodesia's brand of conservatism in a speech he delivered in August 1970.

There are those who criticize us for being Victorian in outlook and isolationist in our attitudes.

I think that in certain aspects this may be a true observation, but many of us do not regard it necessarily as a criticism. Furthermore, I think it is to be expected, as it must be borne in mind that a fair degree of isolation has been forced upon us.

Being a landlocked country, even today in this era of rapid air travel, we are still at a considerable distance from the major concentrations of population in the Western world.

However, this distance can also be fortuitous and our isolationism is at certain times quite deliberate. The trends in world society towards anarchy and permissiveness amount to a sickness and although we cannot put the whole outside world in quarantine, there is no reason to expose ourselves unduly to the risk of infection. . . .

We, in Rhodesia, with our tradition of a common sense approach must strike a happy balance between permanence and change. We must not turn away from the outside world—and in fact we have no desire to do so.

At the same time there is no reason or intention on our part to abandon the true heritage of our past merely to follow the fashions of a world in which values become meaningless.

One of the best aspects of the life of our early settlers was their belief in principle. They were men who coupled the strong fundamental ideas with a practical spirit of adventure. I believe that this spirit is still with us today.

PROCEDURES

Rhodesia has an active, selective policy for recruiting immigrants, mostly from the United Kingdom. Like South Africa, Rhodesia proselytizes less vigorously in the United States but will take as settlers Americans who qualify.

The main requirements are good health, good character (meaning no felony convictions, or, if a criminal record, evidence of a pardon), literacy in a European language (Hebrew included), evidence of a skill or capital, and a valid U.S. passport.

There are two sources of information on settling in Rhodesia: Rhodesian Information Office, 2852 McGill Terrace N.W., Washington, D.C. 20008; The Department of Immigration Promotion, P.B. 7711, Causeway, Salisbury, Rhodesia.

Application for a *residence permit* is a one-two process. The first step is to fill out and mail the form "Details of Prospective Immigrant" to one of the above addresses. This is a preliminary application by which Rhodesian immigration officials make an initial assessment of you and your qualifications. Much of the information requested involves profession or skill, and capital resources.

Twice yearly the Rhodesian National Employment Service compiles a bulletin, "Vacancies Difficult to Fill from Local Sources." The preliminary application is often checked against these current needs, which often include quite a wide range of skills. It is just as likely to include a sewing-machine repairman as a civil engineer. White-collar professions are the most commonly excluded, especially at managerial level.

If the application appears satisfactory and your skill applicable, the Rhodesian immigration authorities will send you a second form, "Application for Residence Permit." If your trade is in the national interest, you may be eligible for assisted passage, up to $480 per person by air, or $240 by sea, plus the cost of rail fare. If you have requested assisted passage, they will send you an additional application.

Should your skill be more difficult to place, they may still invite you to visit Rhodesia. Rhodesia permits and highly recommends entrance as a tourist to look for work. Americans may enter Rhodesia without a visa, requiring only evidence of support and a return ticket.

Rhodesia does not require prior employment as a prerequisite for obtaining a residence permit. If accepted as an immigrant, the Rhodesian government will attempt to help the new settler find suitable work. Rhodesian immigration officials pointedly observe that a number of immigrants arrive in Rhodesia underestimating the amount of money it takes to get started, and some have failed because of it.

The entire application process usually takes at least three months. Residence in Rhodesia implies no obligation for an American to become a Rhodesian citizen. After two years' residence Americans may apply for citizenship, but it means renouncing American citizenship by doing so.

There is a rental pinch in Rhodesia, and the Rhodesian government has recently purchased several large housing buildings for the accommodation of newcomers. Like Australians and New Zealanders, most Rhodesians prefer to own their own homes, and purchasing a house is by world standards inexpensive.

FINDING OUT MORE

The Rhodesian Information Office has a great number of materials available for the prospective immigrant, much of it sent only when specifically requested. Among those of greatest interest:

Summary of Rhodesian Immigration Requirements. A simple, direct three-page statement of their requirements.

Questions You Ask About Rhodesia. One they would probably send you without asking. A pretty skimpy treatment of education, health, shopping, etc.

Rhodesia in Brief. A little sixty-five-page pamphlet that does rather better than the above, except that it still doesn't say much about education. The country's secondary-educational system is modeled on that of the British, with "O" levels and "A" levels. There are both government and private schools, and the quality of instruction, the Rhodesians claim, is quite high. In the employment of teachers, Canadians are favored over Americans because the Rhodesians think that American teachers tend to be top-heavy on the methodology of teaching and short on subject knowledge. As a whole, like New Zealand, South Africa, and most of Europe, there is not the commitment to offer a college or university education to the majority. There are good-quality agricultural, technical, and teachers' colleges in Rhodesia, and the single new university (University College, Rhodesia) enrolls about 1,200 students. About three times that number of college-age students leave the country to attend universities in Europe or South Africa. University College also has a new medical school, with plans under way for a faculty of engineering.

Employment in Rhodesia. A rather too brief fold-out brochure that discusses generally the requirements for practicing professions, working in commerce, and factory work. Has a useful table of wage scales for journeymen in the building, engineering, motoring, and printing trades. Also explains workmen's compensation and medical-aid schemes.

Income Tax in Rhodesia. A single sheet, but detailed enough. The basic income-tax system if you are employed is PAYE style—pay as you earn. Through abatements for children and such (their counterpart of the U.S. deduction system), it is possible to have a tax-free income equivalent to about $4,200 (U.S.) per year, with the tax sliding from approximately ten cents to fifty cents on the dollar on additional earnings. There is an additional two-year abatement for immigrants —about $750 for a married couple, with an additional $150 (approximately) for each child. A single person would receive an abatement of about $600.

Customs Rebates and Concessions. Explains the system whereby permanent residents are given a customs rebate (refund) on household goods, including an automobile. This amounts to a duty-free import.

Farming in Rhodesia. Out of print, but the Rhodesian Information Office will send you a Xerox copy. You are requested not to ask for it unless you are a farmer, and serious about it. It is a lengthy, detailed discussion of different kinds of farming opportunities. Farming is one of the country's priorities because of its role in helping to develop the provinces, and as an agent to help the Africans become productive. Rhodesia's Lowveld region has a wide range of agricultural possibilities.

American Firms, Subsidiaries and Affiliates. A mimeographed list, revised from time to time. The best thing about it is Stateside addresses of the companies operating in Rhodesia, so you can write to them directly.

Teach in Rhodesia. Rhodesia needs primary- and secondary-school teachers, prefers them younger than fifty years of age, and is particularly short-handed in the fields of science and math. This brochure lists in brief the salary scale and the long list of benefits available to teachers.

The Man and His Ways. An interpretation of the customs and beliefs of Rhodesia's African peoples. Published by the Ministry of Information, Immigration and Tourism. The whites in Rhodesia are a one-in-twenty minority, and their relationship with the African, if judged solely on this book, sounds like a rather tolerant, old-fashioned kind of paternalism.

From Other Sources

A Principle in Torment. This is a militant political discussion of the same relationship, published by the United Nations, whose bias slants strongly toward indictment of the white Rhodesians. One Rhodesian called it the most distorted account of Rhodesia that has ever been written. Available from the United Nations Office of Public Information. Sales number: E.69.I.26. Price seventy-five cents.

Richard West. *The White Tribes of Africa.* Macmillan, 1965. An anecdotal look by a British writer at the four million whites living in black Africa.

Rhodesian Perspective. Edited by Theodore Bull. Michael Joseph (London), 1967. A fairly objective look at recent Rhodesian politics and racial problems, slightly favoring the Africans. Bull was the former editor of the *Central African Examiner,* a newspaper that ceased publication in Salisbury after UDI.

Charles Burton Marshall. *Crisis Over Rhodesia: A Skeptical View.* Johns Hopkins, 1967. A short, energetically written book that cuts through the fuzzy reporting and political rhetoric about Rhodesia's independence. Scholarly but stylistically light treatment of a heavy subject. Highly recommended.

The Rhodesian Department of Information suggests the following as possibly helpful for Americans who have decided to migrate to Rhodesia: The Welcome to Rhodesia Association; Box 8364, Causeway; Salisbury, Rhodesia.

SOUTH AFRICA

Area: 472,494 square miles (about twice the size of Texas). Population: (1970) 21,300,000 (white: 3,779,000; colored—Hottentot, Malay, and mixed: 1,996,000; Asian: 614,000; Bantu: 14,893,000). Capital: (Administrative) Pretoria (448,000); (Legislative) Cape Town (817,000). Languages: Afrikaans, English, and tribal.

Most Americans who live in South Africa go as employees of American-owned companies. Despite the formal position of the United States government in opposition to South Africa's internal racial policy, American business has quickened its stride in appreciation of South Africa's potential. When President Johnson put restrictions on United States direct investment abroad, American investors sidestepped the restriction by buying heavily into stocks and shares of South African companies.

South Africa's appeal to American business can be sketched with a few quick facts.

South Africa is a physically rich country—Steel, water power, 90 percent of the continent's mined coal, and half the total number of telephones and automobiles in Africa. Add to that cooper, uranium, diamonds, and South Africa's unique export to the rest of the world —gold, 81 percent of the known production outside of the Soviet Union. There have been fifty years of strong authoritarian government in South Africa, a government that has dealt easily with business while violently opposing Communism and any encroachment upon its borders.

These attributes have not gone unnoticed. Thirteen percent of all U.S. investment in Africa has gone into South Africa—about 750 million dollars' worth. General Motors, Ford, Chrysler, IBM, Polaroid, and some 250 other American companies have a stake in South Africa, and from all indicators find it a congenial, profitable business environment.

Partly due to the labor demands of the booming economy, partly because South Africa wants more white settlers, the country has an active program for recruiting permanent migrants, mostly from Western Europe. The recruiting program does not extend to the United States, although South Africa will accept qualified Americans as permanent residents.

The emphasis is strictly on European (white) ancestry and possession of a high-level skill or needed talent, although the talents are sometimes unexpected ones. South Africa recently attempted to recruit 250 white bus drivers and conductors in Britain and Holland. Opportunities on the land are nil; the agricultural frontier in South Africa disappeared decades ago.

The total number of new settlers going to South Africa averages about 40,000 per year, roughly equal to those going to New Zealand.

Most new settlers come from England or Germany, with smaller numbers from Belgium, Holland, the Scandinavian countries, and Italy. About three in every four stay permanently.

Despite the number of American businesses, the total number of Americans resident in South Africa is modest, slightly more than 6,000 persons in 1971. Few are true settlers or migrants. About 20,000 U.S. tourists a year visit South Africa, and about another 1,000 Americans are admitted each year with "temporary employment visas" that require a prior job commitment. The Americans who actually migrate to South Africa number in the hundreds, and judging from the record, don't appear a very durable lot.

In 1968, 364 Americans were admitted as permanent residents, while about 360 Americans already permanent residents left. In 1969 Americans had an even poorer record—187 settled, 269 already there left.

As might be expected in light of this, inquiries regarding permanent settlement made to South African consular authorities in the United States are treated, initially at least, with courteous reserve. Part of the reserve is because most South Africans suspect that Americans know little about their country, and understand less. The South African Information Service in New York receives numerous inquiries about all the countries in Africa, because, as it turns out, South Africa is the only African country with the word "Africa" in its name.

Among South African government officials it is felt that the U.S. government's condemnation of their racial policies at long distance is undeserved, even a little dismaying. Prime Minister John Vorster once said in an interview that when either England or the United States solves its own racial problems, he would be prepared to listen to advice. Consular officials are sensitive to any slide toward moralizing over their official racial policy.

Given the scope of this book, little can be said about apartheid, which the South Africans call "separate development." As a governmental policy it is clear-cut: racial separateness, not out of any racial hatred, say the South Africans, but because of economic and cultural necessity.

The stated objective of "separate development" is someday complete separate black and white nations, coexisting each in its own geographic territory, each race retaining its cultural identity and language. An often-used government metaphor is "each man with his own house and his own fence around it."

Whatever criticisms there are of apartheid directed at South Africa by the United Nations, the United States, Britain, and the two most vocally opposed black African nations, Zambia and Tanzania, within the country the critics are numerically few and politically weak. Even the opposition United party is termed only "mildly" antiapartheid. If there is powerful sentiment, it is on the proapartheid side. Among members of his own party, Prime Minister Vorster must appear dangerously liberal. He has pushed considerably his "outward-looking policy," which has begun to stir a response from the leaders of some black African nations not so dead-set on isolating South Africa as are Zambia and Tanzania. South Africa trades with Malawi, has offered a massive foreign-aid plan to Madagascar, and Vorster has stated a willingness to receive African diplomats from other nations on a basis of equality. Facing labor shortages due to a strong, long-lasting surge of economic development, the government has even had to relax apartheid to the point of allowing nonwhites to enter the construction industry and nursing.

The key fact to consider is that most white South Africans, while perhaps not in complete agreement with the National party's single-minded, often strict pursuit of "separate development," are in agreement with the principle of keeping the races separate. A *U.S. News & World Report* survey reported that only 9 percent of white South Africans were critical of apartheid.

Most take it for granted, one aspect of a way of life that in many respects is quite appealing.

The typical white South African owns his own attractive home, or aspires to, even if he lives in a rather large apartment in one of the cities. The home would be a spacious single-story bungalow-style with three bedrooms, a living room, bathroom, dining room, and kitchen, with electric appliances not much different from those found in many kitchens the United States. Since temperatures in any climatic region of South Africa are seldom severely hot or cold, houses are without central heating or air-conditioning. It would be on its own lot, which might be as large as three-fourths of an acre. Invariably there would be a garden (in which most South Africans take considerable pride), with separate sections for vegetables and flowers. The house may have cost upwards of the equivalent of $20,000, but in better surburbs homes costing $75,000 or $100,000 are not uncommon; if necessary, it would be bought with the help of a 8½-percent loan from a building society, paid back monthly over twenty years. If the economy continues to expand as it has, the owner knows his home will be worth considerably more than his equity, should he care to sell it.

Whatever his occupation, the South African earns more than his Australian, New Zealand, or British counterpart; he pays less taxes, and due to generally lower prices, has greater purchasing power. In the construction trades he works a standard forty-hour week with a chance of overtime, since South Africa is in the midst of a building boom. In industry he works a forty-five-hour week. In both general categories, whatever his specific trade or skill, he would bring home a pay packet well over a hundred dollars a week, a figure that would be the envy of the workman in Australia, New Zealand, or Britain, as would his salary if in management, perhaps the equivalent of $20,000 to $50,000 per year. Top managers of major firms may earn more than $100,000 per year.

His wife would probably not work. Her main job would be managing the children and supervising the help, although she might dabble in the garden or take a hand in the cooking and housecleaning. She probably would have a Coloured servant (Cape Coloured, i.e., mixed), which would cost perhaps $40 per month. An experienced Bantu servant would cost slightly less. The servant would live in separate furnished quarters on the premises, built according to government specifications and by law a specific distance from the main house. The servant would also receive free meals.

The housewife would shop in different food shops instead of a supermarket, charge most of her food, paying bills monthly. Since there is no national health scheme as there is in New Zealand, Australia, and Britain, the family would be responsible for most of its medical costs, much less expensive than in the United States.

If financially possible she would insist on the children attending a private school, although the public schools are academically quite suitable, because of a certain prestige. Costs might be as high as $700 per child per year.

Like Australians and New Zealanders, the white South Africans' life is oriented toward the out-of-doors. There is a good chance their home has a swimming pool and that the man of the family is a member of a tennis or athletic club. When not on the job, his work will be unthought of. The family will probably spend at least a two-week holiday at one of the coastal South African resorts, or if in the upper echelons of his company, perhaps a month in Europe every year or two.

They get along without television, which has still to come to South Africa due to the complications of its administration under apartheid. South Africans are used to the "blue laws," which stipulate that entertainment, sporting events, and restaurants remain closed on Sundays and public holidays. Most men favor law and order, approve of the large expenditures the government makes on defense, and are probably in favor of the debated death penalty for drug peddlers. Neither their wives nor families have black acquaintances. There is no opportunity to meet them, and besides, to what end?

If there are injustices under the stern South African laws, most white South Africans don't see them. Any more than most Brazilians see the activities of the political police or Americans see the crime that the rest of the world thinks is a daily occurrence in each of our lives. In South Africa the whites live in material comfort. With some justification, they claim to have done more for the economic development of the blacks than any other ruling power has ever done. Apartheid is seldom seriously questioned; it is part of the "South African way of life."

Most Americans living in South Africa rather like the place. The country is spacious and physically attractive, and the climate ideal. They like the suburban outdoor style of living, and most adjust rather rapidly to the moral landscape, once past the initial shock of seeing apartheid in action. To an American many things in South Africa are familiar, the look of the cities more reminiscent of the United States than would be those of Australia or New Zealand. There are the same makes of automobiles (and they drive on the right), recognizable brand names and trademarks. Most are surprised at the widespread use of Afrikaans. In any case, few Americans stay permanently, a smaller percentage than remain in any other people-seeking country.

As to the future of "separate development," novelist Allen Drury called South Africa's situation a puzzle without a solution. "If you want certainties I refer you to the writings and pronouncements of those who have not been there; or who, having been there for a day, or two, or possibly three or four, have come away with the same preconceptions with which they arrived."

In "Finding Out More," I have included a number of materials that take up both sides of the point. If you are considering South Africa, you should probably delve into "separate development," especially the South African point of view.

PROCEDURES

On the whole, South Africa's immigration policies are well defined and strictly administered.

In June, 1969, Deputy Minister of Immigration Dr. P. J. Koornhof restated the immigration policy in a speech before the South African Parliament. He emphasized five points:

(1)   Only skilled immigrants would be brought into the country.

(2)   No immigrant should oust a South African from his employment.

(3)   Every immigrant should be able to integrate easily with South Africans. "He must come to reinforce the white nation here . . . he must fit in with our national circumstances and our national character."

(4)   All immigrants must become fully bilingual, be able to speak and write English and Afrikaans, the two official languages. (This requirement was explained later to me by a consular officer. Immigrants are encouraged to become fully bilingual; permanent residents who apply for citizenship after five years in South Africa will have to pass tests in Afrikaans and English.)

(5)   The recruitment of immigrants from "our countries of origin."

As a result of the emphasis on European Recruiting, there are no Immigration Department officials operating in the United States. The three South African consulates serve as a source of information and as visa headquarters. Applications for establishing permanent residence in South Africa are forwarded to Pretoria for processing.

An initial inquiry to any South African consulate will result in a letter, including a preliminary application form entitled "Details of Training and Experience."

At the outset, you will have to pursue general information about

South Africa from other sources. The South African Information Service, 655 Madison Avenue, New York, N.Y. 10021, has a wide variety of materials available. Write to them, indicating the things you would like to know about South Africa.

The preliminary application asks for brief information about your immediate family. Six of the eight remaining questions concern academic or trade training, work history, present salary, and your intended occupation in South Africa. There is also a question regarding language efficiency. South Africa is a multilingual nation, and about 60 percent of the whites have Afrikaans as their native tongue. Afrikaans is Dutch-derived, and knowledge of either German or Dutch is advantageous in learning it. It is the most commonly used language in the country, followed by English.

The South African Broadcasting Corporation broadcasts programs in nine languages daily—English, Afrikaans, and seven Bantu languages. In the one Bantu state so far created—named the Transkei—a Bantu language has been added to Afrikaans and English as an official language. Many South Africans speak more than one language.

Once completed, the preliminary application is returned to the consulate. This can be done by mail. The consul will then forward the application to Pretoria for assessment.

The assessment process involves mainly a look at the job market. If your skill appears to give you a reasonable chance of finding work, the Department of Immigration advises the consulate. This assessment normally takes a month or more.

In turn the consulate will contact you and advise you of the chances of finding a job and the probable salary you will earn. They will also at this time provide you with the "Application for a Permanent Residence Permit." They will also send you a series of small pamphlets intended for the prospective settler, issued by the Department of Immigration and revised yearly. The booklets:

The Immigrant's Journey to South Africa. Discusses the details of packing and shipping your household goods.

Assisted Immigration to the Republic of South Africa. About 70 percent of migrants going to South Africa have their passages assisted by the government. About $168 (R120) is contributed toward the passage of each approved migrant, regardless of age. Taking this assistance does not obligate the migrant to remain in South Africa for a minimum amount of time, or to repay the grant once in the country.

The Immigrant Housewife. Information on prices of household goods, food, servants (most whites have them), health services, and so forth.

Housing Facilities. Discusses houses, apartments, home-ownership schemes, and costs.

Employment Prospects. Aimed mainly at industrial employment. Has wage scale for a variety of professions.

Land of Sunshine. A booklet about South Africa's climate and its physical regions.

Educational Facilities. A general discussion of the system. No information on specific schools.

Taxation, Licenses, Etc. in the Republic of South Africa. Personal income tax is lower in South Africa than in Australia, New Zealand, or the United States. On a taxable income of 10,000 rand ($14,000), income tax is about 20 percent for a single man, about 13 percent for a married man with two children.

In addition to the application, you will have to provide for each family member: (1) A photograph not less than 1½ " square. (2) Birth certificate. (3) A medical certificate on a prescribed form. (4) A chest X ray. (5) A police certificate on a prescribed form (if over eighteen). (6) Marriage documents. (7) Education and trade certificates, references, a letter from your employer if a job is already offered.

If physically possible, they will try to arrange a personal interview. If retiring or starting your own business, you must also provide documentary proof of financial resources.

Prior employment is not a condition for admittance into South Africa. In this, South Africa is similar to Australia (although the job market isn't as wide as in Australia). The Department of Immigration, however, will endeavor to help you find employment; once the South Africans admit you, they make considerable effort to assure that you become settled and employed. The government pays for transportation between point of entry and new residence, for example. If you are admitted as a permanent resident, the South Africans will do all within their power to welcome you into their society.

FINDING OUT MORE

American Firms, Subsidiaries and Affiliates in South Africa. U.S. Department of Commerce; Commercial Intelligence Division; Washington, D.C. 20230. One dollar prepaid by check or money order.

Information Guide to Doing Business in the Republic of South

Africa. Price Waterhouse and Company; 60 Broad Street; New York, N.Y. 10005. Free. Write on letterhead.

The following are available free from The South African Information Service; 655 Madison Avenue; New York, N.Y. 10021:

South African Quiz. Not a quiz at all, but the answers. A 156-page information booklet.

Prospects and Progress. It is subtitled "An Economic Profile of Africa's Industrial Giant."

South African Tradition. The counterpart of the above book on the South African cultural scene, art, literature, architecture.

A variety of maps and guides are available free from: The South African Tourist Corporation (SATOUR); 610 Fifth Avenue; Fourth Floor; New York, N.Y. 10020. Ask particularly for the *Travel Companion,* a 156-page booklet with regional and factual information, and maps.

About Separate Development (Apartheid)

For: *Progress Through Separate Development.* A booklet available from the South African Information Service. The official government stance and justification.

"South Africa's Side of the Story" in *U.S. News & World Report,* July 15, 1968. An interview with Prime Minister John Vorster.

Against: *Segregation in South Africa.* United Nations (Pub. No. E.69I.15). Questions and answers on the policy of apartheid. Fifty cents.

Apartheid and Racial Discrimination in Southern Africa. United Nations. Includes comment on Rhodesia and South-West Africa.

All of the above have a heavy slant. For something more analytical, consider:

Douglas Brown. *Against the World: Attitudes of White South Africa.* Doubleday, 1968. Brown is against the system of apartheid but not white South Africa. Makes the reader understand there is more to it than being simply for or against. Brown is an English newspaper editor, and lived in South Africa from 1951 to 1956.

Allen Drury. *A Very Strange Society.* Trident, 1967. A thick collage of impressions, newspaper clippings, conversations, and excerpts from official reports.

Paul Giniewski. *The Two Faces of Apartheid.* Regnery, 1961. Much has happened since the date of publication, but still basically sound. A translation from the French.

South African Embassy; 3051 Massachusetts Avenue N.W.; Washington, D.C. 20008.

South African consulates general are located in New York City, San Francisco, and New Orleans.

American Embassy; Navarre Trust Building; Pretorius Street; Pretoria, Transvaal; South Africa.

ARGENTINA

Area: 1,173,700 square miles. Population: 23,364,000 (1970). Capital: Buenos Aires (8,774,000). Language: Spanish.

Of the great cities of the Western Hemisphere, the Argentine capital Buenos Aires is probably the least known to Americans. By Argentine figures it is the third most populated urban area in the world after Tokyo and London, but its size is the least of surprises for Americans who discover the city. Buenos Aires is cosmopolitan, sophisticated, complete. The elegance of men and women promenading a single street, the Calle Florida, might be equaled only by New York's Fifth Avenue or London's Bond Street. But the old-fashioned elegance one can find in Buenos Aires, as in no other Latin-American city, is the slimmest part of the city's character.

Buenos Aires dominates Argentina in a way that no single city influences the United States, Canada, or even Australia or Brazil. It is the capital of the country in every way. The Argentines cling nostalgically to the belief that the soul of their country is the fertile rolling pampas, with its lore, traditions, and sometimes unsavory history, not unlike our own conquering of the pioneer West.

If the pampas is Argentina's soul, Buenos Aires remains its heart and nervous system. It is not the only city, to be sure. Rosario, 200 miles north on the high banks of the Río Paraná, and Córdoba, the restless plains city known for clear air, manufacturing, its university, and its strikes, both have more than a half-million persons each. But Buenos Aires is *the* city; one-third of the people in the entire country live in its myriad suburbs, spreading out onto the pampas unhindered by any natural barriers.

The appeal of the city is owed neither to geography nor to history. Buenos Aires is situated on the south bank of the La Plata River, where the estuary begins to flare like an inverted champagne glass, reaching some hundred miles or so in width, and finally having to

222

confess to itself that it is no longer a river but part of the Atlantic. The site was chosen by the Spanish some 400 years ago for the singularly uninspiring reason that there a small stream cut through impassable mud flats, allowing the Spanish boats to reach shore.

The site, virtually at sea level, has left modern Buenos Aires an unwished-for legacy: drainage so poor that streets remain mired for days after a heavy rain.

For the first 300 years of its existence Buenos Aires was a sentinel, guarding the back door to the heart of the Spanish empire centered in Bolivia and Peru. But if the Spanish were more concerned with the silver of Alta Peru than the rolling plains farther south, so the *porteños,* as the people of Buenos Aires call themselves, were as little concerned with Spain. It was Indians, Brazilians, smuggling, and the British which occupied their time. Buenos Aires and what was later to become Argentina matured behind father's back, an ignored and unprotected child who grew up learning how to take care of itself. One has the feeling today that Buenos Aires is as culturally detached and independent as any modern city in the world. While most Latin-American capitals still look to Paris, Rome, or New York for everything from pop music to their fashions, Buenos Aires seems to need only itself.

Like the other cities of the former Spanish empire, Buenos Aires was designed to a standard royal plan. A simple rectangular pattern of streets with a plaza or square at the center, and on opposite sides of the plaza the two most important buildings, the church and the governor general's office. Part of the old city is still apparent in the regular narrow streets of the easternmost part of downtown Buenos Aires. Traverse them once at midday and you'll forever be convinced they were designed for another age, one without automobiles.

The inhabitants of every major city in the world have at least one thing in common. They all claim they have the world's worst drivers. Except the *porteños.* They claim they are the best, and they may be right. They are without doubt the most devil-may-care. Beneath the most dignified Argentine exterior lies a born competitor, unleashed in its fullness by the simple act of sliding behind the wheel of an automobile, whether it be a Mercedes taxi or a diminutive Fiat.

Driving prowess to an Argentine is something akin to the *machismo* of the Mexican male, summing up unspoken concepts of manhood, courage, and cool. Add to that the fact that most Argentines take it for granted that were it not for circumstance their own name would be there alongside that of their national hero Juan Fangio as one of the great racing drivers of all time. To the *porteño* the narrow streets of Buenos Aires might just as well be the twisting route of the Monte Carlo Grand Prix, the automobile he controls a finely tuned formula-one racer.

There are few stop signs in Buenos Aires, the perfectly rectangular pattern of the old part of the city such that streets cross each other at right angles. Each driver approaches an intersection at speed, and upon sighting a competitor vying for the right to cross first, each makes flawless mental calculations, taking into account comparative auto size, momentum, and the willingness to bluff. One occasionally sees automobiles off the road totally demolished, but seldom a car with a scratched fender.

One of the most distinguishing aspects of the urban landscape of Buenos Aires is the numerous plain restaurants, invariably jammed with people and emanating the same aromas of frying potatoes and meat cooked next to an open fire.

In the United States the restaurants are at extremes, either coffee shops or rather expensive places reserved for the expense-account lunch or the rare occasions we go "out to dinner." In Europe, Latin America, and much of Asia, restaurants serve a different purpose. The majority are designed for people who as a habit eat a meal or two daily in a restaurant. They are low-priced, have attentive service (what other kind would a Latin expect?), and often surprisingly fine food. But the Argentine doesn't care for fine food; he cares for beefsteak.

The Argentines and their neighbors the Uruguayans are the greatest meat eaters in the world. Each country consumes well over a pound per day per person, figuring in every man, woman, and infant. To an Argentine, his beefsteak is as taken for granted as tea is to an Englishman, eaten as compulsively as Americans drink endless cups of coffee. Without his *lomo* or *filete* the Argentine man is sure his body will decay, his mind dull, and his sexual powers fail. Find a gang of workmen repairing a street or constructing a building, and there won't be a lunch pail in sight. But off to one side patiently building a fire of scrapped lumber will be a man whose sole purpose on the job is to prepare and cook the meat eaten for lunch.

Many world travelers claim that the best beef in the world after American, which without question is the finest in texture and taste, is the Kobi beef of Japan. Those that do have surely missed Argentine beef. Part of the reason is that outside of Argentina itself, one seldom tastes their finest, as is also true of Argentine wine.

For more than a century Argentina has been the chief exporter of beef to Britain, clinging to the best quality for home consumption. When a butcher in Britain refers to "chilled beef," he means Argentine, and invariably there is condescension in his voice. Argentina still depends chiefly on exports of beef for foreign exchange, but in recent years the increased appetite for their own beef has cut disastrously into exports. In desperation, a recent military government instituted "meatless days" in an attempt to conserve beef for export.

The move struck the Argentines' most vital spot. When the government was quietly removed, most Argentines felt good riddance. Improved balance of payments is too abstract a concern for him to worry about. At the expense of taking meat from his table, increased reserves of currency mean as little to an Argentine as real estate on the moon.

Few Americans, in any case, take to Buenos Aires quickly. The weather can be extreme, cold and penetratingly damp in winter and as steamy as Charleston in summer. Many Americans find the *porteños* reserved and distant, even to each other. I once attended a party where the wives of two long-time business associates met each other for the first time.

Buenos Aires is one of the most expensive Latin-American capitals, the cost of living less than Caracas, Panama City, or Rio, and slightly less than Mexico City, but more than Quito, Santiago, Bogotá, or La Paz. By United Nations figures, Buenos Aires is about on a par with Lima and San José, Costa Rica, which is still considerably less for an American than any major city in the United States.

For many years Buenos Aires had proportionally the lowest rents on the continent. In 1943 rents were frozen by a military dictator named Pedro Pablo Ramírez, and no ruler since has had the courage to take off the freeze. For years the rents crept up due to taxes and maintenance salaries, but the basic rates stayed the same; inflation skyrocketed the price of everything else. Until early 1971 it was possible to find comfortable large apartments and a few older houses for less than $100 per month. The Argentines paid a smaller proportion of their income in rent than any other *latinos*. It couldn't last. The same government that rationed beef also took the lid off rent controls, due now to spiral upward by steps until 1976.

One American who moved to Buenos Aires in 1969 estimates that a family of four needs at least the equivalent of $400 per month after taxes to live at any standard of comfort, which would be a good salary for an Argentine.

But the appeal of a place can never be reduced simply to dollars and cents. If so, Paris and New York would be ghost towns. Buenos Aires takes hold of you slowly, as does Argentina itself. At some point, without really knowing why, you are reluctant to leave.

And so it is with many Argentines. Young and professional people come to Buenos Aires from the provinces to study, and once there, never return home to live. There are movies (the largest movie industry in Latin America), the arts, books, excitement. The city also attracts the poor. In the *barrios* of the south and southeast grow tin-roofed shanty towns, *villas miserias,* crowded with rural workers and their families. In the city there are at least television, bright lights, movement, and the slenderest thread of chance.

The paradox is that while the city swells, Argentina remains one of a handful of countries in the world with growing space and chronic underpopulation. The country is large, about equal in area to the United States east of the Mississippi River. Yet the total population is slightly more than California and Arizona combined. Except for the purposes of development, the people are all in the wrong places.

Argentina even has what might be called a frontier, several of them in fact. South of the city of Bahía Blanca is the Patagonia plateau, a cold dry region nearly unpopulated that extends southward to Tierra del Fuego.

In the far north, stretching from the city of Corrientes to Salta, is an arid scrub-covered lowland, part of a single geographic region shared with Bolivia and Paraguay. It was in the Bolivian part of this region that Che Guevara tried his guerrilla campaign and failed.

Throughout its history as a country Argentina has tried to fill its space with people and never quite succeeded; economic pressure always welled up to force the country to consolidate, before pushing on again to populate. Argentina is at the moment in a stage of consolidation. Like the United States, it is a nation of immigrants. Several million Spaniards and Italians arrived between 1880 and 1930. The British built Argentina's railroads and the beef industry; one by-product is a number of Anglo-Argentine descendants, apparent in the names on diplomatic-corps rolls and in commerce.

There are smatterings of other immigrant groups. Welsh in the cool south. Japanese growing flowers near Buenos Aires. Koreans, Lebanese, refugee Poles and White Russians, Belgians from the Congo. Hundreds of thousands of Jews fleeing Europe in the 1930's headed for Argentina, as did a large number of ex-Nazis fleeing a collapsing Reich a few years later. Their both choosing Buenos Aires as a destination is one of recent history's more peculiar ironies.

Buenos Aires has the largest Jewish population of any city in the Western Hemisphere except New York City, some 400,000.

Toward the end of the 1950's, in the face of incipient depression, real immigration dried up. Now Chilean workers come into Argentina to work, but go home to have their children. Numbers of the Chilean aristocracy, who always put down the *porteños* as brassy, are drifting to Buenos Aires rather than face Chile's uncertainty. Paraguayans, Bolivians, and Uruguayans sneak across the border to find work, because at the moment Argentina is more prosperous than home. The Argentine government periodically mounts campaigns of deportation against them. The 6,000 or so Americans in Argentina work almost exclusively for American companies; a few teach in private schools. A number of them have quietly married Argentincs and melted in. Opportunities are few that can't better be capitalized upon by nationals. Argentina, as a nation, is literate (86 percent: the highest rate in Latin America), energetic, cosmopolitan; the people already know most of the tricks Americans come to teach them.

Still Argentina remains as it was one hundred years ago. A country underpopulated, a place with potential.

PROCEDURES

Argentina's immigration procedures are liberal and fairly uncomplicated. But they'll consume time.

There are two general types of nontourist visas, temporary and immigrant. Both use the same basic application form, available from any Argentine consulate. Depending on the kind of visa required, different materials must be submitted with the application, and they are processed in different ways. Generally, temporary visas may be given by the local consul. Visas given to immigrants are granted, except in special circumstances, only by the Migration Department of the Ministry of the Interior in Buenos Aires.

Temporary Visas. There are two kinds. There is a special category of temporary visas for Americans only, to promote culture and business. This is the most common kind of visa for an American with a job already in hand; in this case the visa is applied for in Argentina by the employer. This class of visa also covers newspapermen on assignment, students, artists or writers with a firm commitment of work in progress, which they wish to complete in Argentina. It is issued initially for one year and can be renewed indefinitely. If applied for at an Argentine consulate in the United States, with all necessary documents in order, this visa can be "issued in minutes."

Missionaries wishing to visit Argentina must have their temporary visas applied for by a sponsoring group in Argentina.

The second type of temporary visa is issued worldwide. It is intended for athletes, technicians servicing contracts, and so forth. It is usually given for six months.

Immigrant Visas. Immigrant visas are granted immediately if your wife or brother is Argentine, your parents are Argentine, or if you are the parent of an Argentine citizen. In most other cases, your application and documents will be forwarded to Argentina before the visa is issued. A word here about the application.

The application covers both sides of a single page. In addition to name, birth date, nationality, civil status (married, single, divorced), the questionnaire also asks where you have lived during the last five years, and information you might have should your family live in Argentina. The last four questions on page one are as follows (translation mine): Place where you will locate in Argentina. Object of the trip. Do you own land in Argentina? What means of making a living do you possess?

The last two questions are most important. Owning land bought at some prior time, or bought by the issuing of power of attorney, is a good reason for issuing a permanent visa, as in the case of a man intending to farm, for example. Don't run out and buy land just to qualify here. If you have that kind of money, you can qualify just as easily under the last question, "means of making a living." If the "means" are a bank balance, you should have a letter from your bank documenting the amount. The consulate will refuse to tell you how much is enough; the remark that several thousand dollars is a lot of money in Argentina was heard several times, but it is not uncommon for the serious migrant to have 30 or 40 thousand dollars ready for investment. Putting up bond is necessary for migration to Argentina.

In the case of application for voluntary migration, you will probably be asked for an interview with a consul, if it is physically possible. The bottom half of the last page of the application is reserved for comment by the consul, ending up with the crunch question: Is your migration in the interest of the country or not? If the consul judges no, you can appeal. In practice, except in the cases of misunderstood information, appeals seldom win out. The consul is not out to get you, but he will probably ask you a number of questions about your political ideology, to find out if below your capitalist exterior lies a pent-up Marxist.

In addition to the application, either for temporary or immigrant visas, you will need the following: (1) A valid passport. (2) International smallpox-vaccination certificate. (3) A police good-conduct certificate (not required for children under sixteen). (4) Health certificate issued by a doctor recommended by the consulate (ask them for the names). (5) Two signed photographs, 1" × 1", three-quarter profile. (6) Birth certificate, marriage certificate, divorce certificate, etc. You need the original or a certified copy. (See chapter on "Rules of the Game.") (7) Diploma or document stating knowledge or skill. This is discussed a bit more under "Working in Argentina." (8) Letter from the firm where applicant is engaged. In the case of a newspaperman on assignment, for example. (9) Other documents as required. For a writer, a book contract would serve here.

Processing of the immigrant visa should take up to three months. In practice, the application may stretch out to six or nine months. If approved, you will be given a single green sheet of paper, which is your permission to enter Argentina. Once there, you will have to register with National Registry of Persons. Everyone in Argentina, citizen and alien alike, has a *cédula de identidad,* an I.D. card. Once permanent residence is obtained, you must report in once a year, or with any change of address or occupation. This is fairly standard as an alien in any country, including foreigners in the United States. If you leave for more than twenty-four months, you'll have to reapply all over again.

Once admitted as an immigrant, you have nearly all the rights of an Argentine citizen, including the ownership of land, except within a stipulated distance from the borders. You cannot vote. Under a treaty of Friendship, Commerce, and Navigation signed between Argentina and the United States 120 years ago and still in force, "citizens of the United States residing in the Argentine Confederation . . . shall be exempted from all compulsory military service."

A treaty of extradition exists between Argentina and the United States. And Argentina, as do most countries, reserves the right to expel you if you become undesirable, mainly by entering illegally to begin with or by partaking in "activities that affect social peace, national security, or public order." The entire range of admission of foreigners, their residence and "expulsion," is detailed in Decreto Ley 4804, June 17, 1963. If you actually apply for immigration, ask the consul to give you a copy.

Immigrants are allowed to take in free of duty $1,500 worth of household goods, automobiles excluded, plus an additional $150 worth for each person included in the total migrating. It is recommended not to bring furniture, since this is available rather cheaply in Argentina.

WORKING IN ARGENTINA

Government officials and the American Chamber of Commerce in Argentina will all try to discourage you about the employment possibilities in Argentina. Though there are 270 American companies operating in Argentina, they utilize a large number of Argentines in their operation, although Argentine labor laws are nonrestrictive in this respect. It's that most Argentines are just as talented, skillful, and sophisticated in business practices as Americans. In Buenos Aires commerce a large number of locals are bilingual, thanks to a long-standing close connection with Great Britain.

Professional persons have a greater bind. Argentina has shortages of neither doctors nor lawyers. Any professional person wishing to practice for the public must have his foreign diplomas legalized and validated. This requires thorough examination *in Spanish,* equivalent to Argentine graduates in the same field.

Teachers who are not citizens of Argentina are forbidden to teach in national schools, even foreign languages. A list of private schools, mostly around Buenos Aires, is available from the consulate. Teaching positions are very difficult to obtain at long distance.

Entering Argentina as a tourist, then applying for permanent residence while remaining in the country, is legal, but complicated. The duty-free import exemption would have to be waived. If you do this, see a lawyer.

The prospects may sound grim, and for a person without something unique going for him, it probably is. But Argentina at least has room for the unique. It is a sophisticated, urban country, moving into new things: wildlife management, environment-protection research, tourism within Argentina. It has large publishing and fashion industries. As one young Argentine said, "It is hard to say what we need. There are undoubtedly ideas that would work. It's just that nobody here has thought to try them yet."

The United States and Argentina have a mutual treaty to secure investments, but it protects only AID-approved projects, with some stiff criteria. For the smaller speculator, the Argentines are not in the habit of guaranteeing anyone's future. But they are trying to promote small-scale development.

In 1969 the government passed a law aimed at encouraging immigration to Argentina of people willing to invest in infant industries and developing areas. It was not aimed at big companies, but rather at individuals and small combines "expert in carrying out rural, industrial, mining, and fishery tasks."

The incentive is a per-person customs exemption of 18 million pesos' (about $46,000) worth of goods needed in the project—cattle, seeds, levelers, prefab houses, tools, scientific equipment, vehicles (except automobiles), and other machinery. The mechanics of this process include the submitting of a plan evaluated by the relevant administering authority in Argentina, before approval. The consulates know little about the details of this promotion, but a recently translated version has been issued by the Argentine government, which the consul can give you. Ask for "Promotion of Immigration to Argentina. Decree N. 194/69." As yet, no success stories under this scheme have been reported.

Jim Wassel is from Texas originally, and owned a sporting-goods store in New Jersey. His wife, Joy, and their three-year-old son, Woody, went to Buenos Aires in January, 1971. The Wassels are in their mid-twenties.

We got the idea over a couple of drinks. Joy's mother is from Italy, and her brother had gone to South America nine years ago, first to Paraguay and then to Buenos Aires. He was up on his honeymoon, and we were having a few drinks and began talking about it, him chattering away in Italian, me in English, but mostly with a lot of sign language.

He raised chinchillas. His partner and best friend was American, an older guy, from Texas too, originally. The partner handled the actual raising side, especially processing the pelts, while Joy's uncle did most of the sales. The partner who handled the pelts kept most of the processes in his head, sort of trade secrets, but he'd had three heart attacks, and both of them had started talking about bringing somebody into the business that he could teach these processes to. He didn't want to pass them on to just anyone. Joy's uncle thought we ought to come to Argentina, and me learn that side of the business. Right then we started talking about it seriously.

Joy and I had already been looking around. I'm basically a sportsman. That's why I got into selling sporting goods. As far as I'm concerned, the East is too crowded. We looked in California, and Arizona, and still hadn't found a deal that sounded right. So Argentina didn't sound that crazy. Joy's father was in the Army, so she grew up moving every three years and has been a lot of places. Me, I've never been out of the country. So when we got to the point of realizing her uncle was serious, we said go ahead.

Back in Argentina, her uncle filed papers requesting us as immigrants, and we got a letter saying we'd be notified by the Argentine consul in New York.

Then the waiting began. After a while both Joy and I started to get cold feet. All the uncertainties started to mount up, from what kind of electric current they have, to schools. We read every book we could get our hands on, and that helped some. What we were really worried about was Joy's uncle. I kept thinking that maybe all his talk about wanting us to get in business with him was some sort of Latin polite act, that he really didn't think we'd take him up on it. And we still hadn't heard anything. Finally I wrote him a letter and asked what was happening. A day or two later, even before he could have received my letter, we heard from him. He told us his partner and best friend, the Texan, had walked in front of a bus and been killed. It had thrown the business into an uproar. Three days later, while they were trying to sort things out, they had all their furs taken in an armed robbery. With all the problems, he hadn't been able to write, but he still wanted us to come.

Well, that was the worst time for me and Joy. The uncle had no family in Argentina. And with his partner dead with all those processes in his head, the business was uncertain. We were already set on going to Argentina, and if we hadn't been we probably would have given up the idea right there. After a couple more letters we decided to give it a try anyway, just that simple.

The whole business of getting the documents, physicals, and that entry permit took longer than I thought. I must have run up a hundred-dollar phone bill a couple of months in a row, just in phone calls between Jersey and the consulate. But we finally got it. I've sold the business, and we're going to Buenos Aires.

I really don't have any big worries. We know the schools are all right, and we think it's great that Woody will grow up speaking two languages. I had two years of high-school Spanish and I can't remember any of it, but I'm not worried. I've already made up my mind it will be tough. We're looking forward to Buenos Aires. It's a big city with some night life, we found that out. Sometimes in South Jersey we wanted to get dressed up and have a class night out, I mean tux and all. You do that, and people look at you like you're nuts.

It's all the little things I'm sweating. I'm having trouble getting my hunting stuff allowed into the country. Pan Am won't ship it, because the Venezuelans won't even let the plane land on the way with guns aboard. I had to cable Buenos Aires for permission, and I still haven't received it. Going as immigrants means we can take household things, but what do you take? The stereo is going, that's for sure. I guess thinking about getting the house in shape, all the problems of not knowing what things cost, or when we're getting screwed. It's the not knowing that makes you worry the most. I've got the worst part taken care of. I have the job, and we've got Joy's uncle and his new wife our age to help us around the first month. After that we'll be all right. I'm basically a businessman, although I've spent enough time out of doors to know the opposite ends of a chinchilla. But what I'm really looking forward to is finding out if there are new things

I can do. One of my friends said I'm crazy to sell a good business. I'm not going to Argentina to get rich, because I figure you can do that better here. We have an opportunity, that's all. To see a new country, to try something different. We're young. We don't have a thing to lose.

FINDING OUT MORE

George Pendel. *Argentina.* New York, Oxford University Press. Pendel knows both Argentina and Uruguay first-hand. A historian with a fast-paced style.

American Firms, Subsidiaries and Affiliates in Argentina. U.S. Department of Commerce; Commercial Intelligence Division; Washington, D.C. 20230. One dollar prepaid by check or money order.

Establishing a Business in Argentina. U.S. Department of Commerce, Overseas Business Report. Fifteen cents, from the U.S. Government Printing Office. Dated. No mention of Decreto 194/69.

Information Guide for Doing Business in Argentina. Price Waterhouse and Company; 60 Broad Street, New York, N.Y. 10005. Free. Write on letterhead.

Chamber of Commerce of the U.S.A. in the Argentine Republic. Av. R. Sáenz Peña 567; Buenos Aires, Argentina.

Comisión Católica Argentina de Inmigración (CCAI). Laprida 930; Buenos Aires, Argentina. Not part of the government. An affiliated organization of the International Catholic Migration Commission. Supposed to be helpful in counseling migrants, especially Catholics. No first-hand information here.

For information about Decreto 194/69 regarding incentives to promote immigration you can write directly to: Señor Director Nacional de Migraciones; Departamento Técnico; Avenida Atártida Argentina 1355; Darsena Norte–Capital Federal; *Argentina.*

Argentine Embassy; 1600 New Hampshire Ave N.W.; Washington, D.C. 20009. (No consular section; write directly to the consulates.)

Argentine consulates are located in the following cities: Los Angeles, San Francisco, Miami, Chicago, New Orleans, Baltimore, Boston, New York City, San Juan, Houston.

American Embassy; Sarimiento 633; Buenos Aires, Argentina.

BRAZIL

Area: 3.3 million square miles (slightly smaller than continental United States). Population: 90–95 million (1971 est.). Capital: Brasília. Language: Portuguese.

Brazilian writer and sociologist Gilberto Freyre once likened Brazil to a tropical China.

In Brazil's size and diversity there is much to the comparison. Brazil is the largest country in Latin America, occupying just under half the total land area of the South American continent. Greatest too in numbers of people—more than 90 million, more than half under twenty years of age; and by 1990 there will be twice that number.

The people of Brazil are as racially diverse as any country in the world. Black Brazilians, mainly slave-descended, concentrated in the old sugar areas along the northeast coast. White Brazilians—Germans and Italians mainly—in the farming and cattle states of the south. Indians, Portuguese, Swiss-descended Brazilians, even Japanese—a quarter of a million—doing everything from growing pepper in the Amazon basin to driving taxis in São Paulo.

One of the first of many incongruities I witnessed in Brazil occurred at busy Congonhas airport in São Paulo. An apparently typical group of Japanese businessmen, square baggy suits, cameras dangling, disembarked from a Varig Airlines Electra and made straight for a coffee bar in the terminal en masse, passing me, chatting alternately in guttural Japanese and flowing Portuguese, as linguistically a mixed bag of sounds as you can imagine.

In common with other Latin-American societies, Brazil has a highly developed social caste system, informal as it may be, not readily apparent to the newcomer. Yet races and nationalities mix with little friction. Perhaps the archetype of the modern Brazilian is an amalgamation of blood strains and national customs, part European in culture, part African in temperament and ability to enjoy life, part American in energetic pursuit of the material. Tolerance of racial difference was once explained in a sentence by Brazilian novelist Jorge Amado. "We're all mulattoes here."

The China-like diversity grows ever more incongruous.

Brazil has seven cities of more than a million persons, two of them great by any continent's standards. São Paulo has a population of six million plus. Rio de Janeiro (always just "Rio" to a Brazilian) has something over four million. As counterpoint against that is the Amazon basin, one of the world's few remaining undeveloped frontiers.

While Rio and São Paulo struggle, some say unsuccessfully, with unbelievable traffic jams and archaic sewage and communication systems, Brazil's military government announces with a fanfare that Brazil is going to conquer the Amazon, and promptly commits several billion dollars over the next few years to do it.

The partially paved highway from Brasília north to Belem at the mouth of the Amazon is still considered something of a wild hare, yet the government announces that the first step in developing the Amazon will be a Transamazonian Highway, from the easternmost point on the continent, west, eventually to hook up with the Peruvian highway system some 4,000 miles distant.

While the cities seem ready to burst with people, a Brazilian folk hero remains the papa grinning proudly from the pages of a Recife newspaper surrounded by his twenty-three children, the twenty-fourth still with mama and a midwife. Looking toward the empty Amazon, toward the unpopulated interior, the Brazilian government is unwilling to consider population control measures of any kind. Brazil is underpopulated, they say. Brazil needs people. Too many children is still a wife's problem, not the country's. The richest rich, the poorest poor, the most ambitious and rapidly growing middle class—Brazil has the extremes and manages to fill the space between them.

But then Brazil always provokes strong reactions from Brazilian and foreigner alike.

From a Brazilian trade official in New York, paroxysms of pride mention that Brazil sells small steel products to Solingen, Germany; exports Brazilian-built G.M. buses that compete with those made in the U.S. on the world market; has twelve auto manufacturers, including the biggest Volkswagen plant outside of Germany; and has largest shipbuilding, iron and steel, and electronic industries in Latin America.

From a Brazilian small businessman in Rio, come a grimace and a sharp comment that he's lucky to survive at all. The GNP may have grown 9 percent, but 13 percent inflation has just about kept him even. His operating expenses are extraordinary. In addition to his secretary, a lawyer, and an exceptionally busy accountant, he needs an office boy to hold the telephone off the hook—listening attentively for a dial tone. If he gets one, he hands the phone to the secretary, who dials a call. Sometimes it takes forty-five minutes; sometimes the boy can't get a dial tone at all, in which case he delivers notes around Rio by hand while the secretary listens at the phone. The standard excuse for everything from avoiding people to broken love affairs is: "I tried to get you on the telephone. . . ."

To that, add bales of government red tape, bureaucratic boondoggling, and useless procedures that date back to the early 1800's, when Portugal moved the capital of the empire to Brazil and brought shiploads of court hangers-on with nothing to do and no place to do it, except to work for the government.

Every businessman's overhead demands a bevy of *despachantes,* specialized expediters skilled at unraveling or weaving through the horrendous procedures that are part of everyday business. One *despachante* knows Itamarati, the Brazilian foreign office; his specialty is visas and exit permits. Another maneuvers imports through the most complicated customs rituals in the world. No graft necessary, nor patent dishonesty. All you need is a *despachante* with the patience of a sphinx and plenty of *jeitinho* (Brazilian for a little know-how).

Everyone complains about inflation and the high cost of housing, while at the same time admitting São Paulo is one of the most vibrantly alive metropolises in the world, and that Rio without doubt has the most beautiful women one could imagine. The Carioca, the inhabitant of Rio, lives constantly aware of undrinkable water, yearly floods, power failures, and crazy taxi drivers. Yet put the Carioca in São Paulo for a day and he suffers immediate, specific nostalgia for his decaying, chaotic city, all summed up by the Brazilian word *saudades.* An American in Rio notes after a few complaints that from his house, the likes of which he couldn't afford in the States, "our little boy can walk to his riding classes at the Hipica Club; it is a six-minute drive from his school in Leblon; a six-minute drive from the beach in Ipanema; and about eight minutes from the Yacht Club."

I have never met an American who has been to Brazil, even for the briefest of visits, that somehow doesn't share with most Brazilians the feeling that the country has a special destiny. The Brazilians have a number of sayings that reflect this feeling, among them that "God is a Brazilian." But perhaps the most pertinent here is *ninguem segura Brasil.* No one holds Brazil back.

Brazil has been a land of the future for a long time, however, attractive not only to Americans. In the scheme of things, we were fairly late arrivals.

For more than a century Brazil has been the great immigrant-receiving country in South America, greater than either Argentina or Venezuela. Between 1850 and 1950 some five million new settlers arrived—Italians, Germans, and Portuguese, many part of massive governmental immigration plans. Even throughout the 1950's about 40,000 new settlers arrived each year, swallowed by Brazil's apparently insatiable ability to assimilate people. But the appetite wasn't insatiable, and as Germany and Italy began to prosper in the postwar period, Brazil found problems of its own, and the immigration dried up.

America really discovered Brazil about the same time, when the present economic boom was making a few feints in the right direction. "When we built Brasília," jokes one consular official, "then you realized Brazil wasn't a city in Argentina."

It could easily have been the other way around. Many Americans still tend to confuse the great cities at the southern end of the continent—São Paulo, Rio de Janeiro, Buenos Aires—often mixing city and country around with impunity. In a similar manner Americans tend to forget the language of Brazil isn't Spanish but Portuguese, and as such is spoken by about half the people in South America.

In print Portuguese may have a disarming similarity to Spanish, but the similarity stops at the ear, or the tongue if you are trying to bend your rudimentary Spanish around to Brazilian Portuguese. The odd thing is that Brazilians will understand you tolerably well, although it doesn't work in reverse. For years American businesses have irked Brazilians by continuing to send sales literature printed in Spanish, because "it'll do." Times are changing. An American banker for a large American bank in Santos, Brazil's great coffee port, says flatly that fluent Portuguese is an absolute requirement for employment in Brazil—let alone survival.

Individual Americans discovered Brazil long before it was discovered by official America—government and business. Probably the only planned movement of a large group of Americans to Brazil came on the heels of the American Civil War. Several thousand ex-Confederate officers and southern planters went to Brazil, settling in two or three separate places. The longest-lasting of the settlements is a town still with many of their descendants, named Americana. It's still there, a stop on the rail line from São Paulo to Ribeirão Preto, a city of about three thousand that has the Fourth of July as a city holiday and a fair number of Brazilians with names like Shaw, Yancey, and Lane.

But official America really began to understand the potential of Brazil not much more than a decade ago. Since then, the money invested by business and spent by the U.S. government on foreign aid to Brazil has been fantastic. Throughout most of the 1960's Brazil never received less than a quarter-billion dollars a year in loans, military grants, and technical help. The AID building in downtown Rio would look at home on Chicago's Loop or L.A.'s Century Plaza. Many Americans had their first look at Brazil thanks to the U.S. government; many have found the country irresistible. A few have stayed on or returned there, somehow moving sideways into business, either with Brazilian or American companies.

In 1971 about 18,000 Americans unconnected with government were living in Brazil, the greatest concentration near São Paulo and its satellite industrial city, Campinas; next is Rio, and lesser numbers in the cities along the coast to the north: Salvador, Recife, Fortaleza —missionaries, teachers, mostly businessmen, many vowing that next year they'll move back to the States, but equally as many knowing they'll stay in Brazil as long as they can.

PROCEDURES

Brazil traditionally has had some of the most liberal laws of any of the Latin American countries for allowing foreigners to establish residence.

Emphasis should be on the word "laws." There was no single immigration law, but a series of decree laws enacted by presidents over the years to account for changes in government policy, or the need of Brazil for people, or just whimsy of the moment. In Brazil it is easier to create new laws than to abolish old ones. Between 1967 and 1969, then Brazilian President Costa y Silva signed some 4,000 new laws into being. One of them was a new immigration law (Decreto-lei No. 941), with the enabling statutes signed in mid-1970.

The new immigration law is more restrictive than previous laws. It is aimed mainly at the poor or the illiterate immigrant that still might prefer the newness of Brazil to the poverty and sameness of his own country. In practice it has become slightly more specific in the various ways a person may enter Brazil.

Under the new law there are six classes of visa given to enter Brazil, from tourist to diplomatic. Only two classes need concern us here, temporary and permanent.

There are five categories of temporary and one of permanent residence, although there are a number of different ways to qualify for a permanent residence visa. All temporary and permanent residence visas use the same application form and require many of the same documents.

If you are a native-born American citizens you can obtain either category of visa very quickly, once you have filed the application, complete with the proper documents—about a week. Unlike many countries, Brazil gives the power to issue permanent visas to the consulate general. If you are a nationalized American, however, it may take a month; they have to forward the application to the Foreign Office in Brazil.

There are no quotas for Americans going to Brazil. It wasn't until 1971 that Brazil decided to compile on a national basis the number of Americans who do go there. In 1970 about 1,400 temporary and permanent visas were granted Americans through the Brazilian consulate general in New York; the U.S. total was probably something over 3,000.

Temporary Residence. Permission for temporary residence in Brazil is given to members of cultural missions, businessmen on official business trips, artists, and sportsmen (all of these up to a limit of six months); and to students or persons with scholarships, and professors or technicians under contracts.

All admittance on temporary status requires the following documents to be submitted with an application (in duplicate): (1) valid passport; (2) two passport-size photographs; (3) smallpox-vaccination certificate; (4) health certificate issued within the last six months by *any* doctor, stating you are in good health—no contagious diseases, etc; (4) good-conduct certificate furnished by local police; (5) polio-vaccination certificate.

The temporary visas differ with the nature of the visit, which in each case must be documented by either a work contract or a letter of explanation, including financial arrangements. The exact requirements are explained in the mimeographed memo the consulate will send you, called *Requirements for Temporary Residence in Brazil.* Note carefully the words "registered" and "legalized": make sure you understand the extent of both from the consulate before you go about gathering the information.

Permanent Residence. Applying for permanent residence is still not difficult by South American standards, but will require more of you—if not in time, in effort.

The preliminary requirements are the same as for a temporary visa: application form (this time in triplicate); *three* passport-size photos; smallpox-vaccination certificate; police good-conduct certificate; health certificate (for a permanent visa it must be completed by an official consular physician, the name supplied by the nearest consulate general); polio-vaccination certificate. You also must have a copy of your birth certificate, proof of marriage, and so forth.

In addition, there must be one of the following:

(1) A letter from the American or Brazilian firm employing you in Brazil, describing the job and the financial arrangements, plus a labor contract registered at the Ministry of Labor in Brazil. Your company should know the ins and outs of this if you have prior employment. This requirement has been tightened considerably over the years.

(2) Proof of three years' experience in a desired field of engineering, electronics, or other specialized technical field *officially* listed as desired by the government. In this case you escape the labor-contract clause. Every six months the Ministry of Labor issues a bulletin of critical skills to the consulate. In February, 1971, it included the whole spectrum of engineers, electronic technicians, and machinery designers. The list may change radically or slightly in any six-month period. One recent study published in Brazil foretold of a glut of engineers on the market in Brazil by 1975. But right now they still appear to be in demand. There is no language or certification requirement.

(3) A certifiable income of at least $150 per month (which in the major cities doesn't go far) if you are retired.

(4) If you are a member of a religious institution, a letter from the organization stating your mission in Brazil.

(5) Remittance of $25,000 to Brazil through the Banco do Brasil or any American bank with branches in Brazil. This is evidence of self-support, and is yours to spend. A receipt has to be presented with the application. (In 1967, the figure was $10,000.)

A list of household things taken into Brazil by a permanent resident must have prior legalization by the Brazilian consulate before departure.

The details of obtaining a permanent-residence visa for Brazil are contained in the mimeographed bulletin *Requirements for Permanent Residence in Brazil,* available from any consulate.

It is possible to go to Brazil as a tourist (for up to three months, with a three-month renewal) or on a temporary visa, and change it once you are in the country. You will need the same documents, so if this should ever be your intention, such things as the police good-conduct certificate will have to be secured beforehand. You will also need the help of a *despachante,* since the red tape is enormous. The cost may be four or five hundred dollars before you are finished. It is possible, however.

In most cases you'll find Brazilian consular people open and helpful throughout the process. It's just that there is a lot they don't tell you. The consul will allow you a permanent-residence visa if you possess one of the officially needed skills, but it is not within their realm to help you find a job in any way (nor will the American consulate once you are in Brazil).

Another item they usually neglect to mention is the necessity of obtaining an identity card within fifteen days of arrival in Brazil. This isn't done out of meanness. Identity cards *(cartera de identidade, modêlo número 19),* the "green cards" as they are called, are issued by the federal police, not the Foreign Office. A small demonstration, perhaps, but one illustrating a valid point for Americans newly going to Brazil—you are on your own.

FINDING OUT MORE

Gilberto Freyre. *New World in the Tropics.* Random House, 1959. A development of his "Brazil as a tropical China" theme, with a good deal of material from his earlier pioneering works, *The Mansions and the Shanties* and *The Masters and the Slaves.*

Charles Wagley. *Introduction to Brazil.* Columbia University, 1963. The smoothest, most understandable introduction. By an American anthropologist who knows Brazil well.

William Lytle Schurz. *Brazil, the Infinite Country.* E. P. Dutton, 1961. Good treatment of Brazil just prior to the current boom. A historian able to write from more than one point of view.

The American Chamber of Commerce for Brazil (Rio de Janeiro). C. Postal 916–ZC–00; Rio de Janeiro, GB; Brazil. Publishes a number of bulletins for members, among them weekly *Brazilian News Briefs* and an employment bulletin. They also have a wide range of cost-of-living information and tips for people moving to Brazil, especially Rio.

The American Society of São Paulo; Rua Formasa, 367; 29th Floor; C. Postal 8109; São Paulo, SP; Brazil. Publishes a *Family Guide* yearly, and for a modest membership fee can include you quickly in São Paulo's American community. There is also a "Newcomers Club" which does its best to ease the shock for Americans new to Brazil. Can be contacted either through the American consulate in São Paulo or the American Society.

American Firms, Subsidiaries and Affiliates in Brazil. U.S. Department of Commerce; Commercial Intelligence Division; Washington, D. C. 20230. One dollar prepaid by check or money order.

The Brazilian Education System: A Summary. 1970. Available from the U.S. Government Printing Office. Twenty-five cents postpaid.

Chase Manhattan Bank; 1 Chase Manhattan Plaza; New York, N.Y.10015. *A Businessman's Introduction to Brazilian Law and Practice.*

Information Guide for Doing Business in Brazil. Price Waterhouse and Company; 60 Broad Street; New York, N.Y. 10005. Free. Write on letterhead.

Brazilian Government Trade Center; 551 Fifth Avenue; New York, N.Y. 10017. Best single source of information about Brazil's economy, etc. Not visa information.

Brazilian Embassy; 3007 Whitehaven Street N.W.; Washington, D.C. 20008.

Brazilian consulates are located in the following cities: Los Angeles, San Francisco, Washington (consular section of the embassy), Chicago, New Orleans, New York City, Houston, Seattle.

American Embassy; Av. Presidente Wilson 147; Rio de Janeiro, GB; Brazil. Also a large consulate general: Consulado General Americano; Rua Padre Joao Manoel 20; São Paulo, SP; Brazil.

COSTA RICA

Area: 19,700 square miles (half the size of Virginia). Population: 1,800,000 (1970 est.). Capital: San José (182,961). Language: Spanish.

To many people Central America conjures up visions of "banana republics," hot tropical lowlands, and governments that change hands with the seasons.

Such images, built upon a few shards of truth, have never been better than distortions. For Costa Rica the images are farther from reality than one might anticipate.

Costa Rica does grow bananas. But the country's most important crop is a mild, high-grade coffee, with bananas second, and close behind, a European-style mixed farming and dairying unique in Central America. Agriculture is an important aspect of Costa Rica's developing economy, as it is in all Latin-American countries.

Costa Rica has tropical lowlands, most of the east coast, in fact. But the capital city, San José, is situated on a central *meseta* at an elevation of 3,800 feet, receives one-third the rain of the lowlands, and enjoys cool nights most of the year. Houses in San José need neither central heating nor air-conditioning.

The myth of violent political change has little basis either. Costa Rica is the most politically stable country in Latin America. The army was abolished in 1947.

The tranquillity of the country seeps down to the personal well-being of the man in the street. Petty thievery is common throughout Latin America, with Costa Rica no exception. But crimes of violence are rare and seldom mindless. A Costa Rican who had lived in New York and was returning home said that was the difference between his country and the United States. When a Costa Rican acted violently there was a reason, a motive. In New York people seemed to act for no reason at all. Americans in Costa Rica seldom worry about leaving their children unattended, and women are able to walk the streets alone, even late at night. An elegantly dressed Costa Rican woman attached to the embassy in Washington, D.C., admitted that she had never been able to adjust to the tensions she felt walking anywhere in our capital city.

Additionally, the Costa Ricans (*ticos* as they are called locally), for reasons founded upon nothing tangible, like America and Americans. One American who has lived in Costa Rica for ten years said, "The country is the most pro-American in Latin America. They've adopted *us,* so to speak." There has also been a bit of the reverse. More than a century ago Costa Rica was one of the two countries favored by disaffected southerners after the collapse of the Confederacy, Brazil the other. More Americans live in Costa Rica than in Sweden, Portugal, Denmark, or Iran—about 6,000 in 1971.

Americans who visit Costa Rica for the first time come away with three impressions at least: the friendliness and dignity of the people, the comparative prosperity of the economy, and the attractiveness of the women, who are said to outnumber the men by a fair number.

This abundance of females is a constant topic of conversation, among men at least. In San José I've heard the ratio of women to men given as five to three, and sworn to as official. I later heard a number of different figures, all equally testified to as official. Among foreigners who have taken Costa Rica for their own, there is little mention of the subject. One suspects that they are content to enjoy quietly the situation, which, if you are male anyway, is distressingly to your advantage.

Costa Rica treats foreigners well in a number of other ways. Tourism is considered an industry and approached conscientiously, instead of as something that no one really wants but must put up with to bring in foreign exchange. Resident aliens have the same individual and social rights under the constitution as nationals, including the right to own land, without the border and seacoast restrictions of Mexico and Panama.

Political privileges are withheld from foreigners. Aliens cannot vote or intervene in the political affairs of the country, political parties, or trade unions. Article 31 of the constitution stipulates that "the territory of Costa Rica will be an asylum for all persons persecuted for political reasons." However, political refugees must come dressed to standards acceptable to Costa Rican custom. In Costa Rica, as in a number of other places, long hair is considered more a symbol of Western decadence than of independence from the system. Haircuts are often demanded by airport customs officials, and people who didn't conform to local cultural standards of dress have been known to be sent off on the next outward flight.

Such idiosyncrasies detract little from the appeal of Costa Rica to Americans who have discovered the country. Part of the appeal is that Costa Rica seems manageable, a small, simple country with a reasonable pace of life. Compared with Brazil's complexity, or the stresses of daily existence in Mexico City or Caracas, Costa Rica and its capital, San José, might seem as far removed as a Piper Cub from a Concorde.

Add a certain appeal to more base economic instincts, stimulated by Costa Rica's conscious effort to lure investors. As a member of the Central American Common Market (CACM), Costa Rica offers liberal fiscal incentives "to be applied to the establishment or amplification of manufacturing industries which effectively contribute to the economic development of Central America." Costa Rica additionally has an attractive tax structure, with a personal income tax greater than neighboring Panama but low by European standards. An earned income of $10,000 would be taxed 18 percent, with the rate scaling up to a 30-percent maximum.

The impression, at first glance, is that Costa Rica is one of the few remaining places where the small investor can speculate and make a fortune. Almost any successful American resident in Costa Rica will tell you stories of other Americans who arrived, mouths watering, with modest nest eggs and speculated in stocks, real estate in the developing northwest, or in get-rich-quick business enterprises, and not so slowly watched the nest eggs dwindle away. Writes one American who has spent more than a decade in Costa Rica: "The chance here for a person with drive but undercapitalized is practically nil today . . . the coffee shops in San José are full of men with ideas and schemes just needing 'a little capital.' "

Writes another American who has preferred the humdrum of a daily job to speculation: "It is even more difficult for elderly people with a bundle to come here and expect to place it without losing their shirts."

George Curtis, an American in the mortgage and loan business with eleven years experience in Costa Rica, has his own advice for Americans considering investments in Costa Rica. "In a nutshell, invest cautiously and live comfortably on the income. Government bonds, reputable commercial and industrial stocks, mortgages arranged through well-known banks—they all pay well."

Particular caution is urged for retired Americans considering Costa Rica.

Costa Rica is one of the growing number of countries interested in attracting retired people who have a fixed income. The basic requirement is a minimum monthly income of $250 for the applicant and an additional $75 a month for each dependent person over fifteen years of age who will actually reside with the applicant. Such income is untaxed in Costa Rica. Admittance under these *pensionado* visas allows $5,000 worth of household goods admitted duty free, one time, plus an automobile. Information is avilable from any Costa Rican consulate. Ask for "Instruction Manual for Persons Interested in Taking Advantage of the Benefits of Law 4064." The booklet is in English. It is also available from the Institute of Tourism, as is other tourist and immigration information: Costa Rican Institute of Tourism; P.O. Box 777; San José, Costa Rica.

Obtaining a pensioner's visa is a much easier process than obtaining the standard resident visa. Despite their friendliness and interest in foreign investment, application for residence in Costa Rica requires considerable documentation.

PROCEDURES

Without sufficient money to invest, your skill or profession will attract considerable attention in the application for permanent residence. A prior job offer is the surest way to ensure that your application will be accepted. But the Commercial section of the U.S. embassy in Costa Rica warns: "Job opportunities for Americans are very limited in that there is a 10-percent ceiling on the number of Americans who may be employed by any particular firm."

It is impossible to obtain employment unless admitted to Costa Rica with *permanent-residence* status. You will be allowed to change status from tourist to permanent resident inside the country, but all the necessary documents must be with you.

Applications for permanent residence or pensioner's visa are made with the Costa Rican consulates general in the United States. The applications, together with the proper documents, are then forwarded to the Ministry of Foreign Relations in Costa Rica for processing. Processing normally takes three to four weeks.

Application for permanent residence must include the following information, and must be translated into Spanish: Applicant's name, including mother's maiden name. Profession or occupation. Present nationality. Purpose of desired residence in Costa Rica. Names of the members of the applicant's family who will accompany him. Present address. Pertinent details which may help in determination of the case (a job offer, for example).

In addition, the application must be supported by the following:

(1) Certificate of solvency, or any other satisfactory guarantee (person, company, bank, etc.) for the cost and expenses of residence and repatriation of the person desiring to establish residence.

(2) Birth certificate: two copies.

(3) Certificate of good conduct: two copies, issued by the corresponding authority of the place or places of residence during the last five years, showing, if the case is that, the criminal record.

(4) Certificate of marriage: two copies.

(5) One photograph: front view, taken recently, individually.

(6) Medical-examination certificate consisting of: smallpox-vaccination certificate; blood test for venereal diseases; lung examination, including X ray, with its respective medical interpretation. These documents must be presented when the application is being made through a consulate. If such application is being done through the Ministry of Foreign Relations, all of the medical examinations *should* be done by a doctor in Costa Rica.

(7) A statement or affidavit specifying the reasons why the person desires to establish residence in Costa Rica.

All documents must be duly legalized as follows: For all areas of the United States except Washington, D.C., by notary public or county clerk. For Washington, D.C., notary public or Department of State.

All documents *must* be translated into Spanish before submitting them to legalization by the consular office.

As the Costa Rican consulate adds: "All the above documents are to be prepared in accordance with these instructions. When everything is in order they will be mailed to Costa Rica. The cost of the airmail must be paid by the individual. There is also a *strong suggestion* to have an interview with the consular officer before mailing all the documents to Costa Rica."

Fees for consular legalizaton may run as high as $10 per document.

FINDING OUT MORE

Investor's Guide to Costa Rica. A fifty-three-page booklet that is something more than its title implies. Complete business laws and regulations, and a good deal of general information as well. Should be available free from U.S. Department of Commerce field offices. Also from a principal source of business information: Export-Investment Promotion Center; Post Office Box 5418; San José, Costa Rica.

Information Guide for Central America. Price Waterhouse and Company; 60 Broad Street; New York, N.Y. 10005. Free. Write on letterhead.

American Firms, Subsidiaries and Affiliates in Costa Rica. U.S. Department of Commerce; Commercial Intelligence Division; Washington, D.C. 20230. One dollar prepaid by check or money order made payable to the Department of Commerce.

Four tourist and immigration information: Costa Rican Tourism Institute; P.O. Box 777; San José, Costa Rica, CA.

Costa Rican Embassy; 2112 S Street N.W.; Washington, D.C. 20008.

Costa Rican consulates are located in the following cities: San Francisco, Los Angeles, Washington, Miami, Tampa, Chicago, New Orleans, Detroit, New York City, Houston, Seattle.

American Embassy; Calle 1, Avenida 3; San José, Costa Rica. Write to them for "Information Concerning Costa Rica"—a valuable seven-page bulletin.

LIBERIA

Area: 43,000 square miles (about the size of Ohio). Population: 1.15 million (1969 U.N. est.). Capital: Monrovia (80,992). Languages: English (official), twenty-eight native dialects.

Liberia is Africa's oldest republic, and the only black African country that permits immigration in the traditional sense.

Liberia was founded in 1824 by former slaves from the United States. It is their ancestors today, though less than one-tenth of the population, who rule and manage the country. Unlike many of the newer African countries, carved and subdivided out of former European-governed colonies, within Liberia's borders are resources—rubber, iron, and timber—rich enough to finance the building of a small nation. Former State Department adviser C. M. Wilson, who knows Liberia first-hand, calls it a beautiful land of beautiful people, with resources as well, most of them unaccessible.

For almost three decades now Liberia has opened the door of its economy to foreign investment in an effort to get at the country's buried wealth. Liberia's late President William V. S. Tubman instituted the "open-door" policy very soon after his first election as President in 1943. Liberia remains a poor country; 70 percent of the people are farmers. The per-capita income is about $185 a year. Like many other developing countries, it is going through a "Liberiaza-tion," that is, pushing forward its own people into positions of employment with foreign-owned companies. Labor laws are very strict in regard to the employment of aliens, white or black, and the immigration policies are not uninfluenced by them.

For example, under the Alien and Nationality Law of the Republic there are four ways an alien may enter Liberia other than as a tourist: visitor, diplomat, resident, and immigrant.

Any alien who goes to Liberia on either a tourist or visitor's visa and stays more than fifteen days must report to an immigration office and make arrangements for a continued stay. After fifteen days an exit permit is required before leaving the country. Anyone going into Liberia under these statuses will be deported immediately if he tries to change his status to allow him to work. If you come as a visitor, you must leave as a visitor.

Other than tourists or visitors, most foreigners go to Liberia on a residence visa. Before a residence visa will be issued, an employer within Liberia must apply for a work permit. The residence visa and the work permit go hand in hand.

Liberian labor law prohibits the employing of foreigners except in administrative, supervisory, and technical capacities, unless there is a shortage of qualified Liberians. An employer must prove this is the case when he applies for a work permit. An employer who hires foreigners also must periodically document to the government what they do, their nationality, how long they have worked for him, and so forth. In certain technical positions the government requires the employee to train a Liberian in his job.

There are a number of shortages in Liberia's labor market, and in actual fact the majority of Americans living in Liberia work for either foreign companies or missionary societies. Even those who propose eventual naturalization usually qualify first as residents. Having Negro ancestry is the only blanket requirement. In 1971 the total number of American citizens living in Liberia was about 4,000, more than in any other black African country except Nigeria.

A person attempting to qualify as an immigrant must surrender a good measure of control of his life to government administration.

PROCEDURES

The first step in the process of receiving immigrant status is to write directly to the Immigration Board in Liberia, stating in as much detail as possible your reasons for wanting to migrate to Liberia, your professional or technical qualifications, and your personal background.

President Tubman established the Immigration Board in 1967, made up of seven high-ranking government officials. Their duties include:

(1) Determining, within the limits of the constitution, laws of Liberia, and the policies of government, conditions under which aliens seeking admission into Liberia as immigrants will be allowed to enter and reside in Liberia.

(2) Interviewing immigrants who wish to reside permanently in Liberia, checking their qualifications, and cataloging their professions and vocations.

(3) Selecting areas within the country for the immigrants to settle, assigning them to the areas selected, and assuring that the assignments are adhered to. In the selection and assignment of the immigrants, the board shall endeavor to locate them in all parts of the country to ensure their fuller knowledge of and participation in the communities of Liberia.

(4) Assisting the immigrants to find jobs, locate houses, and generally get settled.

(5) Working with the immigrants to effect their rapid and harmonious assimilation into the Liberian community.

We'll come back to several of those points in a moment. The first thing the board does is review the letter of the applicant.

If on the surface the applicant appears suitable, they will return the letter to the Liberian embassy in Washington or the consulate general in New York, to make additional inquiries into the substance of the letter.

The Immigration Board has designated a number of occupations in the category of "desirable immigrants." It includes professional occupations such as physicians, dentists, engineers, agriculturists, pharmacists, and teachers. It also includes others needed in Liberia's developing economy—carpenters; nurses; business secretaries; dieticians; motor mechanics; and hat, shoe, and dress makers.

After the consulate has made inquiries, they usually request a personal interview. The Commissioner of Immigration and Naturalization, Edward S. Jones, assures prospective immigrants that such applications will be handled speedily, and that delays usually are the fault of the immigrant-to-be. Consular officials refuse to be pinned down on just how long the processing requires, but several months is the general rule.

Receiving an immigrant visa implies several things. Immigrants should be prepared to be employed by the government. They should be prepared to live in localities assigned by the government; Subsection 13 of the Nationality Law requires immigrants to be assigned to different sections of the country. The Liberian government is trying to prevent overcrowding of the capital city of Monrovia.

If the immigrant is willing to file a declaration of intent to become a Liberian citizen, the government is prepared to provide additional help. In actuality, declaration of intent does not necessarily mean automatic, immediate Liberian citizenship. There is a two-year-residence period as a requirement.

But when such an intent is filed, the President may offer the immigrant free lodging at government expense for a period of up to three months, and the allotment of specific tracts of public (government-owned) land.

The fact is that during the past decade fewer than 200 American citizens have gone to Liberia initially as immigrants. Most black Americans living in Liberia came on residence visas, changing their status after they had become familiar with the country.

Of those that chose immigration directly, a group of black Americans coming originally from Chicago is best remembered. One hundred and seventy-three members of a black Hebrew group arrived in Liberia between July and December, 1967, a number of women and children among them. They first attempted clearing and farming a 300-acre tract of land in central Liberia, about eighty miles from Monrovia. Problems with malaria, the fact that most of them were city people rather than farmers, and an increasing insistence by the Liberian government that they assimilate more into the stream of Liberian life all frayed the effort from the beginning.

Early on, some of the younger members of the group returned to Chicago, reportedly because they had been misled as to what Liberia was really like. Some drifted to Monrovia, the capital. In November, 1969, the Liberian government nearly ousted the remaining number as "unwanted aliens," but eventually relented. About twenty-five of the original group have become Liberian citizens. Most of the others have left, expressing a desire to settle in Israel.

The experience was apparently illuminating for the Liberian government. The idea of Americans leaving the United States primarily because of racial reasons is fully understood by the Liberians. Late President Tubman's great-grandfather was a slave, which is not an uncommon heritage for the Liberian ruling class. What befuddles Africans is the reluctance of most American blacks who return to Africa to relinquish American citizenship. Trying to have it both ways is an irritant.

Commissioner of Immigration Edward S. Jones emphasizes the desire that people coming to Liberia be prepared to join in Liberian society. "Most American Negroes coming as immigrants don't seem to be willing to assimilate into our society but attempt to form their separate groups, which makes them strangers for as long as they stay here. If they are willing to freely mix with the Liberian citizens met, they will have no problems whatsoever."

FINDING OUT MORE

In Liberia, the address of the Immigration Board is as follows: The Chairman; Board of Immigration; Department of Internal Affairs, R. L.; Monrovia, Liberia.

Information on visas, health, agriculture, and foreign private investment is available from the board and from: Embassy of Liberia, 5201 16th Street N.W., Washington, D.C. 20011; and: Liberian Consulate General, 1120 Avenue of the Americas, New York, N.Y. 10036.

Establishing a Business in Liberia. Overseas Business Report, U.S. Department of Commerce. U.S. Government Printing Office; Washington, D.C. 20402. Fifteen cents a copy.

Business Firms in Liberia. U.S. Department of Commerce; Commercial Intelligence Division; Washington, D.C. 20230. One dollar prepaid by check or money order.

American Embassy; United Nations Drive; Monrovia, Liberia.

GREAT BRITAIN

Area: 88,764 square miles (a little smaller than Oregon). Including Northern Ireland it becomes some 94,000 square miles. Population: 54,021,000; with Northern Ireland, 55,534,000 (1969). Capital: London, 8,194,480 (1969). Language: English.

The first thing any British consular officer will try to impress upon you is that Britain is not an immigrant nation.

What he means is that there is neither a need for more people nor a mechanism for handling a vast influx of aliens and assimilating them smoothly into British society.

People do migrate to Britain, considerable numbers in fact, mainly from other Commonwealth countries. Except for the Australians and New Zealanders who generally come for a look, stay a few years, and then go home where the sun is shining, many of the others try to stay.

Immigration over the past several years has become something of a hot issue in Britain. It was touched off by the influx of Indians and Pakistanis (called "Asians" in Britain) from East Africa in 1968, and the thought that with "Africanization" in the countries of East Africa a large number of the 150,000 "Asians" living there holding British passports might all come home in a rush to mother England.

The country is already having problems blending in the "Asians" already there, as well as the numbers of migrants arriving from the Caribbean. The plumber and the charwoman are likely to be the most vocal critics of the migrants, muttering about the "colored," mainly because they are new in Britain's social makeup and compete in the lower end of the labor market. A few of the suburbs around the major cities that were all white ten years ago have become populated with large numbers of "Asians" and Caribbean blacks. Wander down a side street in Brixton, for example, and you are likely to find houses painted blue and pink and the sound of a Caribbean steel band wafting from windows and pubs. A spicy contrast to the sameness of London's fringes, perhaps the drabbest suburbs of any city in the world.

But in typical fashion the British have handled migration sensibly but with a firmness that has angered a few. The country has dedicated itself to becoming a multiracial, multinational society, and is probably as close to succeeding with a minimum of friction as any country might hope.

Caught up in the swirl of new arrivals are about 19,000 nontourist Americans who enter Britain each year, mainly as employees of American-owned companies, students, and teachers. One in three will try to make Britain home when his assignment is through.

Next to the American businessman, the largest definable segment of Americans resident in Britain are those living on pensions. As of August, 1971, the consular section of the American embassy distributed monthly about 12,500 government and Social Security pension checks. Most Americans drawing pensions have found London too expensive, but an hour or two from London by train are myriad country towns where the cost of living is cheaper by a large percentage, with the added amenities of the nearby English countryside.

There have been a few well-publicized American movie people who have moved to Britain, and the country has probably overtaken Switzerland as the place for fashionable exiles. André Previn now directs the London Symphony Orchestra; the ex-director of CBS News writes and edits a weekly newspaper in a small country town; and S. J. Perelman, the humorist, has made a widely reported exit from the United States in favor of Britain.

One of Perelman's comments hits upon one aspect of life in Britain that most Americans living there sooner or later come to appreciate. "In Britain," he said, "they still have the taste for eccentricity."

This willingness of the British to remain individuals, doing their often odd individual things, has given rise to a number of refreshing aspects of daily life, among them the most amusing magazine writing in the world, probably the last existing radio talk shows with spark, and a miscellany of happenings guaranteed to assure you that in Britain the individualist still has a chance.

Several years ago, for example, the British Parliament voted that the country would abandon Greenwich Mean Time for an experimental run with what the government called British Standard Time. The point was that British Standard Time was the time of the rest of Continental Europe. With eyes toward eventual entry into the European Common Market, British Standard Time, among other things, was good for business.

Now there are very few places left on earth where things that are good for business don't eventually become good for everybody, whether they like it or not. The trouble with British Standard Time was that it left people in the dark, literally. Farmers got up in the dark. The Scots, who are close to the Arctic Circle and have short enough days in winter as it is, found sunrise closer to midday than morning. A feisty British writer named A. P. Herbert wrote a letter to *The Times* of London, whose letters-to-the-editor column is the epitome of literate public letterwriting, in which he noted that the British Parliament had superimposed the time of eastern Poland and Yugoslavia upon not only the English but those in the west of Ireland as well.

By the time Parliament met to vote whether to continue on British Standard Time, the public debate was at a vigorous peak; to quiet smiles of triumph from the ordinary man on the street, Parliament decided to return to Greenwich Mean Time by the lopsided vote of 366 to 81.

Whether it is the knowledge that the local "bobbie" on the beat lives in the neighborhood he patrols (and still doesn't carry a pistol), or that the saving of a rare species of field bird was accomplished by a single ornithologist, one has the feeling in England that the battle of man against the impersonality of conscienceless institutions is not being lost so rapidly.

I once lived in an apartment building not exactly elegant, but homely in a peculiar Edwardian way. We tenants learned one day that the entire building was likely to be sold and demolished, and that negotiations were at that moment in the last stages of discussion with a major hotel corporation. Recently a parcel of land several blocks away had been bought for a Hilton Hotel, and the intention was to begin turning the residential neighborhood into a western London haven for businessmen and tourists, closer to the airport than central London. Through concerted action the tenants were able to petition and convince the Borough Council that several hundred people, and an entire neighborhood, would be very unhappy to see such a change. They prevailed. The Council forbade the sale of the property, thereby dooming a second hotel.

Of course, a few other aspects of life in Britain are less promising, thoroughly convincing most Americans that the United States doesn't have a franchise on the world's problems.

Strikes, for example. Britain is one of the most strike-prone nations in the world. In 1970 some 11 million man-days were lost in strikes, and early in 1971 the country withstood a mail strike that lasted six weeks. Rail strikes (travel by train is more common in Britain than in the United States), dustmen's (trash haulers') strikes, automobile workers' strikes, harbor strikes, ambulance drivers' strikes—any group in the labor force that can organize has struck and will eventually strike again. Chancellor of the Exchequer Anthony Barber summed up what most people realize, even the strikers themselves, that with Britain's lagging economy they can hardly afford the luxury. "We are cutting our own throats," said Barber, knowing full well that the strikes will continue if for no better reason than custom.

There are many Britons who claim the country in some vague way is getting "just as bad as America." Frequent newspaper headlines (employing the favored words "shock," "horror," or "scandal") claim an abrupt rise in crime. One Scotland Yard inspector provoked nods of agreement with his statement in a *Sunday Times* interview that London was "going the way of Washington and New York."

Crime *is* on the upswing in Britain, just as it is in every industrialized country, the Soviet Union included. In 1970 Britain recorded some 367 cases of murder and manslaughter; in the same period the United States registered some 15,810 according to the FBI, a proportional difference that can't be explained away by a four-times-greater population. Some countries seem almost to have the habit of violence. Britain does not. The overall increase in violent crime is between 2 and 3 percent a year, a figure in line with most other European countries and far less than most countries in the Western Hemisphere.

Others claim that Britain is going down the drain on the cloak of the "permissive society." Pornography is flourishing, as anyone who has browsed a newsstand can attest, though nowhere is it as blatant as Copenhagen or Times Square. Nor is it spreading without firm resistance. Britain has legalized abortions, and London has acquired the tabloid label "the abortion capital of Europe." Some 80,000 abortions were performed in Britain in 1970, about half of them in London. And a good thing too, says the Family Planning Association, which claims that 35 percent of Britain's brides are pregnant at the altar.

A rapidly increasing cost of living, some 11 percent between September, 1970, and September, 1971, provoked one American who has seen prices rise over the past five years to say, "Yeah, it's still cheaper than Stateside. But it ain't cheap." Add urban congestion, a growing awareness of pollution, increasing drug problems, and one must admit that Britain has the same catalog of problems as the United States, but not yet of equal magnitude. In some way, the problems seem far more visible in Britain, due in part at least to the tendency most Britons have of being harsher critics of their own country and society than the Americans who have moved there and found comparative peace.

And the weather. Technically the climate of Britain is classified (by Koeppen and others) as a "Marine West Coast Climate," distinctly milder than the harsher Continental climates and without undue extremes. Springs and summers are cool, and comparatively warm autumns are not uncommon. Hot days are rare, but so is the other extreme; London has never recorded a temperature below zero degrees Fahrenheit. The yearly averages range from the low sixties in the summer months to the mid-forties during the winter. The fact is that Britain shares the weather of that part of Europe lying west of an imaginary line drawn between Stockholm and Marseilles, not unlike the Pacific Northwest of the United States. That's the official story, anyway.

Most Americans initially find the weather appalling, and knowing it is just as appalling in Brussels or Amsterdam makes it no more endurable. The winters are damp, cloudy, and dark. The summers may decide to be summerlike or may be reminiscent to Americans of a bad eastern spring. I remember one summer that would have made the Riviera proud, with day after day of bright cloudless weather. The next year had the coldest summer recorded since 1936. London averages about 1,480 hours of bright sunshine a year, as compared to 2,200 hours for Washington, D.C.; 2,740 for Lisbon; and 2,750 for southern California. Perhaps the best one can hope for is that the weather will be surprising. The jokes made about Britain's weather, like so much of British humor, are only funny because based on rather painful truth. But the Americans that stay get used to it. Away from England for six months and one can seldom remember the weather as anything but that described by the most favored of British adjectives, "pleasant."

Another thing that irritates some Americans is British politeness, although irritation is seldom the initial reaction. It comes only after an American realizes that the British use the surname, always preceded by a courteous "Mr." or "Miss," as a technique to keep people at a distance. As a nation the British tend to discourage familiarity. Where Americans will be calling a total stranger by his first name within minutes of meeting and consider it admirable to do so, the British will feel perfectly comfortable Miss-and-Mistering casual acquaintances for years.

Their ability to indulge in polite conversation seems inexhaustible. This "superficiality" bothers Americans, who take it personally: there is something about *me* that makes *them* unwilling to "open up." With time, most Americans realize that British reserve was firmly in place long before their arrival. They learn to play the social game by local rules. It is never bad advice. Besides, as one American woman said forthrightly: "I don't care if their politeness is superficial. I like politeness of any kind."

Of course, the main problem for Americans that would like to live in Britain, as it is in every other European country, is finding a place for your talents. The unemployment rate in Britain is usually quite a bit below the American level, which most British people would consider scandalous in their own country. But is has been creeping upward, and the job market throughout the early 1970's will probably be tighter, even for those with a unique skill, than at any time during the past decade.

FINDING WORK

There are few shortages in the British labor market. The so-called "brain drain" of a few years back has been plugged. There are even signs that it is reversing, with British engineers and scientists going back. Selected scientific fields are still open to the qualified foreigner, and there are shortages of doctors, teachers, and trained nurses. In these fields there is still a drain, but it might better be called a "skill drain." There is a reason. British pay scales are comparably low. The average weekly wage for skilled labor is about $86. Less than one-tenth of the nonmanagerial labor force earns more than $115 per week.

According to the *Financial Times* the median salaries of professional and executive people are: aged twenty to twenty-five, $3,480; aged forty-one to forty-five, $6,840. By one survey British executives are the worst paid in Europe. In 1969 only 250,000 persons in the entire country had incomes greater than $7,200 a year. That's one nice thing about Britain; everyone else is poor too.

TAXES

Another good reason why people have little money is taxes. By U.S. standards British taxes are appallingly high. Income tax begins at a standard rate of 38.5% (as of April, 1971), with an increasing surtax on segments of income over £2,500 ($6,000). Actually the standard rate has been creeping down over the past twenty years. During World War II it reached 50 percent.

Taxes are withheld from wages, similar to the American system. The U.K. income tax return is more in the nature of an information form, from which the Board of Inland Revenue assesses the tax. If you are an American resident in Britain you must file with Inland Revenue yearly, whether you have taxable income or not. I dwell on this because there are two wrinkles in British tax laws that affect many Americans. Capital is not taxable, and may therefore be brought into the country without liability (although you must meet several criteria for what constitutes capital). Because of this, it is possible for an American to live temporarily in Britain on money brought in from an unsecured loan from a relative, or a secured loan, as long as the loan is not paid back while you are in Britain. "Temporarily" is generally defined as up to three years, but in actuality can be considerably longer.

Additionally, money you earn outside of Britain is taxed only if it is remitted into the country. Wages paid into a U.S. bank account, for example, can accrue untaxed. For these reasons there are perfectly legal ways for an American with certain types of income to avoid much of the damage done by high taxes on income. The maximum of 91.25 percent combined standard and surtax is reached quickly, on taxable incomes of £15,000 ($36,000) per year or more.

For this reason too, Britain is the best example I can think of on the advisability of obtaining tax advice before leaving the United States.

From other taxes there is no hope of relief. There is a value-added tax called "purchase tax" that adds from 13 ¾ to 55 percent onto the wholesale price of almost everything except food, books, fuel, and medicines. Automobiles are tagged 36 ⅔ percent, furniture and carpets a mere 13 ¾ percent, pet foods up to 22 percent, and phonograph records the limit—55 percent.

Also free of purchase tax are most goods subject to other taxes on expenditure, such as beer, wines and spirits, and tobacco.

An excise tax equivalent to $3.30 is tacked onto each bottle of spirits. There is enough tax on a pint of beer to drive the price up to the equivalent of forty cents. Twenty-ounce pint, though, and stronger beer. Ah, you say, but they do have the National Health Service. True, but you still pay a token weekly fee.

Despite low salaries and high taxes, the balance between them and the rising cost of living has remained in better proportion in Britain than in most European countries; certainly in better proportion than most developing countries. People in Britain live with fewer of the extravagances Americans consider necessities, with the possible exception of the growing passion for color television (of unparalleled technical quality, I might add). Frozen foods are favored less than products from the "greengrocer." Electric can openers are rare. Many housewives, owing to a cool yearly climate, do perfectly well without a refrigerator, shopping daily with a shopping bag instead of weekly with the station wagon.

Still, most Americans try to obtain employment with American companies or their British subsidiaries, because the pay is better. Even the American-owned companies use British personnel wherever possible, or transfer people to Britain from home base. Americans with general management experience are generally considered difficult to place. Scientific, technical, or specialized or unique talents may have an easier time, although finding a job in Britain from scratch is considered difficult.

Two directories might help. *The Anglo-American Trade Directory,* published by the American Chamber of Commerce in London, 75 Brook Street, London W.1. This is a large-format volume with quite a list of British subsidiaries and the names of personnel. At $12.50 it is expensive. Your local British consulate should have a copy.

Something more British caused quite a stir in the boardroom when it was first published a couple of years ago: *Who Owns Whom,* published by O. W. Roskill and Co. Ltd., 14 Great College Street, London S.W.1. This book is even more expensive, about $20.00. Try Department of Commerce field offices and the British consulate and Trade Office. As its title suggests, the book lists the owners of British companies, and was one of the first to highlight the fact that a large number of British companies, particularly publishing and automotive, are controlled by Americans. There are the first stirrings of debate, which suggests that foreign ownership of key British industries might be a topic of discussion during the 1970's, as will immigration.

The two best newspapers for employment advertising (called "Appointments" in Britain) are the *Times*, both daily and Sunday, and the *Daily Telegraph*, especially on Thursday, for some reason.

The largest group concerned with turning up qualified people is Management Selection (Group) Limited, 17 Stratton Street, London WIX 6 DB. They aren't head-hunters, though, and do not handle placements. Usually they are retained by a company to screen possible people whom they contact through the use of newspaper advertising. MSL has a number of associated companies in the United States. Occasionally they will circulate the qualifications of Americans in their "North American Register," which makes the rounds of British companies.

A number of teaching appointments are advertised in the *Times Educational Supplement.* The American School of London has a few openings yearly for qualified teachers, but almost always a personal interview is required before employment. (Teachers see also "Finding Out More.")

Despite warnings, it is possible (though not according to regulation) to enter Britain as a tourist, find a job, and have your employer apply for a work permit for you. In Mexico or Switzerland it is near impossible. Even with the "books of regulations," the British remain flexible. Individual cases are treated as such, and often, if you are a decent person with reasonably honorable intent, you can "get on," as the British say, in a manner rare in other countries.

That may sound old-fashioned. To Americans it is this tolerance, a certain humanity, and a great range of experiences available to even the modestly employed that is part of Britain's appeal. As Anthony Lewis commented in the international *Herald Tribune*: "Almost without exception they express delight, wonder, relief at finding themselves again in a country of civility and good nature."

If you balance that against "Sod you Jack, I'm all right," the workingman's comment to those less fortunate than he, you have two poles of British temperament with a measure of good things for the American in between.

PROCEDURES

If living in Britain interests you, the first step is to write to the nearest British consulate (see "Finding Out More" for cities with consulates). In your letter, state simply: (1) you want information about working, studying, retiring, etc.; and (2) your nationality. If a naturalized American, give date of naturalization. Ask the consul specifically to send you the following bulletins if you are interested; otherwise you'll get a form letter and have to write again for more information.

Setting Up Residence in the United Kingdom. This contains information on moving household effects, motor vehicles, and is somewhat a guide to other guides. It also contains a range of factual information that gets down to the reality of living in Britain, such as the fact that wall electrical sockets are of a different type and fewer than you're used to. And that you'll have to wait six months before being joined by your dog or cat, while they sit out quarantine.

Finding Employment in Britain. Begins rather severely by saying the British government will give no assistance in finding employment other than what is contained in the bulletin. It also states flatly that aliens are positively not admitted to Britain for the purpose of looking for a job. It's not quite that forboding.

Admission of Children from Overseas to British Schools. Another guide to guides. Focuses on the British secondary-school system and public schools, which in England means private schools. If London is your destination, you might also write to the American School in London, 6 York Gate, Regents Park, London N.W. 1, for information.

United Kingdom Income Taxes. An explanation in simple language of how tax is determined, and what it amounts to. Read it and weep.

Conditions of Admission to the United Kingdom for Foreigners not Requiring Visas. Since you are an American citizen, this includes you. Visas are required of nationals of Communist, Arab, and a number of Asian countries, and holders of a "U.S. Re-entry Permit."

The consulate would probably send you this bulletin anyway, but it is such an innocuous three-page pamphlet that it might go unnoticed. "We have books of regulations," one consul said. But the most definitive statement available to the public is this three-page pamphlet. The subsections need reading several times, to dig out full meaning.

The pamphlet outlines five ways you can enter England. A sixth way is discussed later.

(1) As a visitor or tourist. In which case the pamphlet notes that you "are readily admitted to the United Kingdom, provided the immigration officer is satisfied you do not intend to stay there." A word here about the immigration officer. He is the first man you meet after disembarking from your airplane or ship. He will be uniformed, efficient, and like British policemen, will have a confident air of polite authority. He will ask you a number of questions to which he probably knows or suspects the answer beforehand. He is near-unfoolable, and his power is inviolate. He can and does refuse landing to people entering England, but usually for a good reason. The best reason is lack of enough money to sustain your visit. The second reason is looking scruffy, to use an English term. That doesn't mean just long

hair. The English started the whole hair business, remember. Once you're in England you can dress pretty much as you like. But it's best not to look worse than you must at Immigration. Especially if in the back of your mind you plan to look for a job, you must arrive looking like a tourist with enough money to behave like one.

(2) As a foreigner wishing to set up a business. The British are extremely liberal about the nature of the business and where you intend to locate. But they require prior application to be admitted in this status. They essentially want to know that *you* know what you are doing, and have made financial arrangements for it. See *Establishing a Business in the United Kingdom,* Overseas Business Report 67–63, U.S. Department of Commerce. Acceptance of your application will result in a letter of official permission to enter the United Kingdom, which is presented to the immigration officer on arrival.

(3) As a foreigner wishing to take up residence in the United Kingdom. This is a limited category for wives and dependents of people already in Britain, or those going to marry a British citizen. Also includes people with enough money to sustain themselves (and everyone traveling with them) for an indefinite period without working. Application required beforehand, resulting in a letter of official permission if accepted.

(4) As a student. They mean a real one. You must prove to the immigration officer that a place in a school has been reserved for you and that you have enough money to live on. You'll be expected to leave when the school term is over. At the moment, students drifting to Britain with only vague ideas about studying are a particular vexation of consular officials. If this is your category, request "Some Notes for the Guidance of Overseas Students Who Wish to Study at British Universities." Despite the wordy title, it is one of their more informative handouts. For *entry* into a British university, U.S. applicants would normally be required to have a degree from one of the more "distinguished" U.S. universities.

(5) To take up employment. This presumes that you have a work permit to present to Immigration upon arrival. Work permits are obtained for you by an employer before you enter Britain by application to the Department of Employment. By world standards the process is fairly uncomplicated once you have a job. There are no quotas in Britain for foreign labor, but entry is tightly controlled through the work-permit system.

There is also provision for entering the country for specialized medical treatment. The pamphlet does not cover, however, the self-employed—a writer or painter, for example.

Entering as a self-employed person requires prior application. The application form is a simple one-page document, submitted in triplicate to a British consul. The only subjective question is the last: "Give full details of your reasons for wishing to reside in the United Kingdom." There are no set answers here, but the reasons should be positive toward Britain, not negative about life in the United States. The consul will probably wish to talk with you before he forwards the application to the Home Office for consideration. Approval will come in the form of a letter of official permission to be presented to Immigration upon arrival. The process takes about six weeks.

Admission as a self-employed person is granted initially for one year. At the end of that year you must present yourself to the Home Office, convince them that you have had good conduct and in fact did make a living. Then you can be given another year.

Again, the prime issue is the ability to earn a living. Any contracts, royalty statements, and information about work in progress should be brought to the attention of the consul at the time of application. Unpublished poets and artists in spirit should not attempt to qualify in this category unless they have "ample funds."

Except for going to Britain as a tourist, you must take prior action —file application; find a job; be admitted by a college—before leaving the United States.

FINDING OUT MORE

The best single source of information about Britain is: The British Information Service, Sales Section, 845 Third Avenue, New York, N.Y. 10022. They publish materials and distribute those of Her Majesty's Stationery Office. Most of the following pamphlets and bulletins are available free or at a modest cost. *Do not write to the B.I.S. for tourist information;* write to the British Tourist Authority, 680 Fifth Avenue, New York, N.Y. 10019.

Britain 1971, An Official Handbook. Just what it says, more than 500 pages of information about British institutions, from law and order to sport. About $6 postpaid.

Notes on Some Prices in Britain. Essential. Sixty cents.

Health Services in Britain. A sixty-three-page booklet with more than you'll ever want to know about doctors and nurses, and what they can do for you. $1.60.

Advice to Teachers Who Wish to Teach in Great Britain and Northern Ireland. Long name for a brief leaflet. Free.

The Double Taxation Conventions Between the United Kingdom and the United States. A heavy document intended mainly as business advice. Free.

Immigration into Britain. Factel No.588. Discusses immigration and immigration control. Written during the crisis resulting from large numbers of Indians descending on mother England's doorstep from East Africa. Good background. Likewise, *Race Relations in England. Factel No.600.* A limited number available free on request.

Anthony Sampson. *The New Anatomy of Britain.* Stein and Day, 1972. A revision of a very successful study of institutional Britain, government, politics (in Britain they are different things), schools, communications, finance, and industry. Essentially a look at Britain's modern predicaments.

David Frost and Anthony Jay. *The English.* Stein and Day, 1968. Somehow does better by the spirit of the place than Sampson's book. Approaches such favored British subjects as the "classless society" and the "English way of life" in a light but enlightening way.

Skeff Ardon and Nancy Zager. *Hang Your Hat in London.* A factual book dealing specifically with the settling-in problems of Americans coming to live in London. Sections on food-shopping, manners, and all sorts of things that a person stumbles on his first year in a place. Available for $1.50 from First National City Bank, 17 Bruton Street, London WIX 8AA, England.

Britain's closest equivalent to *Time* magazine is the *Economist*, published weekly. An airmail edition is available widely throughout the United States.

Arthur Andersen and Company. *Guide for U.S. Citizens to Taxation and Other Formalities in the United Kingdom.* Second edition. Good information on what to do before you leave the United States. Basic.

British Embassy; 3100 Massachusetts Avenue N.W.; Washington D.C. 20008. Has a consular section.

British consulates are located in the following cities: Los Angeles, San Francisco, Miami, Atlanta, Honolulu, Chicago, New York City, San Juan, Houston, St. Thomas, and Seattle.

American Embassy; 24/31 Grosvenor Square, London WIA IAE, England. The consular section is one of the busiest abroad, handling, among other things, the problems of most American tourists on their way to Europe through the narrow neck of the bottle (London), including about one American death a day. Has probably the most comprehensive up-to-date set of bulletins of any American consulate in the world, almost two dozen on such topics as estate agents (realtors), private detectives, domestic employment agencies. All offered without assuming any responsibility. Write to them. Tell them what you need.

MEXICO

Area: 780,000 square miles (about one-fourth the size of the United States). Population: 48,313,438 (1970 est.). Capital: Mexico City (7,005,855; 1970 est.). Language: Spanish.

As a step toward understanding what is happening in Latin America today, one could do worse than study the history of Mexico since 1910. Mexico has been through a number of things ahead of its Latin-American neighbors, and learned from them.

Since 1910 and through the 1920's Mexico not only went through a long violent revolution but a subsequent "Mexicanization" as well, first in a social sense, then economically. Mexico recognized the Indian elements in its society in those years, then embraced them. Brazil went through a similar process of recognizing its African roots, but much later. Peru has still to come to terms with its Indians.

In the 1930's Mexico set about industrializing. Former President Cárdenas saw Mexico as a country of small rural landholdings and lightly industrialized hamlets producing goods at a local level, aimed at satisfying the immediate needs of the people. It was an idealistic vision, one that depended on Mexico nationalizing the sources of industrial power within the country, owned at that time mostly by foreign companies.

In 1938 Mexico threw out American oil interests, resisted the veiled threats to call out the marines, and, spurred by the unexpected boom following World War II, proceeded to industrialize in a manner never dreamed of by Cárdenas. But always the strong hand of the government kept itself dealt firmly into the country's economic development.

In one sense, the current headlines about nationalization in Chile and to a lesser extent the moves in Venezuela, Peru, and Bolivia all ring of an earlier era of Mexican history, save for the emergence of a unique Mexican-grown kind of capitalism. But for a number of years now, Mexican government and entrepreneurs have managed to do something rare in the history of Latin America's dealings with the United States. They have managed to encourage American investment while retaining control, as historian John Womack observed—to keep the investment flowing, without the flood. Mexico has managed to do this even while continuing to nurture a diplomatic friendship with the United States, which one government writer says is as good these days as it has ever been.

It isn't the purpose here to sketch Mexico's recent history, even if it could be done in several paragraphs. Or even to launch into a glimpse of Mexico's entrepreneurs, industrial barons fully as flamboyant and fascinating as their Greek or Brazilian counterparts.

The purpose is to establish in a couple of broad sweeps several reasons for Mexico's caution in dealing with the United States, a caution that has paid off. Its attitude of protectiveness is now backed by an enormous governmental self-confidence. Mexico is in control, and nowhere does it show better than in its labor laws and restrictions on the residence of aliens within Mexico's borders.

Mexico's labor and immigration laws are among the most restrictive in the Americas, only easier, perhaps, than our own. They are a forerunner, perhaps, of what might be expected from other Latin countries in the 1970's. They combine a succinctness rare in Latin America with the usual complications of administration, but without the usual flexibility in their execution. The laws are specific, and the Mexican government applies them strictly.

Three examples particularly relevant to Americans:

(1) Aliens are virtually excluded from practicing a number of professions. Mexico's Law of Professions reserves practice to Mexican citizens with degrees granted or legalized in Mexico. There is a provision for exceptions, but it is seldom used—in the case of an American accountant employed by an international accounting firm, for example. Restricted professions include architecture, dentistry, social work, medicine, teaching in primary and secondary schools, engineering, nursing, and law.

(2) By law, 90 percent of the workers in any establishment must be Mexican. Americans coming into even American-owned companies must either possess skills unavailable in Mexico or be in certain positions of trust—managers and directors, for example. Even then the 90-percent rule holds, and such personnel seldom receive permanent-residence status, of which there are probably no more than a hundred given to aliens by the Mexican government in any one year. Most Americans working in Mexico generally live in a limbo of

renewals of their temporary-residence *(visitante)* status.

(3) Under the law Americans *can* own land. The ownership of land is not a right of aliens, but a permission granted to an alien by the government. To do so, an alien must formally forfeit the right to complain to the United States, should the land end up legally appropriated—once a very real hazard in Mexico, now a distant possibility only. Article 27 of the Mexican constitution prohibits alien ownership of land within sixty-two miles of a frontier or within thirty-one miles of a seacoast. An alien must have immigrant status of some sort to be seriously considered for ownership of land. Mineral rights stay with the government in any case. The Americans that do obtain land outside of these restrictions have usually had a lawyer or bank make the purchase in its name, on their behalf. Since Americans who obtain land in this way have no legal title, trust is an essential part of the transaction.

Despite such restrictions, many Americans have discovered the country to the south, and a large number of them live there—if not permanently, for lengthy periods of time. Officially, the U.S. State Department calculates that about 98,000 American citizens live in Mexico, a figure bettered only by the number of Americans resident in Canada.

In reality, the figure is probably much greater. Access to Mexico is only slightly less easy for the tourist than access to Canada. Tourism is Mexico's biggest dollar-earning industry, and the treatment of tourists at border and airport has eased to the point of near joviality in recent years. Rather than go through the legalities of some sort of formal resident status, many Americans go to Mexico as tourists, do not register with the American consulate, stay for a short or long period of time, and eventually return to the United States.

The closeness of Mexico allows a greater diversity in types of Americans than found, say, in Brazil. As in Brazil, a number of Americans are in business in Mexico, mainly in Mexico City, Guadalajara, and a few other urban centers. Many are in Mexico temporarily, their visas secured at great expense and explanation by the Mexican lawyers retained by their companies.

There are a large number of Americans with independent incomes, a few expatriate rich, and many more retired people. *Business Week* reported that the American consulate general in Guadalajara received for distribution in 1970 on the order of 4,000 Social Security and government pension checks a month, and the number is on the increase. There are also a few Americans living in Mexico married to

Mexican citizens, and there are a fair number of students. At Guadalajara University almost 800 Americans are studying medicine, many avoiding the draft or attracted by the easy entrance requirements.

It is difficult to guess how many of the total number of Americans in Mexico are hard-core permanent residents; the best guess is far less than half.

A young Mexican-American woman living in Guadalajara views with a certain sadness the reasons Americans come to Mexico to live:

> Most Americans come to Mexico because the weather is appealing and because it is still a little cheaper to live here than in the United States. The Mexican people are not taken into account; they simply are a part of the whole picture. These Americans think of Mexico and its people as "colorful"—and I don't blame them. Tourism is Mexico's number-one industry, and "colorfulness" is a wonderful gimmick. The result is of course many Americans fall for it and come to Mexico with false hopes. Without understanding the crux of the culture, they react to cultural differences with negative feelings of superiority. So many leave, disillusioned, because Mexico is not such a paradise after all.

In a sense, of course, this could be written about a percentage of Americans (or Germans, or British) who go anywhere. Only Mexico seems to bring out the extremes of American behavior, from vocal to quiet American; from those who live without dipping beneath the surface of Mexico's culture to those who have completely submerged themselves in it.

Some Americans choose to live in the cliquey, highly visible "gringo clusters"—a label given by one English-speaking Mexican to such places as Puerto Vallarta, Cuernavaca, San Miguel de Allende, and Vera Cruz. The longest-standing and largest American colony in Mexico is the concentration at Ajijc, by Lake Chapala near Guadalajara. Here there are American churches; a weekly newspaper —the *Colony Reporter;* an English-language radio station; and a comfortable, well-oiled style of expatriate living.

Another kind of American is the complete antithesis, difficult to find to the point of being invisible. They share no similarities as a class except that somehow they have reached beneath the surface of Mexico, found something they liked, and have managed to hang on.

Jon Rose is from Los Angeles and has lived in Mexico eight years. He works for a Mexican company with no international affiliation, something rather rare for most Americans.

I came to Mexico originally because I was offered a job by an American company. Previously I had scouted Europe for several years halfheartedly, but I never came up with a way of earning a living. When Mexico was offered to me, I readily accepted. Without a job offer I would never have come, and I don't readily advise it for others. Most foreign countries, including Mexico, have an unemployment problem with their own citizens. Americans have no special genius which makes them more attractive than natives, whatever you have heard.

As a people, Mexicans are mentally healthier than Americans, despite their complexes. They can relax, enjoy a fiesta, take a three-day weekend, and not feel guilty of any sin. The sooner Americans moving here accept that attitude, the sooner they get over the rest of the problems that come their way from being in Mexico.

Beyond that, any American will have a problem at being accepted. During the first year working for the American company I traveled a lot, had nothing in common with the Mexicans I met in my daily work, and didn't take the time to see the Mexican business contacts I made outside of working hours. So I knew Mexicans, but I visited socially with few. Things had to change when I went to work with the Mexican company; about six months later I found myself being accepted by my Mexican co-workers. I am now married to a Mexican girl, and her family and friends totally accept me, as much as any in-laws accept the man who robs them of their daughter. It's the same way in the small Mexican town I live in, about an hour from Mexico City. If there are any reservations of acceptance, they come now from the foreign colony. Part of the reason for the acceptance is now I try to learn from my Mexican friends and family instead of trying to teach them the "right way." I don't do it out of condescension, either. I'm an outsider, a foreigner, and I am interested to know how people live and act and think here. I don't judge much, although I'm hardly a total convert.

My own feeling is that Mexico is no place for expatriates without independent means. It is no place to do your own thing. Or to wear sandals and sarapes in the big city, because that is a cruel joke to those who have struggled hard to put away such clothing and make a new life away from the farms. It is no place for political activity by foreigners. It's a great place to speak and think in a different language, or to learn some different history, or to study anthropology, archaeology, or architecture. It is still a very human environment. Even five years ago I might have been tempted to comment on the poorness of public services, but now that railroads, airports, post offices, and trash collectors everywhere don't work well anymore, there aren't any differences worth mentioning.

I suppose if I couldn't earn a living here I'd go back to the States and try there. But I've always managed to make my hundred a week, always paid my taxes, and tried to enjoy what I'm doing while I'm doing it. I know how tempting that must sound to Americans who dream of a new life down here. Unfortunately, if you don't have some special talent and find a job before you get here, and if you don't have a command of the language, you're worth less than you are in the States. Some come here and try some sort of a hustle. If the government catches you, there is no leg to stand on. If you know how to really hustle for a living you ought to do it in the States. At least there it's a way of life.

PROCEDURES

There are several ways an American citizen may enter Mexico legally and live there.

(1) As a tourist. This requires neither a passport nor a visa, although you do need some proof of American citizenship. A tourist card, good for unlimited multiple entries, can be obtained from any Mexican consulate, at the Mexican border, or by an airline serving Mexico. You may enter Mexico anytime within ninety days of receiving the tourist card, the six-month duration of the card beginning the day you cross the border.

As a tourist you can live anywhere in Mexico, rent an apartment if you wish, but you cannot work or partake in any lucrative activity while in Mexico. Aliens caught working illegally are treated harshly by the Mexican authorities, to the point of being held incommunicado until deportation can be effected. Anyone deported from Mexico ends up on a permanent black list and will be refused entry into Mexico again.

A large number of Americans live in Mexico year after year as tourists very satisfactorily. Once every six months they take a trip to the border, cross over, and reapply for another tourist card on the way back to Mexico.

Most people who eventually decide Mexico is for them at least become acquainted with the country as tourists. One good reason is the difficulty of obtaining status as an *inmigrante*.

(2) As a student. If you intend to study in Mexico for a period greater than six months you should apply at a Mexican consulate for permission to enter as a student. This requires a letter of acceptance from an accredited school in Mexico, six front-view photos and six in profile, a health certificate certified by the nearest Mexican consulate ($4 fee), and written certified proof that you have an income of at least $100 per month for the duration of your stay in Mexico.

(3) As a short-term visitor on business. There are several kinds of visitor's *(visitante)* visas, including a *visa de cortesía* issued by the government to newsmen on short-term assignments, covering the Olympics, for example. The two most common visitor's visas are one

called a *técnico,* the other a *negocios.* The *técnico* is given for a period not greater than thirty days to machinery installers, technical assistants, and the like. This differs from the category *inmigrante-técnico* given to technical people going on a lengthy assignment. A *visitante-técnico* is strictly short-term and requires a request from an established concern in Mexico, validated by a Mexican consul. Expensive, too: $41.50 for the visa, and it's due for an increase. That's dollars, not pesos. The *visitante-negocios* is given primarily to people visiting Mexico to establish business contacts, a traveling salesman, for example. The prime requirement is a letter from his employing firm stating the purpose of the trip, dates of travel, and that the firm is financially responsible. This must be supported by a letter from the company's banker indicating that the company is financially solvent. A *visitante-negocios* is good for up to six months and may be renewed, with considerable documentation, three times only.

(4) As an immigrant. There are six categories of immigrant, each differentiated mainly by how you earn your living. Here things begin to get difficult. Briefly, the six categories are: an investor in business *(inversionista);* an investor in securities; a professional; a person assuming a position of trust; a technician or specialized worker; and a recipient of a fixed income *(rentista).*

Each of these categories has its own specific requirements and rights, but they have a number of things in common.

They use the same application form, which is perhaps the least difficult part of the process. It is a single page and asks only basic information, the most exceptional question being the name and address of a person in Mexico who can give you a reference.

In addition, you will need as a starter: twelve photographs 2″ × 2″, six profile and six full face; a valid U.S. passport; a standard health certificate from your own doctor; a police good-conduct certificate. You will also need certified copies of key personal documents, which in turn must be certified by the consulate. Each category of *inmigrante* has separate financial requirements.

Another thing you'll need is plenty of time. *Inmigrante* status is given only by the Secretaria de Gobernación in Mexico City. Approval of applications sent through the Mexican consulate takes six to ten months, with the average on the high side. It is strongly recommended after initially contacting a Mexican consulate to acquire a competent immigratiom lawyer.

Any of these *inmigrante* statuses may be legally applied for in

Mexico, but the same documents, properly certified, are still required. A lawyer is an absolute necessity, still with no guarantee that one of the *inmigrante* statuses can be acquired. In Mexico a list of lawyers is available from the American consulate, or in the United States from the nearest Department of Commerce field office.

Once *inmigrante* status is granted, it is necessary to leave Mexico in your present status (tourist) and reenter in the new category. Aliens who become *inmigrantes* cannot leave Mexico for more than ninety days during the first two years after entry, nor for more than eighteen months during the first five years, otherwise *inmigrante* status will be lost.

Information on the requirements for all classes of *inmigrantes* can be obtained at any Mexican consulate. Let me elaborate slightly on the sixth category of *inmigrante,* the recipient of a fixed income *(inmigrante rentista).* It is a good illustration of why most Americans who go to Mexico on their own go initially at least as tourists.

The *inmigrante-rentista* is a category designed for Americans with a permanent fixed income derived from outside of Mexico. A minimum of at least $240 U.S. per month for the family head is required, with another $80 per month for each dependent member of the family over fifteen years of age. You'll have to prove that such income is sustainable for five years from the time of entry into Mexico.

You'll have to go through the standard application procedure, including the above-mentioned documents, and wait the prescribed amount of time. The main advantage of this category is that you can import a car duty-free, as well as household goods on a one-time, one-shipment basis. A list of the household goods also has to be authenticated by the Mexican consulate before shipment. There is a fee for authentication.

There is a nonimmigrant variation of the *inmigrante-rentista,* called a *visitante rentista* (also a *no-inmigrante-rentista).* In this case the requirement for fixed income derived from outside of Mexico is $160 U.S. per month for the head of the household, who must be fifty-five years or older. Each dependent over fifteen years of age needs the same $80 per month. The visa is given for six months at a time up to a total of two years; then it must be applied for again. A car is permitted duty-free, as long as you don't sell it in Mexico; household goods are not permitted.

Under both *rentista* categories there is an exemption from Mexican income tax on all fixed income earned outside of Mexico.

FINDING OUT MORE

There is no scarcity of information available about almost every facet of Mexico. Don't overlook the books of Oscar Lewis: *Five Families, Children of Sánchez, Pedro Martínez,* and two lesser-known, more anthropological works—*Life in a Mexican Village* and *Tepotzotlan, Village in Mexico.* John Womack's *Zapata* is a recent treatment of the revolution. A well-known introduction to Mexican culture and history is Leslie Byrd Simpson's *Many Mexicos.*

M. Truett Garrett. *A Guide to Retirement in Mexico.* Far superior to the usual kind of retirement book. Good sections on rules and regulations, and investments. Highly recommended. New edition due early 1972 no price fixed yet. The previous edition was $3.95. Order directly from the publisher: The Gary Press; P.O. Box 655; Brownsville, Texas 78520.

American Firms, Subsidiaries and Affiliates in Mexico. U.S. Department of Commerce, Commercial Intelligence Division, Washington, D.C. 20230. One dollar, check or money order, prepaid.

Establishing a Business in Mexico. Overseas Business Report (OBR 70-41). Available from the Superintendent of Documents, or from any Department of Commerce field office. Fifteen cents. Mexico is one of the better ones of this series. Takes into account the new labor law.

Information Guide to Doing Business in Mexico. Price Waterhouse and Company; 60 Broad Street; New York, N.Y. 10005. Free. Write on letterhead.

Tax and Trade Guide for Mexico. Arthur Andersen and Company; 1345 Avenue of the Americas; New York, N.Y. 10019. Free. Write on letterhead.

American Chamber of Commerce; Lucerna 78; ADPO Postal 82 bis; Mexico 6 D.F. Also in Guadalajara at: 16 de Septiembre 730; Despacho 301; Guadalajara; Jalisco, Mexico. The American Chamber is not in the business of helping Americans find work. Their function is to provide information. They publish a number of pamphlets and bulletins, including a directory of English-speaking persons resident in Mexico, English translations of most Mexican laws, and a volume of practical information for anyone thinking about business, called *Business Mexico.* Ask for their publication list.

Mexican Embassy; 2829 16th Street N.W.; Washington, D.C. 20009.

Mexican consulates general are located in the following cities: Los

Angeles, San Francisco, Chicago, New Orleans, El Paso, San Antonio, and New York City. In addition, there are Mexican consular offices in a great number of cities.

American Embassy; Cor. Danubio and Paseo de la Reforma 305; Colonia Cuauhtemoc; Mexico City, Mexico.

COUNTRIES IN BRIEF

BELGIUM

Since the end of World War II the business of Belgium increasingly has been business. Geographically at the crossroads of Western Europe, its location, liberal government incentives to business and manufacturing, and the Common Market headquarters in Brussels make Belgium a prosperous small nation. As long as it remains prosperous its policies toward residence of aliens are likely to remain liberal. Presently about 690,000 aliens reside in Belgium, more than 15,000 of them Americans. Low corporate and personal income taxes have helped Brussels become a new center for multinational companies. Whereas a decade ago the decision to locate centrally in Europe might have meant a choice among Geneva, London, and Paris, Brussels has added itself firmly at the front of the list. By comparison with the others it may be a gray, charmless city, but available office space, better facilities for housing, and ease of operations account for the increasing number of foreigners in Brussels. There are essentially three conditions that allow residence in Belgium. Americans working for companies established in Belgium may apply for an *autorisation de séjour provisoire,* a temporary residence permit which allows them to stay in Belgium for an indefinite period. It may be applied for in the United States, requiring the usual valid passport, police good-conduct certificate, brief application, photographs, but more important, the possession of a work permit. The work permit is applied for in Belgium by the employer and is sent directly to the prospective employee in the United States. Presentation of the work permit with the necessary documents at a Belgian consulate usually brings forth the temporary residence permit in about twenty-four hours. A similar residence permit is issued to the self-employed. In place of a letter from an employer in this case one must apply for a *carte profession-nelle.* This "professional card" is issued to anyone who proves to the

Ministère des Classes Moyennes that his activity will be profitable to the Belgian economy. This is proved in two ways: you must demonstrate increasing exports, or you must use a high proportion of Belgian labor. Americans are usually restricted from practicing a number of professions, among them law and medicine. Application from the self-employed usually takes at least three months for government consideration and is usually applied for with a lawyer's help. People with independent means may obtain a *visa d'établissement,* the principal requirements being ability to prove sufficient funds to avoid being a burden upon the community, and references from Belgian citizens. Application usually requires a month to process. Details are available from the Embassy of Belgium; 3330 Garfield Street N.W.; Washington, D.C. 20008. Consulates are located in Los Angeles; San Francisco; Washington, D.C.; Chicago; New Orleans; and New York City. The American embassy in Belgium is located at 27 Blvd. du Regent; Brussels, Belgium.

FRANCE

Most Americans who live permanently in France agree that it is difficult, that existing in Paris, as in New York, is fraught with impossibilities, then usually end up reluctantly admitting that they could no longer be happy living anywhere else. Whereas in Australia, Canada, or New Zealand one might be awed by the physical aspects of the country either in shcer spatial extravagance or visual impact, in France it is the French themselves who overwhelm, beguile, or repel. Their indifference to foreigners, Americans especially, is legendary. American writer Mary McCarthy once commented on her own early false start at settling into France by remarking simply that the French were hard to know. For a foreigner the first three years in France are the hardest, largely because without a command of French one can scarcely begin. It's not that the French dislike foreigners. Some three million live in France, and the country has opened its borders to a number of political refugees and foreign workers. It is rather that they withhold acceptance. French journalist Sanche de Gramont observes that the French workingman lives in a cocoon made up of his family, his cronies, and his set habits, from which he cannot be induced to emerge, nor which the foreigner can easily penetrate. His protectionism starts on his doorstep. What is known in English as a "welcome mat" is called in French a *paillasson,* which has the connotation not of welcome, but rather, "if you must come in, at least wipe your feet." It is this reluctance to allow foreigners social admittance that causes the most distress to new American residents in France; we are a more egalitarian nation than most of us realize, and Americans quickly observe that despite the slogan of the French Revolution, equality is not an aspect of French character that has yet blossomed into maturity. Notes Gramont:

> In every aspect of French life there is a Masonic division between the initiated and the uninitiated, from the few favored customers for whom the restaurant owner saves his hidden store of wine to someone who has been "recommended" and gets special treatment in government offices. Belonging is everything, the barriers of suspicion fall, and one is allowed into the magic circle, protected from a hostile world.

Students and artists have a somewhat easier time in France, in large part because they already belong to an easily defined and much privileged part of French society. More Americans study in France than in any other European country, and Paris still remains something of a minor mecca for painters, writers (although, as one writer said, they no longer write about Paris), and political exiles. Some 20,000 Americans live in France, considerably less visibly than the roughly equal number that live in Spain, for example. The figure has edged downward over the past several years, the single Western European country that has had a decrease of American residents.

As a tourist, an American can remain in France for up to three months. If you remain more than three months you are automatically classified as a temporary resident and must apply for a *carte de séjour* from the local prefecture or commissariat of police before your initial three months expires. The principal requirement for obtaining a *carte de séjour* is either a student registration card or proof of financial resources. A *carte de séjour* is not a work permit, but rather a permit to stay awhile. To work in France one needs a work permit, a *carte de travail,* issued by the Ministry of Labor. It will not be issued without evidence of prospective employment, and that, without special skills and a good knowledge of French, is the problem. There are a number of good sources of information about France available to Americans. *Enjoy France* is a booklet packed with names and addresses of organizations and tips to women, published by the American Women's Group of Paris, 49 Rue Pierre Charron, Paris 8°, France. The most comprehensive booklet on schooling in France is

Elementary and Secondary Schools in France, published by French Cultural Services, 972 Fifth Avenue, New York, N.Y. 10021. They also have information about studying in France. School and housing information, and a list of English-speaking lawyers, are available from the American Embassy, 2 Av. Gabriel, Paris 8°, France. *Helpful Hints for Living in Paris* is published by the American Church in Paris, 65 Quai d'Orsay, Paris 7°, France. A directory of members of the American Chamber of Commerce in France is available for $5 postpaid from the Chamber's office at 21 Avenue George V, Paris 8°, France. Embassy of France; 2535 Belmont Road N.W.; Washington, D.C. 20008. Consulates are located in Washington, D.C.; Boston; Chicago; Denver; Detroit; Houston; Los Angeles; New Orleans; New York City; Philadelphia; and San Francisco.

GREECE

Greece has some quickly observable similarities with Italy: a low cost of living, especially outside of the cities; immigration laws that are vague about just how long a person may live in the country as a tourist; and an American population living there permanently, a large number of whom are former immigrants to the United States who have returned to live on Social Security payments. The Greek National Tourist Office in New York City estimates they have dealt with some 15,000 Greek-Americans on their way back to Greece in the past ten years. "And why not?" said a Greek official leaning back in his chair and gazing at a map of Greece on the wall. "They live beautifully, especially in the villages. The country is warm, you know. When they die, they die peacefully." Of course, a number of foreigners have lived beautifully in Greece for a long time. While the "American-Americans," as one Greek called them, prefer Athens, Rhodes, and the islands south, the long-standing British colony centers on Corfu, north near the Yugoslavian border. Next to Finland, Greece has had the slowest rise in its cost of living of any country in Western Europe. Most Americans now living in Greece had been there before, some retired from the Diplomatic Corps or private business. The problem for those below retiring age, as in Italy, is finding work, and like Italy, it is in this concern that the Greek government is likely to become brusque with foreigners, especially if they attempt to compete with locals for jobs. Americans may visit Greece, even on business, for up to two months without a visa, after which time they must renew their visitor status; there is apparently no limit to the number of renewals allowable as long as a visitor doesn't threaten to become a burden upon the community. To work requires a work permit from the Ministry of Labor and a residence permit from the Ministry of the Interior. Generally they are issued sparingly to foreigners for specialized work not available locally, and then only for one-year periods. *The Greek Tourist Guide,* containing residence information, is available from the National Tourist Organization (EOT), 565 Fifth Avenue, New York, N.Y. 10036. For insights into the Greece of the generals see Herbert Kubly's *Gods and Heroes.* Doubleday, 1969. Embassy of Greece; 2221 Massachusetts Avenue N.W.; Washington, D.C. 20008. Consulates are located in San Francisco, Chicago, New Orleans, Boston, and New York City. American Embassy; 91 Queen Sophia Avenue; Athens, Greece.

IRELAND

As in Greece and Italy, the largest components of the American population living in Ireland—in total about 9,000 persons—are former Irish immigrants, naturalized Americans, or their immediate descendants, who have returned with pensions and a heavy nostalgia for the old sod of Ireland. Although the country is small, about equal in size to the state of West Virginia, with about 4.5 million people, Ireland has had millions of its own emigrate over the past century and a half to populate, and enliven, a number of other countries. One estimate puts the figure of Irish emigrants and their descendants living abroad at about 20 million. As in Britain, there are generally two ways, other than as a tourist, that an American can reside in Ireland. He must either demonstrate sufficient income to support himself and those dependent on him or have a firm offer of employment, in which case his employer must apply for a work permit *before* he enters the country. Ireland is amenable to the retired. The cost of living has doubled in the past fifteen years, but it is a cheaper country to live in on the whole than Germany, Switzerland, the Scandinavian countries, or Britain. U.S. Social Security payments and pensions derived from sources outside of Ireland are usually untaxed. The problem is trying to find work. Ireland is still one of the most agriculturally dependent nations in Europe, with about 30 percent of the work force involved in farming, compared with 18 percent in France and 8 percent in Germany. Industry grows slowly, and jobs are in short supply. Ireland favors the return of any Irish with needed skills. Given equal talents, government regulations favor the employment of an Irish citizen in a position over a foreigner. There are occasional shortages in the labor market, and Ireland's tax laws are extremely lenient on artists and writers who reside in Ireland but earn their money elsewhere. Employment in the professions is limited. For information on current labor needs, write: National Manpower Service; Central Clearing Section; Room 203; Department of Labor; Mespil Road; Dublin 4, Ireland. For information on tax liabilities, write: Revenue Commissioner's Office; Dublin Castle; Dublin 2, Ireland. For cost-of-living and residence information, write: Embassy of Ireland; 2234 Massachusetts Avenue N.W.; Washington, D.C. 20008. Or to an Irish consulate general in Boston, Chicago, New York City, or San Francisco. The American Embassy in Ireland is located at 42 Elgin Road; Ballsbridge; Dublin, Ireland.

ITALY

Ah, Italy. Into the 700-mile-long boot dangling beneath the subcontinent of Western Europe there has not been a single new wave of people since the Middle Ages. That is, if one ignores what journalist Luigi Barzini calls in *The Italians* "the peaceful invasion," the millions of tourists that yearly flood into Italy "driven by some unknown urge." In point of fact Italy has been one of the great emigrant nations of the past century, contributing a great number of migrants not only to the United States but also as far afield as Brazil, Chile, Argentina, Ethiopia, and Australia. Today Italians work throughout Europe even while their own economy, statistically at least, is one of the fastest-growing in the world, exceeded throughout most of the 1960's only by Japan and West Germany. While many Italians look outward for places where they might avoid the poverty and boredom of the provinces, many Americans as well as other Europeans see Italy as the epitome of a country with a sense of life. The great cities seem the quintessential Europe, rich in history and tradition, decorated with striking architecture, and spiced by the touch of Mediterranean climate. As many Americans live in Italy as in France and Britain combined, about 74,000 in mid-1971. By far the largest segment of the American population are former Italian immigrants, naturalized Americans who have returned to the places of their birth to live on slim pensions. But the whole spectrum of the overseas American is there: young and old who have discovered Italy, or more often Rome or Florence, and have scrambled for a way to stay on; a few artists and writers who find that Italy and their modest and varying incomes mix nicely; and the top-level managers and technical people working for American-owned companies. The range of life styles available to the foreigner is probably greater in Italy than in any other European country. You can live well on a few hundred dollars a month if you choose, or go broke on ten times that amount. As it is with a growing number of Italians, finding work is the problem. Americans already living there, the staff at the American embassy, and Italians themselves all offer their various equivalents of the sad Latin shake of the head when asked: "But how does one get a job?" The American embassy in Rome, like American embassies everywhere, will not help Americans find work. They do publish a bulletin titled "Employment in Italy," pointing out that competition for any job is high, and ending with the plea not to come to Italy without either a prior offer of work or sufficient money. Equipped with one or the other, Italy is as amenable a country to foreigners in its midst as presently exists. All foreigners are classified simply as *tourists* or *residents* without sub-categories or further classifications. An American with a valid U.S. passport may enter Italy as a tourist without a visa. All foreigners, even tourists, however, are required within three days of arrival to appear at a local police office *(questura)* or town hall *(municipio)* and apply for a *permesso di soggiorno,* a permit to stay. If staying at a hotel or *pensione,* the *permesso di soggiorno* can easily be obtained for you by the management. It is good initially for three months, and is renewable, usually without question, for another three months. What happens after that, as is so often the case in Italy, depends. Italy has no law that limits the stay of a tourist to six months, and as in Mexico, there are many Americans who stay lengthy periods of time, renewing their tourist status periodically. A *resident* is any foreigner living in Italy not considered a tourist. It generally means anyone working in Italy, studying at an accredited school, or living on a fixed independent income. Applying for a residence visa under one of these circumstances while still living in the United States is done through an Italian consulate. If you have a job waiting, your employer applies in Italy for an *autorizzazione al lavoro,* a permit to work, which when approved is mailed to you. Presentation of the *autorizzazione* to an Italian consul, along with a simple application in quadruplicate (plus a photo), will result in issuance of a residence visa in a matter of days.

Students must show proof of admission to an accredited school, and their sources of support. Those moving to Italy with a fixed income likewise must demonstrate its nature and source to the satisfaction of consular officials. For details, write: Embassy of Italy; 1601 Fuller Street N.W.; Washington, D.C. 20009. Consulates general are located in Los Angeles, San Francisco, Boston, Chicago, New Orleans, New York City, and Philadelphia. The American embassy has information on schooling, and some brief bulletins on work and moving to Italy. Write to: The American Embassy; Via Veneto 119; Rome, Italy.

JAMAICA

Those who know the Caribbean well vouch for the uniqueness of each island. From pancake-flat Barbados, set apart geologically east of the Lesser Antilles, north and westward to Jamaica and Cuba, no two islands are the same. The Bajian dialect of Barbados is as unintelligible to the Patois-speaking St. Lucians nearby as both would be to the Spanish-speaking Cubans, or the Jamaicans with their own mellifluous brand of the King's English. Among the islands of the Caribbean, only the problems are the same: overpopulation, one-crop economies, unemployment, and net emigration often of their brightest and best-trained people. All suffer the hangover of former colonial rule (or in the case of Martinique and Guadeloupe, continuing colonial rule by France), and all reluctantly cater to tourism that juxtaposes comparative wealth with their own poorness more blatantly than anyplace else in the world. Whether driven by economic problems or growing racial awareness, the Caribbean is changing. Even Ian Fleming, who, in the James Bond books painted as lopsided a view of Jamaica as anyone has in recent years, knew that change was in the air, as the dialogue between Strangeways and his colleagues in the opening scenes of *Dr. No* attests. Of the islands, Jamaica has a little more of everything than most: more land, more people (about half the number of New Zealand), a few minerals, more industry, and more underlying political problems than perhaps any Caribbean island except Tobago. With regard to new foreign residents, almost all the islands are protective, Jamaica's policies being fairly representative. Ideally, Jamaica would like the talented and skilled Jamaicans living abroad to come home. Secondly, they want people who can bring skills noncompetitive with Jamaicans but who are willing to work at the same wage levels. Even while Jamaicans emigrate to the United States and Canada, the Jamaican government searches in both countries for people to fill positions in the Civil Service. Jamaica has a stated need for doctors, nurses, dentists, engineers, accountants, and architects. Americans cannot work without a work permit, which, British-style, is applied for by the prospective employer prior to entry into the country. Americans desiring residence, or with prior employment, need a valid passport, a medical certificate, a police good-conduct certificate, a visa from a Jamaican consulate, and a financial statement showing enough funds to support the purpose of the visit. The island is interested in investors. But like Britain, those drifting to Jamaica with the announced purpose of looking for work will not be looked upon kindly by immigration officials. For commerical information, write: Jamaica Industrial Development Corporation; 200 Park Avenue; New York, N.Y. 10017. The Jamaican consulate general in New York is at the same address. There is also a consular section in the Jamaican embassy, 1666 Connecticut Avenue N.W.; Washington, D.C. 20009. The Personnel Development Unit of Jamaica's Ministry of Finance and Planning publishes a monthly leaflet called *Jobs Jamaica*, available from either the consulate general or the embassy. For additional general information, write: Jamaica Information Service; 10 South Avenue; Kingston 4, Jamaica. Probably the most informative book on the entire Caribbean is *The West Indian and Caribbean Yearbook*, published by Thomas Skinner and Company (Publishers) Ltd.; 30 Finsbury Square; London E.C. 2, England. The American embassy in Jamaica is located at 43 Duke Street; Kingston, Jamaica.

JAPAN

Japan has a complex set of immigration procedures, including sixteen separate visa classifications, and a recently tightened "Immigration Control Order" aimed mainly at the large number of Koreans living in Japan. Japan in no way needs people, yet it remains one of those distant mystical countries, like Australia or Nepal, that titillate the imagination of many Americans, who get little closer to the country than a letter to the American embassy asking how they can live there. The embassy's reply is not encouraging, noting the necessity of having a knowledge of Japanese and prior employment. About 20,000 American civilians live in Japan nonetheless, and opportunities to visit the country for study are equaled by no other Asian country. Even tourists need visas, available from any Japanese consulate. Visas are given for a particular reason, and normally cannot be easily changed once in Japan. A small booklet, *Foreigner's Guide to Immigration Procedures*, is available from *The Japan Times*; 5–4, Shibaura 4-chome; Minato-ku; Tokyo, Japan. They also publish an English-language newspaper available in an airmail edition. The American embassy also distributes the booklet, along with a detailed list of school facilities. Schooling in Japan for many international people is the counterpart of Switzerland in quality and variety. The book *Living in Japan* is published by the American Chamber of Commerce in Japan; Room 701, Tosho Bldg.; 2–2 Marunouchi 3-chome; Chiyoda-ku; Tokyo, Japan. Price $8 postpaid. They also circulate a newsletter among their members in Japan listing people available for employment (usually already in the country). For insight into the Japanese business environment see Howard Van Zandt's excellent article "How to Negotiate in Japan," in *Harvard Business Review* Nov.–Dec., 1970. The Council on International Education Exchange (CIEE), 777 United Nations Plaza, New York, N.Y. 10017, produces a well-done information report, revised yearly and free, called *Japan: Study, Travel and Work Opportunities*. Embassy of Japan: 2520 Massachusetts Avenue N.W.; Washington, D.C. 20008. Consulates are located in Los Angeles; San Francisco; Honolulu; New Orleans; New York City; Portland, Ore.; Houston; Seattle; and Chicago. The American embassy is located at 2 Aoi-cho; Akasaka; Minato-ku; Tokyo 107, Japan.

MICRONESIA

Writing in the periodical *Natural History,* anthropologist Margaret Mead observed: ". . . the smallest islands of the earth are almost all in trouble . . . resources, overpopulation, dependent on distant and outside money." Yet she sees in the islands a training ground for the new professions in ecology needed to inhabit the earth as a whole. "For older students who wish to make a career of the development of man's environment, a year on an island, learning the language, mastering the intricacies and the interrelationship of its living population and all its plants and creatures, would be perfect preparation for thinking about wholes." The United States Department of the Interior presently administers perhaps the largest expanse of small islands in trouble on the face of the earth, the Trust Territory of the Pacific Islands—three of the four major island groups of the Anthropological-Geographic region of the Pacific called Micronesia. The islands themselves were dragged into the twentieth century by World War II, with Peleliu, Truk, Guam, Saipan, and Kwajalein battles memorable to an older generation of Americans. The *Enola Gay* took off from the Micronesian island Tinian. Another Micronesian island, Bikini, is in the midst of being resettled after decades of forced abandonment. Following the defeat of the Japanese, who had once administered the islands, the United Nations gave them in trusteeship to the United States. For the next twenty years they remained virtually sealed to the outside world and forgotten. I researched the islands in the early 1960's for an article I later wrote for *Focus*. In late 1970, through chance, I had the opportunity to island-hop the Trust Territory from one end to the other aboard an Air Micronesia 727, a service then in its second year. The change was phenomenal. The islands are still in trouble, but add to Miss Mead's comments about the study of environment, the study of almost visible social change. For better or worse, I'm not qualified to comment. But whatever change there has been is the result of a revitalized American interest in the islands and the slow, unobtrusive economic reinvasion of the islands by the Japanese. With the beginning of the Air Micronesia flights has come tourism, administered in an improvised way that I thought had disappeared from what has become a mass-production industry. There are a growing number of Americans working in the Trust Territory, ex-Peace Corps volunteers or government types who have stayed on after their assignments, and having sampled the enormous difference in the islands, have picked the place that suits their temperament best: Saipan, with its gloomy shadows of World War II and flat empty land eyed by Japanese entrepreneurs who claim they can make the island into a garden and return their investment the second year; Yap, an anthropological backwater, whose people stubbornly fend off tourists and businessmen alike, taken advantage of only by the wily Palauans from the islands west of Yap; Truk, whose people have a history of dealing with outsiders and getting a shade better of the deal; Ponape, whose open and sincere island dwellers are somehow dominated by the almost embarrassing beauty of their island; the Marshalls, some two dozen atolls which instantly repel or attract, but where the absolute limit of available land was reached long ago. Between these islands, a hundred more inhabited, a thousand more empty, spread over a portion of the Pacific as great in area as the United States itself, islands not particularly wanting outside help, but no longer able to live in this century without it. The amount of money spent by the

United States government in the Trust Territory is increasing, and so too is the staff. The best bets are employment with the Department of the Interior, which hires a number of teachers. Write to: Education Officer; U.S. Trust Territory of the Pacific Islands; Saipan, Mariana Islands. The Peace Corps also has several hundred volunteers in the islands. Considerable information about all Pacific islands is found in the periodical the *Pacific Islands Monthly*, or from Continental Airlines, the operators of Air Micronesia. The most comprehensive guide to the entire Pacific is *The Pacific Islands Yearbook and Who's Who*. Available from Pacifica Publications Pty, Ltd; 29 Alberta Street, Sydney, Australia; priced at $A7.80 (that's Australian dollars.)

MOROCCO

Despite the *Late Show* image of Casablanca as a mysterious city with every street narrow and bustling, and the rather rakish, trendy reputation of Marrakesh, Morocco remains a conservative Islamic country, friendly to America, and more important to Americans, trying to diversify its largely agricultural economy and suffering the usual growing pains of a developing nation. Although it is the closest African nation to Europe, Morocco is a giant step into the Arab world, which is part of the appeal for the European population of the country, some 150,000 of a total 15 million people. French influence is strong. Most Moroccans speak Arabic, and French as a second language, with Spanish spoken in the north. English, even among the well-educated, is pretty much unknown. About 1,000 Americans live in Morocco, a great many retired, preferring Tangier in the far north, a ferryboat ride from Spain, to either Rabat, the government center, or commercial-industrial Casablanca, facing the Atlantic. The Americans one is likely to see on a casual visit most probably won't be the residents. The rather easy accessibility of a number of unlawful delights has made Morocco particularly attractive to some of the international subcultures, who have found drugs and sex of a remarkable variety available at far below the Stateside prices. Most Americans, resident and otherwise, find other living costs predictably more expensive, apartments averaging anything from $150 per month on up. An American may visit Morocco for up to three months as a tourist without a visa. To stay longer requires either leaving the country and returning again as a tourist with a new three-month stay ahead of you or establishing permanent residence at the nearest police office and obtaining a Moroccan identification card. Permanent residents, Americans included, must apply for exit and reentry visas (also obtainable through the police) for visits outside of the country, which take at least three weeks to obtain. The main requirements for establishing permanent residence are either evidence of enough money to live on or proof of employment. An American citizen can go to Morocco, find work (theoretically at least), and change his status from tourist to resident with few complications. The country is amenable to writers and artists as long as they can demonstrate some modest source of support. Embassy of Morocco; 1601 21st Street N.W.; Washington, D.C. 20009. The American embassy in Morocco is located at 6 Avenue de Marrakesh; Rabat, Morocco.

PANAMA

Panama does not belong to the United States. It is the smallest Latin-American republic, carved out of Colombia during the first decade of this century and pressured toward independence by the prospect of the Panama Canal. The ten-mile-wide strip of land accommodating the present canal was leased to the United States in perpetuity. The Canal Zone *is* U.S. territory and under its total jurisdiction, almost a country within a country. Outside the zone, Panama runs its own affairs, not uninfluenced by the United States, but often stubbornly independent. The attraction of Panama stems from its location, a freewheeling business environment, and a receptive attitude toward foreign investment. Income taxes are low, restrictions on the movement of money nonexistent, and incorporation and other business procedures easily and quickly managed. In this respect Panama is more akin to Singapore, Switzerland, or the Benelux countries than either of its neighbors, Colombia and Costa Rica. There are problems. The country is ruled by a junta, but the wheels of commerce roll on. The country wants foreign investment, but has labor laws like Mexico and Costa Rica demanding that a high percentage of workers be Panamanian. The government encourages those interested in the country to visit as tourists, since formal immigration is a long, document-filled process. Application for permanent residence can be made once in the country, handled smoothly by one of many reputable local lawyers. Panama has a newly instituted "retirement visa" obtainable by anyone who can demonstrate a fixed income of $400 per month, but unlike Mexico, people with this status can engage in business, as well as buy land. Residence information is available from any Panamanian consulate or from the American embassy in Panama. There is a small, business-oriented international community in Panama, of which about 5,000 are American. A *Directory of Commerce, Industry and Tourism* is available from the publisher: Sati de Panama, SA; Ave. Justi Arosemena y Calle 35; Apto 7600; Panama 5. Embassy of Panama; 2862 McGill Terrace N.W.; Washington, D.C. 20008. Consulates are located in Los Angeles, Augusta, New Orleans, New York City, Philadelphia, Dallas, Houston, San Antonio, and Miami. The mailing address of the American embassy in Panama is Box 2016; Balboa, Canal Zone.

PHILIPPINES

From 1898, as a prize for the United States winning the Spanish-American War, until just prior to World War II, the Philippines were a U.S. territory similar in status to American Samoa, or Guam, or Hawaii before statehood. After World War II the United States and the Philippines bound themselves together with a long list of defense and trade treaties, the most important of which was the Laurel-Langly Agreement whereby a number of American bases are maintained in the Philippines. Due to expire in 1974, it is the cause of some anxiety in the State Department becuase of the "bastion in Asia" role the country plays in military affairs. Seventy years of American presence have created not so much an American community, as, similar to Panama and Guam, a melding over the years of a number of Americans into local society. Almost 25,000 civilian Americans unconnected with the U.S. government reside in the Philippines, many married to Philippine nationals. In a smaller measure than either Greece or Italy, there arc also many naturalized Americans, native-born in the Philippines, who have been returning home in recent years with Social Security or pension checks to lead relatively affluent lives enjoying politics, cockfighting, and the other less volatile entertainments of the Filipinos. Other than marrying a Philippine national or having been born there, it is difficult for Americans casually to take up residence. Since the Philippines is one of those nations with a large percentage of unemployed and underemployed (an increasing number of Philippine nationals are immigrating to Hawaii and the West Coast), an American must have a firm offer of employment before he will be encouraged to reside in the country. Americans who do reside in the Philippines find themselves almost automatically enjoying the upper-class luxuries of the home-grown aristocracy simply because there is very little middle class between rich and poor. English is considered the country's only common language, bridging the communication gap among about seventy-five different languages and dialects, but only about 40 percent of the people speak it throughout the islands. As a latecomer in the bid for the tourist dollar, the Filipinos have only recently made it easier to visit the islands as a tourist. They have abolished the need of a tourist visa for stays of up to twenty-one days, provided confirmed reservations and return tickets are in evidence. From twenty-one days to six months, all visitors, tourist or business, need visas. A booklet, *Introducing Manila*, is published by the American Association of the Philippines; 1422 A. Mabini Street; Manila, Philippines. Both a monthly journal and a weekly newsletter are published by the American Chamber of Commerce of the Philippines Inc.; Shurdut Building; Intramuros; P.O. Box 1836; Manila, Philippines. Embassy of the Philippines; 1617 Massachusetts Avenue N.W.; Washington, D.C. 20036. Consulates are located in Chicago, Honolulu, Los Angeles, New York City, New Orleans, San Francisco, and Seattle. The American Embassy; 1201 Roxas Blvd.; Manila, Philippines.

PORTUGAL

Portugal has a reputation for being one of the least expensive, "unspoiled," quaintly charming countries in Europe. An American journalist living in France claims that that is precisely why he finds the country dull: no brassiness and little vice. Some 4,500 Americans reside there nonetheless, many of them retired, proving apparently that one man's definition of dullness can be another's description of paradise. Beyond the attraction of a slower, more manageable way of life is a sunny, mild climate similar to that of southern California, and a low cost of living. In 1969 the average yearly income in Portugal was slightly more than $500 per capita, and higher wages paid elsewhere in Europe have made Portugal, like Italy, an emigrant nation. Some quarter of a million Portuguese live and work elsewhere in Europe. But the price spiral has hit Portugal too. The cost of living increased about 6 percent in 1970, and the rate of increase is the fourth-fastest in Western Europe, trailing only neighboring Spain, Denmark, and Britain. Another appeal is low income taxes for the few foreigners who manage to find work in Portugal; money earned abroad—including Social Security and most pension payments—is generally untaxed. For reasons the Portuguese themselves don't quite understand, Portugal has recently acquired mystique. Even among people who have never been to Portugal, the idea that it is one of the few remaining inexpensive, climatically appealing places attracts many. One Portuguese consular official mentioned a not atypical case of an American who had visited the consulate. "He said he wanted to buy an apartment building in Estoril or Cascais," said the consul. "He had the money and was planning to buy something right away. I asked him if he had owned an apartment building before, in this country. He said no. I asked him if he spoke Portuguese. He said no, he had never been to Portugal. I told him to go have a look first. Rent an apartment and see, but to leave his money here. It's no good to take all your money to Portugal. The interest the banks pay is nothing." In general, Portugal's policy regarding the residence of foreigners is similar to Italy's: an open attitude toward persons with independent income, restriction on those who compete with nationals in the labor market. For practical purposes, foreign doctors, journalists, engineers, and architects may not practice in Portugal. Unlike the Italians, however, the Portuguese have none of the laissez-faire attitude toward administering their immigration laws. From the Moors the Portuguese inherited a rather highly developed sense of administrative procedure, a passion, if you will, for bureaucracy. Their customs regulations are among the most detailed in the world, and anyone moving a household to Portugal should retain a customs broker beforehand. Unfortunately, the printed information regarding residence offered by Portuguese consular offices in the United States is sometimes vague and lacking in detail. This mustn't be misinterpreted as a reflection of imprecise laws that are easily manipulated. Taking up residence in Portugal is like guiding a ship through a reef-strewn channel. The chart is detailed, the passage narrow, with a fair share of snags for those who vary from the course. An American with a valid passport is allowed to enter Portugal as a tourist and remain sixty days; an extension of thirty days may be applied for by application written in Portuguese on legal paper, and presented to the international police at least seven days before the original sixty days expires. If this is too much trouble, it is possible to visit nearby Spain for a few days and return to Portugal. Normally foreigners are granted a sixty-day entry visa even though they have been gone for only a short time. Unlike Mexico, Italy, or Britain, you are not allowed to rent (unfurnished) or buy a residence in Portugal as a tourist. Americans who wish to reside in Portugal need visas. In practice, such visas are easily obtained by those who have a definite job in Portugal (the employer having proved that no Portuguese can fill the position), have sufficient means of support, or have people in Portugal willing to assume financial responsibility for them (including their possible expatriation). Application for a residence visa is made to a Portuguese consulate. You must have a valid passport, fill out a single-sheet application stating name, address, marital status, the reason for wanting to settle in Portugal, means of support, and the names of two people in Portugal who will vouch for your character. If you do not have a job, you will also need a police certificate, two passport photos, and documented proof of funds. Processing an application takes from two to six weeks. A helpful guide, much broader than its title implies, is *Guide to Investment in Portugal*, distributed free to those who write on business letterhead by the Casa de Portugal; Commercial Services Division; 570 Fifth Avenue; New York, N.Y. 10036. The Embassy of Portugal; 2125 Kalorama Road N.W.; Washington, D.C. 20008. Consulates are located in Los Angeles, San Francisco, Honolulu, Chicago, Boston, Newark, New York City, Providence, and Houston. Bulletins on customs, schools, realtors, and a helpful guide, "General Information on Living in Portugal," are obtainable from: American Embassy, Avenida Duque de Loule, 39; Lisbon 1, Portugal.

SINGAPORE

Singapore is an independent country, a single large island about one-third the size of Oahu in the Hawaiian Islands, and some forty odd islets strewn across the Singapore Strait toward nearby Indonesia. The city of Singapore is situated on the southern edge of the large island; once the administrative center for a large portion of the British empire, it has since become one of the fastest-growing, dizzyingly modern cities in Asia. Flying into Singapore from Madras or Calcutta, one has the feeling of bridging centuries of time and landing smack in the middle of the most modern of worlds. High-rise apartments, bright lights, new automobiles, and everywhere the signs that Singapore has never been more prosperous. The basis of the prosperity is a mixture of the old Singapore and the new. Its wealth in large measure is still based on the idea of Singapore being a strategically located *entrepôt*, a commercial middleman—processing, packaging, and assembling the goods of other nations. And with that the inevitable accessories to commerce—banking and shipping. One hundred shipping lines still call on Singapore. The new Singapore aims at attracting the high-technology industries and has already made a running start in electronics. In place of the ship-repair facilities once manned by the British, there is a growing locally owned shipbuilding industry. The banks of Singapore see themselves as a prime force in the development of Southeast Asia, particularly Indonesia; in 1970 Singapore took another step toward making itself something of an Asian Switzerland by establishing the practice of numbered bank accounts. It is already one of Asia's more important traders of gold. Though late in discovering Singapore, American businesses now seem to find it one of the favored sites for headquarters of Southeast Asian operations, more so than Hong Kong, Taiwan, or Manila. Both Esso and Mobil have refineries in Singapore, and the number of Americans totals about 7,500, a jump of 115 percent in two years, due largely to another interest of Singapore in which Americans are playing a part—oil explorations near Indonesia. Singapore's once strict immigration laws have been eased to allow the importation of skilled and professional people. Though Malay is the official language, Chinese, English, and Tamil are widely used. Americans may enter Singapore in three ways. A tourist or a temporary business visitor will be admitted "for a short stay"—anything from a day to three months—upon presentation of a valid U.S. passport, proof of immunization against both smallpox and cholera, an onward or a return ticket, and sufficient funds. A *professional-visit pass* is commonly issued to employees of American companies upon application by the company or the individual directly to Singapore's Comptroller of Immigration, provided there is a *bona fide* need for an American in a job that cannot be done by a local. It is good for one year initially, and is renewable. A *social-visit pass* is designed to allow the family of an American citizen who are American citizens themselves to reside in Singapore while he may be doing his business elsewhere. It is easily obtained if some person or company resident in Singapore will guarantee support and repatriation if necessary. The Singapore embassy recommends that applications for both the *professional-* and *social-visit passes* be made while still in the United States by writing directly to the Comptroller of Immigration in Singapore. For trade and commercial information write to: Singapore Economic Development Board; 745 Fifth Avenue; New York, N.Y. 10022. Embassy of the Republic of Singapore; 1824 "R" Street N.W.; Washington, D.C. 20009. The American Embassy; 30 Hill Street; Singapore.

SOVIET UNION

Yes, you can go and live permanently in the Soviet Union. But you must first become a Soviet citizen. They have no provision for status as a resident alien. The only other nontourist status is a special "invited" category that implies family, professional, or cultural ties to the Soviet Union; the party in the Soviet Union does the inviting. Forms for Soviet citizenship can be obtained from the consular section of the Soviet embassy. You are required to fill out the application in quadruplicate, answering such questions as nature of your profession, object of the journey, relatives in the Soviet Union, and whether you have been there before. The answers must be translated into Russian, for which there is a fee. The application is then submitted with six passport photos, one for each copy of the application and two extra for the Soviet passport when, and if, issued. The exact number of Americans who become Soviet citizens is small. The Soviet embassy will confirm no figure, but suggests that most have family ties or sound reasons for doing so. The Soviet Union has no interest in taking in those disaffected with American political life, and they strongly encourage anyone interested in the Soviet Union to make a pilot trip. Applications for citizenship are forwarded by the consulate to Moscow, each acted upon separately by the Supreme Soviet. The Soviet Union does not demand proof that you renounce citizenship, but the application form contains a statement whereby you swear allegiance to the Soviet Union and no other nation, which would probably be good evidence for the U.S. State Department to doubt your intent to remain an American citizen. Receiving Soviet citizenship means accepting the rights and obligations of all Soviet citizens. But if you are accepted as a Soviet citizen, the government virtually guarantees a job for you. That is what their system is about, they say. It is unlikely that a serious application for citizenship would be approved without extensive consultation between you and the Soviet consul, and qualifications very attractive to the Soviet Union. If accepted, you receive a Soviet passport in the United States, which allows you to travel. They do have a procedure whereby if you change your mind you may reapply to the Supreme Soviet for renunciation of Soviet citizenship and a subsequent exit visa. There is usually a fee for renunciation. The Soviet consular authorities make it clear that they are not interested in people seeking novelty, and only the sincere, well-informed need apply. Embassy of the USSR; Consular Division; 1609 Decatur Street N.W.; Washington, D.C. 20011. For information on scholarly exchange programs: International Research and Exchange Board; 110 East 59th Street; New York, N.Y. 10022. See also the bulletin, *Travel to the Soviet Union*, available free from the Passport Office, Department of State, Washington, D.C. 20524.

SPAIN

If one were to map the international population living in Spain, one would find that the majority reside in a minuscule part of the land area. The second observable fact would be that with the exception of the concentration of foreigners in Madrid, most foreigners live, if not within sight of the sea, at least within inhaling distance of a sea breeze. A narrow but concentrated swath of foreign settlement sweeps south from Barcelona along the eastern edge of the Iberian peninsula to Alicante. A less dense concentration is found along the entire coast from Alicante to Cartagena, and from there continues west past Málaga and the tourist hot spot Torremolinos to British-controlled Gibraltar. Barcelona remains Spain's most international city, though fading as the great commercial center it once was prior to the Spanish Civil War. The Franco government has consciously given a hard-sell to Madrid at the expense of the Catalans of Barcelona, to the point that Madrid has finally begun to glow quite brightly as an international city, considerably more so than it did even a decade ago. By Spain's calendar, Madrid is a young city, not yet five centuries old, a planned capital, as are Washington, Canberra, and Brasilia. Of the four, Madrid has come the closest to becoming an effective central city of the nation, with most of its development in the last twenty years. The chief tangible appeal of Spain for Americans (of which there are about 24,000 without connections to our large military establishment there) has long been low prices. They may be rock bottom no longer, but Spain is still less expensive to live in day-to-day than the majority of Western European countries. It remains a favorite of Americans with modest fixed incomes and of artists and writers, since the residence policies for the self-employed are fairly easily negotiated (as long as some money is coming in). A small American business community exists, mainly in Madrid, part of it dealing with Spaniards, the other part dealing with the U.S. military establishment. For a literate, easily digestible look at Spanish character, see Fernando Díaz-Plaja's *The Spaniard and the Seven Deadly Sins*, Scribner's, 1967. See also the books of Gerald Brenan. Spain's regulations concerning permanent residence are much like Italy's. Americans can stay as tourists in Spain for up to six months without a visa, holding only a valid U.S. passport. Six months from the last entry into Spain a foreigner must apply at the Alien Office of the Director General of Security for a *permanencia,* a three-month extension, which can in turn be extended for an additional three months, totaling a year. Failure to extend these documents before they expire results in not being allowed to leave the country without an exit permit, which is obtained by paying a stiff fine. If a foreigner wants to stay on in Spain indefinitely, he needs a permanent-residence permit (which is not the same as a work permit). A residence permit will generally be granted if there is obvious proof that a person intends actually to live in the country, such as a labor contract, a business, a rented house, property, a fixed income coming from abroad, or regular pensions. As in most European countries, the difficulty is finding work, with the principle being that you will not be given a work permit if a Spaniard can be found to do the job. Summer jobs are nonexistent. In practice, most American companies operating in Spain have few Americans on the staff. Self-employed people still need a special work-identification card *(Tarjeta de Identidad Profesional),* which, if approved, involves a yearly tax at renewal time of the card, depending on estimated earnings. These regulations also hold for the Balearic Islands—Majorca, Minorca, Ibiza, Formentera—which have been favored retreats for expatriate artists and writers for years, even before their popularity as an inexpensive vacation spot for Europe's young working class. See Robert Graves's and Paul Hogarth's *Majorca Observed,* Doubleday, 1965. Sources of information about Spain are excellent. The American embassy in Spain publishes two bulletins, *General Information on Spain* and *General Information on Employment in Spain,* as well as a number of other information sheets on everything from attorneys and adoptions to schools and translators. The American Embassy; Consular Section; Serrano 75; Madrid-6, Spain. There is also an American Club of Madrid, Desengaño 12, Madrid; and an American Women's Club, Plaza Ecuador 6, Madrid. The American Chamber of Commerce in

Spain is located at San Agustin, 2; Madrid. The Ministerio de Hacienda publishes an excellent booklet in English called *Taxation Regulations for Foreigners,* available from the Spanish embassy in the United States, Spanish consular offices, and Spanish national tourist offices in major U.S. cities. Embassy of Spain; 2700 15th Street N.W.; Washington, D.C. 20009. Spanish consulates are located in Los Angeles, San Francisco, Chicago, New Orleans, Boston, and New York City.

SWEDEN

Sweden was once a very poor country. From the last decades of the nineteenth century until the beginning of World War I, a million Swedes left for a better life in the United States, nearly one in five of the population. Sweden is poor no longer, having a per-capita gross national product second only to the United States. Nor has it been an emigrant nation since the early 1930's—just the opposite, in fact. Its apparent prosperity has attracted between 300 and 500 thousand foreigners since the end of World War II. Thirty percent of the factory workers in Sweden are Finns, Yugoslavs, Italians, and Greeks. Foreigners make up about 6 percent of the entire labor force. In many aspects Sweden projects itself as a model of enlightenment. It managed to stay neutral in two world wars, it sponsors the Nobel prize, was one of the first countries to protest American involvement in Vietnam, and gives a larger proportion of its national budget in aid to poor countries, without conditions, than any other nation. Sweden has as national priorities both better housing and full employment. Although it has been determined to make room in its society for the large number of aliens who have come to Sweden (over 300,000), the country has little in its heart for outsiders who think they have found in Sweden some sort of social Utopia but who aren't willing to contribute to the future as well. The American deserters who have gone to Sweden have found that political asylum and social acceptance are not the same thing. Their first problem was language, their second not enough skill in a very skilled society. From those two problems stemmed the others—boredom, separateness, the need to find a hustle, drugs, and for many, finally ostracism. The few American deserters who are likely to remain in Sweden have dug into the language, got out of Stockholm, cut off their connections with other deserters, and set about learning some skill. Competition for employment is fierce in

Sweden. Restrictions on foreign permanent settlement are not likely to ease. In March, 1967, "free" immigration stopped. To settle in Sweden today requires a work permit *before* entering the country, which means having a job, and an added wrinkle: because Sweden has an acute housing shortage, a foreigner must also have written proof of living accommodations. In 1969 the country additionally revised its laws so that it is no longer possible to obtain Swedish citizenship by marrying a Swede. Other than in factories, there are few opportunities for non-Scandinavians, and such positions would be closely tied to knowing Swedish and a number of other "primary qualifications." American companies operating in Sweden rarely hire Americans, partly because of language and partly because there are qualified Swedish managers available. American visitors may enter Sweden for three months without a visa, and after that renew their temporary residence at the discretion of Swedish authorities. Write to the Swedish embassy for their bulletin *Employment in Sweden*, guaranteed to dampen the casually interested. Embassy of Sweden; 2249 R Street N.W.; Washington, D.C. 20008. Also consulates in New York City, Minneapolis, San Francisco, Chicago, and Houston. The booklet *Travel, Study and Research in Sweden* is available from the American Scandinavian Foundation, 127 East 73rd Street, New York, N.Y. 10021; price $3 postpaid; many facts and addresses. The American Embassy; Strandvagen 101; Stockholm, Sweden.

SWITZERLAND

In the mid-1960's Swiss immigration officials realized, apparently quite suddenly, that there were 800,000 aliens resident in Switzerland, almost one in six of the entire population. Given Switzerland's reputation as a millionaires' haven and tax shelter, one might expect this figure to include a large number of the world's rich taking refuge in Switzerland's noted civility, sound currency, and lenient income tax on fortunes gathered elsewhere. In reality, most of the aliens were farm and construction workers from Italy, Portugal, Yugoslavia, and Spain. The increasing presence of aliens caused a touch of xenophobia to nudge the Swiss conscience. The result was that in 1965 two stiff new laws were passed designed to restrict the number of aliens in Switzerland; in June, 1970, a plebiscite was held over the issue of how many foreigners ought to reside in Switzerland, and even tighter restrictions were narrowly avoided. All companies and organizations in Switzerland now have a strict quota on the number of aliens they may employ. Aliens wanting to work in Switzerland (Americans included) must have a work permit *before* they enter the country, and the process of obtaining the work permit for an alien by his prospective employer has been made intentionally more tedious and time-consuming. Often the permit is not granted at all. There is a loophole to avoid the quota system whereby an employer can demonstrate an "exceptional need" for a particular person, or that the prospective employee has skills not normally available in the country. Via this loophole the construction and farm workers still enter Switzerland and the large American firms in Zurich, Geneva, and Basel are able to bring in key people. In point of fact there are now more aliens resident in Switzerland than in the mid-1960's, about 970,000 according to the 1970 Swiss census. But the Swiss authorities feel that they have the entrance of aliens under firm control. About 19,000 Americans currently reside in Switzerland, one in five gainfully employed. The remainder are dependents, students, a few retired people, and a smattering of the wealthy living on money earned elsewhere. The surest way to become resident in Switzerland is to find a job with an American company located there. The catch is that most assign only top-level management or technical people to Swiss subsidiaries, and since Geneva and Zurich are considered something of a plum among international assignments, most companies have little difficulty making the transfers from within. Employment possibilities with Swiss companies are limited unless you possess a unique skill and can work in one of the official languages—Italian, German, and French. Americans can visit Switzerland as tourists without a visa, needing only a valid passport, and look for work. The tourist may stay initially for ninety days and obtain one extension for an equal period, but cannot work—even if he finds a job—under strict penalty if caught doing so. He must leave the country while his prospective employer applies for a work permit, which, if approved, is sent to the Swiss consulate in his country of residence, who will then issue the documents necessary for entrance into Switzerland. The whole process may take several months. In the case of applying for residence directly through a Swiss consulate in the United States, the applicant must fill out a single-page application, the two most important questions being: "How much money do you have?" and "Where exactly in Switzerland do you wish to live?" The Swiss consulate then forwards the application, with a brief personal assessment, through the Swiss federal authorities to the

Swiss canton (there are twenty-two) where the applicant would like to reside. The Swiss tend to discourage casual inquiries from pensioners, in the belief that high costs of living in Switzerland and cultural and language differences make living too difficult for many older Americans with limited means. Furthermore, the American embassy in Bern suggests that it is extremely difficult to obtain a *permis de séjour* (a residence permit) for the cantons of Zurich and Geneva, which are both suffering a housing shortage. The cantons near Lake Lugano are less congested, but the rule of prior firm employment or sufficient independent income still applies. The cantons have the power to decide whom they will allow to live and work within their borders, and if a canton refuses admittance to a foreigner, it is a closed issue. Swiss consulates in the United States will not assist Americans to find jobs in Switzerland, but for the patient they offer some odd bits of information. Each consulate has a directory of officially licensed employment agencies in Switzerland usable on the premises. They also have directories of professional organizations, and information on summer work for students over nineteen. Such information is subject to change or withdrawal as the Swiss see fit. Embassy of Switzerland; 2900 Cathedral Avenue N.W.; Washington, D.C. 20008. Swiss consulates are located in Los Angeles, San Francisco, Chicago, New Orleans, New York City, and Cleveland. For a number of business publications, write: Union Bank of Switzerland; 14 Wall Street; Suite 2406; New York, N.Y. 10005. For information on Swiss schools, see chapter on "Your Child's Learning." The American embassy in Switzerland has additional bulletins on schooling, work (or lack of it), and living in Switzerland; write: American Embassy, 93/95 Jubilaumstrasse, 3000 Bern, Switzerland.

TURKEY

There is a surprisingly large number of Americans in Turkey, due mainly to the presence of the American military. More dependent families live in Turkey than in either Korea or Thailand. Substantial American communities exist in the capital city, Ankara; in Istanbul, west of the Bosporus in European Turkey; in Izmir; and in Adana. In Ankara there is an American school, an Air Force-operated hospital, and such watermarks of American presence as the Ford Foundation, CARE, and Gulf Oil. Thirty years ago French and German were the most commonly heard languages other than Turkish, and though both are still useful, English has become a popular second language. Thanks to the British presence as well, there are libraries with books in English; English-language churches; and English-speaking doctors and lawyers in most major cities. Middle Eastern Technical University, one of the better engineering schools in the Near East, uses English as a language of instruction, and has, naturally enough, become something of a target for Turkey's own energetic corps of nationalist youth. Still Turkey is a rather permissive country toward foreigners, except for those unfortunate enough to be caught dealing in the country's great illegal export; most of the heroin that wends its way to the United States via Marseilles has its origin in the peaceful fields of European Turkey. An American may visit Turkey for up to three months without a visa. If the intention is to stay longer than three months, a visa good up to a year is obtainable in about twenty-four hours from any Turkish consulate upon presentation of a valid passport and payment of a small consular fee. The visa is not good for working, but it is issued without a formal visa application or proof of financial resources. It can be changed once in Turkey if a job is found. If the purpose of the visit to Turkey is to work or engage in business, a different visa is required. If your profession is in one of the fields of engineering, in a technical field, or in teaching, the consulate can issue the visa quickly upon seeing proof of your work contract. All visa applications involving other professions need approval from Ankara and hence take weeks to obtain. Embassy of the Republic of Turkey; 1606 23rd Street N.W.; Washington, D.C. 20008. Consulates are located in Los Angeles, San Francisco, Chicago, and New York City. The American Embassy; 110 Attaturk Blvd.; Ankara, Turkey. There are American consulates in Adana, Izmir, and Istanbul.

WEST GERMANY

The total number of Americans living in Germany—military, dependent, and civilian—exceeds even those in Canada, something approaching 400,000. More U.S.-government employees are stationed in Germany than in Vietnam. Generally, Germany's residence and labor requirements are among the least restrictive on the Continent. Americans may visit Germany as tourists for up to three months, possessing only a valid passport. After three months, one must apply at the local Alien Registration Office for a residence permit (*Aufenthalts-Erlaubnis*). The permit may be issued for up to twelve months and is extendable yearly if the resident pays his taxes, attends to civil or alien laws, demonstrates means of support for himself and his family, and generally returns the hospitality given him by the German government. Working in Germany is restricted less than in Italy, Spain, or France, although in practice a knowledge of German is near-essential. Germany is just now beginning to have a natural increase in its labor force, making up for the losses of World War II and the low birth rate. With the expanding economy, Germany uses large numbers of Italians, Spaniards, Greeks, Turks, and Portuguese. An American arriving in Germany wanting to find work is advised by the American embassy to visit the local labor office (Arbeitsamt) and apply for the required permit to work *(Arbeitserlaubnis)*. There is no fee for the work permit, and it is given fairly liberally under a Treaty of Friendship and Navigation existing between Germany and the United States. The work permit is usually granted for a specific job, initially for three months and then for a year at a time. There is a German-government Central Placement Office, a monopoly that counsels and places employees in American and German firms mainly in professional, technical, executive, and managerial fields, but also summer work for students. There is also direct hiring of employees, as in the United States. Americans may write to the Central Placement Office beforehand: Zentralstelle fuer Arbeitsvermittlung (abbreviated ZAV); 6000 Frankfurt/M; F.R. Germany. Students should write to: American Student Information Service; Johnstrasse 56C; Frankfurt/M; F.R. Germany. For details of residence requirements, write to the U.S. Department of Commerce, Bureau of International Commerce, European Division, Washington, D.C., and ask for the booklet *Residence and Business Rights of Aliens in the Federal Republic of Germany and West Berlin.* The American embassy in Germany publishes information bulletins for those already resident: American Embassy; Bonn, Bad Godesberg; Germany. Embassy of the Federal Republic of Germany; 4645 Reservoir Road N.W.; Washington, D.C. 20007. Consulates are located in Los Angeles; San Francisco; Washington, D.C.; Atlanta; Chicago; New Orleans; Boston; Detroit; St. Louis; New York City; Philadelphia; and Houston.

VENEZUELA

Venezuela's booming development puts it in the same category as Mexico and Brazil, all countries rich in physical resources and all capable of infecting the outsider with a frenetic sense of movement. In actual fact there is a larger American capital investment in Venezuela than in either Mexico or Brazil, something over three billion dollars, most of it in the single great underwriter of Venezuelan development—oil. Revenues from oil account for about two-thirds of government expenditure, and there is a local saying more common in times past than now that "Oil will pay for everything." Of the many descriptive tags put on Venezuela's development in the past decades, the most common is "dynamic." Venezuelan government officials often speak of the "miracle years," meaning those since 1958 when Marcos Pérez Jiménez, one of the last of the old-style Latin-American dictators, was ousted. It was Pérez, oddly enough, who brought the foreigners to Venezuela. The country had never sought immigrants as had Brazil, Argentina, and Chile, even though the Orinoco river valley is a frontier second in scale only to the Amazon itself and still largely undeveloped. The Pérez regime went after European skilled workers and entrepreneurs. During the 1950's, while immigration in the rest of Latin America was shrinking, about 350,000 new settlers, mainly Spaniards, Portuguese, and Italians, poured into Venezuela, about half into the capital, Caracas. Foreigners came and went freely, national communities flourished, and foreign banks were established with a privileged status. But the open door to foreigners began closing with the ousting of Pérez. Capital flowed out, as did a number of the immigrants. Since then there has been a slow, steady rise in the feeling "Venezuela for the Venezuelans," a brand of economic nationalism that can be seen everywhere in Latin America today. The early 1970's have seen the door close on immigration (although technically the 1936 Law of Immigration and a subsequent 1960 Agrarian Statute are still in effect). In addition, there is increased control over the petroleum industry and a new Banking Reform Act that virtually nationalizes foreign banks. Caracas is probably less cosmopolitan now than it was ten years ago, with the almost complete disappearance of the former national communities. Like São Paulo in Brazil, Caracas is a city without a past, a product of "now," caring less for tradition than glass and concrete, freeways, and the automobile. Americans undoubtedly have a lessening role to play in Venezuela than a decade ago; there are still a considerable number who consider the country a second home. In 1961 the Venezuelan government estimated the number of Americans to be about 53,000. Ten years later the U.S. State Department claims it is about 19,000, though inexplicably the

Venezuelan government puts the figure considerably higher. Visas to enter Venezuela are issued either as tourist, transient, or resident. Americans going to work in Venezuela are given transient visas upon presentation of a work contract and the usual health and police certificates, valid passport, vaccination certificate, and photographs. At the end of one year transient status may be renewed at the authorities' discretion. At the end of two years an American may apply for a residence visa in a joint application with his employer to the Ministry of the Interior. Applications for transient status must be made in person at a Venezuelan consulate. For a wide range of information about the country, write to: Embassy of Venezuela; Institute of Information and Culture; 2437 California Street N.W.; Washington, D.C. 20008. Consulates are located in Mobile; Los Angeles; San Francisco; Chicago; New Orleans; Baltimore; New York City; Philadelphia; Portland, Ore.; Galveston; and Houston. Embassy of Venezuela; 2445 Massachusetts Avenue N.W.; Washington, D.C. 20008. The American Embassy; Avenida Francisco de Miranda and Avenida Principal de La Floresta; Caracas, Venezuela.

ZAMBIA

Zambia is a good example of an African country trying to do things for itself that were once done by foreigners. It is undergoing strict "Zambiazation." Only a Zambian citizen may now own certain businesses, many of them the small consumer shops once owned by Asians. The country is nationalizing insurance, banking, and many key industries. Most aliens can reside in Zambia only as long as they are offering a skill or profession not available in Zambia, and are obviously not displacing a Zambian from a job. Most of the Americans in Zambia are missionaries or work for American companies serving Zambia's rich copper industry. Both require work permits *before* entry into the country, and there are no known cases where a person admitted as a tourist has been given a work permit once in the country. The Zambian government occasionally recruits specialists on its own to fill key positions temporarily. Entrance as a tourist, as in many East African countries, has been eased. Zambia does have a status of permanent residence for aliens, which requires, among other things, four years in the country holding either a residence permit or entry permit. Requests for information should be sent to: Chief Immigration Officer; P.O. Box 1984; Lusaka, Zambia. Zambian President

Kenneth Kaunda's recent speech on his intended plans for Zambia's future development, *Now Zambia Is Ours,* is available from the Zambia Information Services, P.O. Box RW.20, Lusaka, Zambia; or from the Embassy of the Republic of Zambia, 1875 Connecticut Avenue N.W., Washington, D.C. 20009. The Council on International Educational Exchange, 777 United Nations Plaza, New York, N.Y. 10017, produces *Africa: Work, Study and Travel Opportunities,* a well-done information sheet on opportunities, especially for young people, in a number of African countries, including Zambia. The American Embassy; Chester House; Cairo Road; Lusaka, Zambia.

NOTES AND ACKNOWLEDGMENTS

My principal sources have been human, and the main purpose here is to give them my thanks. Until I finally sat down to list those who have offered me advice, information, and above all their time, I had no idea I was indebted to so many people. Without the words of others, most of the thoughts in this book would never have taken shape. For their form and substance I remain fully responsible.

Initial thanks must go to professors Richard F. Logan and Tom L. McKnight, whose friends in many parts of the world gave me initial contacts in countries and places I had never been. Also thanks to Edith Wurtzel and Wes Perry for reading portions of this work in manuscript, and to M. J. Hall, who little suspects the influence her patient research and careful eye have made on the result.

Three articles provided the structure for "A Quiet Exodus": E. G. Ravenstein's original 1889 work, "The Laws of Migration," now available in the Bobbs-Merrill Series in the Social Sciences; Professor Everett S. Lee's "A Theory of Migration," in *Demography*, 1966; and Wilbur Zelinsky's "The Hypothesis of the Mobility Transition," in *Geographical Review*, April, 1971. Particular thanks must go to Professor Lee, now with the Demographic Research and Training Center at the University of Georgia, for his encouraging comments on my rather simplistic treatment of many of his ideas and concepts. Professor Lee makes an additional important hypothesis that I had no room for in the context of this chapter. Writes Lee: "Unless severe checks are imposed, both volume and rate of migration tend to increase with time." In our society as it presently exists, such checks, hopefully, are unlikely. The new emigrants of the past few years may turn out to be in a real sense pioneers, the leading edge that quite a number of others will follow.

Many thanks must also go to Mike Wenk of the U.S. Catholic Conference in Washington, D.C., whose insider's knowledge of where things are found in Washington saved considerable time and pain. And to the good-natured counsel of Professor William S. Bernard, director of the Center of Migration Studies, Brooklyn College of City University of New York.

The starting point for "Rules of the Game" was Murdagh S. Madden and Sherman L. Cohn's article "The Legal Status and Problems of the American Abroad," in *The Annals,* September, 1966, and a subsequent meeting with Professor Cohn at the Georgetown University Law Center. He of course is not responsible in any way for the information I've presented here.

The written sources for tax policies and rates were supplied in most cases by the embassies of the countries mentioned, and from the standard publications of the Internal Revenue Service. There is much movement in the whole field of tax law. Many countries are involved in massive tax reforms, tightening of loopholes in existing laws, and the beginning of a coordinated cracking-down on evaders. The principles of taxation abroad stated here should remain valid for some time; rates and specific regulations may change quickly.

Appreciation to the people of the Office of International Operations of the Internal Revenue Service, Mr. Stanley Nitzburg of McGraw-Hill, Incorporated, and Mr. George Bunge of Arthur Andersen and Company.

Some of the most careful and long-term studies of people adjusting to a new culture have been made by Australian sociologists and demographers. The work of Alan Richardson is found in more detail in "A Theory and a Method for the Psychological Study of Assimilation," in *The International Migration Review,* Fall, 1967. Also for the chapter on "The Culture Leap" I relied heavily on Dr. Charles Price's "Migrants in Australian Society," H.R.H. the Duke of Edinburgh's Third Commonwealth Study Conference, 1968, and R. T. Appleyard's *Immigration: Policy and Progress,* Australian Institute of Political Science Monograph, 1971. Professor Appleyard has done considerable study on why migrants fail.

The entire *Journal of Social Issues,* July, 1963, was given to the subject "Human Factors in Cross-Cultural Adjustment." Particularly useful were John T. and Jeanne E. Gullahorn's "An Extension of the U-Curve Hypothesis," which pretty well documents the culture shock of Americans returning to the United States after prolonged absence.

Kalvero Oberg's description of culture shock from *The Overseas Americans* by Harland Cleveland and others, McGraw-Hill, 1960, now out of print.

The information on Peace Corps volunteers was from Maurice Sill's "The Four Stages of Transculturation," *The Volunteer Magazine,* 1966.

The principal written source for the "Minor Adjustments" chapter was the standard work edited by Sidney Licht, *Medical Climatology,* 4th edition, Licht, 1964. Particular thanks also to the library staff of the American Geographical Society, who have made their small library one of the most pleasant in which to conduct research in New York City.

The estimated apartment rents mentioned in the chapter on "Living Abroad American Style" are from *Business Week,* March 21, 1970, but from experience are still valid despite being several years out of date.

The comparative cost index is taken from *Labor Developments Abroad,* October, 1971. The United Nations statistics are from their *Monthly Bulletin of Statistics,* December, 1971. When local currencies have been converted into dollar figures, exchange rates as of July 31, 1971, have been used throughout.

Many thanks to the Administration and Finance Division of the Peace Corps for supplying me with cost-of-living allowances for volunteers. The figures of estimated family costs are from a Gallup poll released January 9, 1971.

As C. Northcoate Parkinson might have said, experts in any subject tend to disagree. The teachers of language tend to disagree more than most. The experiences of the Foreign Service Institute and the Peace Corps were used here because of their good success in teaching a great number of people a practical command of a foreign language. Special thanks must go to Ed Scebold and his people at the Modern Language Association, who reviewed an earlier draft of this section, and to Dr. John B. Carroll, senior research psychologist at the Educational Testing Service in Princeton, who also added to my modest understanding of what it takes to learn a language.

A parent looking for a more complete criticism of the ills of American-style schooling needn't look far. Others have given the subject a good airing, among them Charles Silberman's *Crisis in the Classroom,* Don Parker's *Schooling For What?,* and the essays and recent works of Ivan Illitch on the much larger subject of institutional reform.

The paraphrase of Illitch's idea of putting learning back into the hands of the learner or his parent refers specifically to "Why We Must Abolish Schooling," in *New York Review of Books,* July 2, 1970.

Many thanks for supplying information go to Porter Sargent; Harry

B. Marcoplos of Calvert School; Dr. John Sly, president of the International Schools Service; and Howard T. Clark of the International Division of Holt, Rinehart and Winston, who has been on the inside of more American schools abroad than anyone else I know.

Early in the research for this book I wrote to approximately 120 foreign embassies (and subsequently to many ministries of immigration) requesting information on immigration policies and procedures. The lists that appear in the "Who Wants Us" chapter are an attempt to deal with what first appeared to be 120 different policies without pattern. The point is that immigration laws are in a constant state of flux. They are not in general becoming more liberal. The next twenty years will probably see increasing restriction on the residence of Americans in many countries.

The tourist too may find his movements more restricted in the future. Even tried-and-true tourist centers are beginning to react to the crush of visitors. Since this chapter was written, the Greek Orthodox Church issued a formal prayer that God may protect Greece from the contaminating effects of foreign tourists. In Madrid the well-read newspaper *ABC* warned that the twenty-five million or so tourists that invade Spain each year were threatening the country with a new colonialism. These may be the first stirrings of things to come. Many places that suffer tourists are beginning to feel much as British writer and traveler V. S. Pritchett when he noted recently that tourism is perhaps the best example of mass human pollution.

Particularly valuable for information on the trends in immigration, and relied heavily upon throughout this book, are three periodicals: the *International Migration Review,* published by the Center for Migration Studies Inc., 209 Flagg Place, New York, N.Y. 10304; *Migration Today,* published by the Secretariat for Migration, Division of Inter-Church Aid, Refugee and World Service, World Council of Churches, 150 Route de Ferney, 1211 Geneva 20, Switzerland; *Migration News,* published by the International Catholic Migration Commission, Information Center, 65 Rue de Lausanne, Geneva, Switzerland.

The chapter "What Can *You* Do?" more than any other is owed to other people. Particular thanks to: Stanford Wilson, Snelling and Snelling (Brazil); Robert J. Malm, president, R. J. Malm Associates; W. F. Williams, First National City Bank (Santos); James Rooney, First National City Development Finance Corporation (Thailand); Michael DeBakey, Lima, Peru; George Curtis, Prestamos Nacionales (Costa Rica); John Dunmar, J. Walter Thompson (Argentina); Jim

Stanley, Fuertejidos (Costa Rica); Bob Geddes, São Paulo, Brazil, and a lot of other places; Gurley Turner, Institute of International Education; Joe Hickey, Council on International Educational Exchange; Jerry Brady and Darcy Neill, the Peace Corps; Paul McCusker, the United Nations; Terry Hokum, Acción Internacional (U.S.A.); James Neil Cavener, the Commission on Voluntary Service and Action; William H. Miller, the United Presbyterian Church (U.S.A.); and Steve Elkington, American Friends Service Committee.

The story about the Harvard grad going to Botswana was told me by an extremely reliable source, ex-Peace Corps recruiter Jim Bullard.

The immigration procedures for separate countries were gathered mainly from official sources. A number of consular and government officials went beyond a routine answer to my questioning. They offered information freely, often with surprising candidness, about their countries, their jobs, and sometimes themselves. Without their help there would have been no book at all.

In particular: Raúl Estrada-Oyuela, embassy of Argentina; Miguel Ocampo and Raúl Street, Argentine consulate general; Lionel Mead, embassy of Australia; Marcello M. de Andrade, Brazilian consulate general; Derek Willcocks, British Information Service; Mr. G. M. Mitchell and Charles Morrow, Canadian Department of Manpower and Immigration; Mrs. Estelle Lorca de Rojo, embassy of Chile; Rogelio Navas, embassy of Costa Rica; Colonel Nachim Golan and George Stanislavski, Israel Aliyah Center; Mrs. Olga Rachmilevitch, Association of Americans and Canadians for Aliyah; Mario Grondona, Italian consulate general; J. Urias Nelson, embassy of Liberia; María Sánchez Gavito, Mexican consulate general; J. Graeme Ammundsen, New Zealand consulate general; José Roberto Luttrell, embassy of Panama; Antonio Azevedo, Portuguese consulate general; Joaquim Vasconcellos, Casa de Portugal; Mrs. Eileen Fox, Rhodesian Information Office; G. Barbour, South African consulate general; Vitali Gorikov, embassy of the Union of Soviet Socialist Republics; Hector Graeber, embassy of Switzerland; Emil Suter, Swiss consulate general; María Hernández and F. J. Lara, embassy of Venezuela; Costain Mweeba, embassy of the Republic of Zambia.

APPENDIX: FINDING HELP
A Guide to Additional Sources

MISCELLANEOUS BOOKS, PAMPHLETS, AND GUIDES

Harland Cleveland, G. Mangone, J. Clarke. *The Overseas Americans.* McGraw-Hill, 1960. 316 pages. A conscientious study done in 1957 on 244 people, men mainly, working in government and business in Mexico, Yugoslavia, Iran, Indonesia, and Japan. Good sections on the hassles of the mature American family abroad, particularly the search for American-style schooling, and what the authors call the "neurotic fear of disease." Also a good section on organizational ability as a prerequisite for the American businessman overseas. A helpful book for businessmen and government workers taking a first overseas assignment.

Harold D. Guither and W.N. Thompson. *Mission Overseas: A Handbook for U.S. Citizens in Foreign Countries.* University of Illinois Press, 1969. 296 pages; almost half is appendix. Developed in response to a questionnaire survey of 598 college professors and 315 of their wives, the preface says, who lived in thirty-nine developing countries between 1951 and 1966. Uses quotes from the questionnaires to illustrate a considerable volume of advice, much of it pretty obvious. On page 138, for example, the reader is advised that "Most commonly used drugs are available in the drugstores." A profusion of "what-they-did" quotes. Aimed at the person going abroad short-term. Less practical than it sounds, but worth a look in the library.

Eleanor B. Pierce. *Living Abroad.* Doubleday, 1968. Sponsored by Pan American Airlines, the book carries a subtitle: "All You Need To Know About Living in 93 Countries." Not quite. The residence and work information is paper-thin. The best part of the book is the first sixty pages, the general information about moving and so forth.

Travel Industry Personnel Directory. The Travel Agent Magazine, 2 West 46th Street, New York, N.Y. 10036. Price $6, check or money order. A miscellany of information for anyone thinking about moving overseas. Complete lists of consulates, foreign travel facilities, shipping lines, and so forth. Published annually.

Guide to Foreign Information Sources. Chamber of Commerce of the United States; 1615 H Street N.W.; Washington, D.C. 20006. Price twenty-five cents. Includes consular addresses, country by country, along with national tourist bureaus. Addresses of organizations. Bibliography. Very handy.

Electric Current Abroad. U. S. Department of Commerce. Available from the Superintendant of Documents; U.S. Government Printing Office; Washington, D.C. 20402. Price forty cents. An eight-page booklet giving the type of current in hundreds of cities around the world.

International Driving Permit. Some ninety-odd countries are party to a 1949 convention that resulted in the creation of an International Driving Permit. Obtainable from any American Automobile Association office in the United States and in key foreign capitals. You need a valid license from one of the U.S. states, a single passport photo, and three dollars fee. By mail, allow a couple of weeks. The permit is good for a year abroad, at which time most foreign countries require you to obtain a local license if you are a resident. The permit is not valid for driving in the country of issue, the United States, for example.

World Holidays Listed. A guide for business travel. U. S. Department of Commerce. Published yearly. Available from the U.S. Government Printing Office; Washington, D. C. 20402. Price twenty cents. Lists commercial holidays for one hundred countries, organized by world religion.

STUDY ABROAD

Handbook on International Study. Vol. 2, for U.S. nationals. Institute of International Education; 809 United Nations Plaza; New York, N.Y. 10017. Price $5. Discusses higher education in 120 countries, government regulations, and organizations of interest to Americans who want to study abroad. Also from the same organization: *Summer Study Abroad,* price fifty cents. Also: *Grants for Graduate Study Abroad,* a forty-page description of the Fulbright-Hays grants, which the institute administers, as well as those grants given by foreign governments, universities, and private donors; revised yearly; free.

Students Abroad. Council on International Educational Exchange; 777 United Nations Plaza; New York, N.Y. 10017. Actually a series of three publications, all available free on request from the CIEE.

Summer Study, Travel and Work Programs, which deals mainly with American-run study programs abroad for undergrads. *Highschool Student Programs,* summer and long-term study for secondary-school students. *Semester and Academic Year Programs,* long-term study opportunities for college undergrads. The CIEE also has information on student travel and work.

Study Abroad. International scholarships and courses, 1971–72. UNESCO. Revised every two years, their trilingual volume labels itself "A Compendium of International Study."

World Study and Travel for Teachers. American Federation of Teachers; 1012 14th Street N.W.; Washington, D.C. 20005. Revised yearly.

John A. Garraty, Walter Adams, Cyril Taylor. *The New Guide to Study Abroad.* Harper & Row, 1969. Aimed mainly at college and graduate students. Mentions a number of programs sponsored by foreign universities, with tuition costs and addresses to write for information. Includes a section on the American teacher abroad.

Shirley Herman. *Guide to Study in Europe.* Four Winds Press, 1969. Good sections on American-university-sponsored programs abroad. Clear layout. Separate sections on France, Germany, Spain, Switzerland, Italy, and Belgium.

U.S. DEPARTMENT OF COMMERCE FIELD OFFICES

Information and advice of interest to U.S. businessmen is available from these offices on: foreign markets for U.S. products and services, economic facts on foreign countries, firms with marketing facilities overseas, trade and investment opportunities abroad, government-financing aid to exporters, foreign-exchange regulations and procedures, export-and-import statistics.

Albuquerque, N.M. 87101, U.S. Courthouse. (505) 843–2386.

Anchorage, Alaska 99501, 412 Hill Bldg., 632 Sixth Ave. (907) 272–6531.

Atlanta, Ga. 30303, 4th Floor Home Savings Bldg., 75 Forsyth St., NW. (404) 526–6000.

Baltimore, Md. 21202, 305 U.S. Customhouse, Gay and Lombard Sts. (301) 962–3560.

Birmingham, Ala. 35205, Suite 200–201, 908 S. 20th St. (205) 325–3327.

Boston, Mass. 02203, Room 510, John Fitzgerald Kennedy Federal Bldg. (617) 223–2312.

Buffalo, N.Y. 14203, 504 Federal Bldg., 117 Ellicott St. (716) 842–3208.

Charleston, S.C. 29403, Federal Bldg., Suite 631, 334 Meeting St. (803) 577–4171.

Charleston, W. Va. 25301, 3000 New Federal Office Bldg., 500 Quarrier St. (304) 343–6181 Ext. 375 and 376.

Cheyenne, Wyo. 82001, 6022 Federal Bldg., 2120 Capitol Ave. (307) 778–2220.

Chicago, Ill. 60604, 1486 New Federal Bldg., 219 S. Dearborn St. (312) 353–4400.

Cincinnati, Ohio 45202, 8028 Federal Office Bldg., 550 Main St. (513) 684–2944.

Cleveland, Ohio 44114, Room 600, 666 Euclid Ave. (216) 522–4750.

Dallas, Tex. 75202, Room 1200, 1114 Commerce St. (214) 749–3287.

Denver, Colo. 80202, Room 161 New Customhouse, 19th and Stout Sts. (303) 297–3246.

Des Moines, Iowa 50309, 609 Federal Bldg., 210 Walnut St. (515) 284–4222.

Detroit, Mich. 48226, 445 Federal Bldg. (313) 226–6088.

Greensboro, N.C. 27402, 258 Federal Bldg., W. Market St., P. O. Box 1950. (919) 275–9111.

Hartford, Conn. 06103, Room 610–B, Federal Office Bldg., 450 Main St. (203) 244–3530.

Honolulu, Hawaii 96813, 286 Alexander Young Bldg., 1015 Bishop St. (808) 546–5977.

Houston, Tex. 77002, 5102 Federal Bldg., 515 Rusk Ave. (713) 226–4231.

Jacksonville, Fla. 32202, P.O. Box 35087, 400 W. Bay St. (904) 791–2796.

Kansas City, Mo. 64106, Room 1840, 601 E. 12th St. (816) 374–3141.

Los Angeles, Calif. 90024, 11th Floor, Federal Bldg., 11000 Wilshire Blvd. (213) 824–7591.

Memphis, Tenn. 38103, 710 First American Bank Bldg., 147 Jefferson Ave. (901) 534–3214.

Miami, Fla. 33130, Room 821, City National Bank Bldg., 25 W. Flagler St. (305) 350–5267.

Milwaukee, Wis. 53203, Straus Bldg., 238 W. Wisconsin Ave. (414) 272–8600.

Minneapolis, Minn. 55401, 306 Federal Bldg., 110 S. Fourth St. (612) 725–2133.

New Orleans, La. 70130, 909 Federal Office Bldg., S., 610 South St. (504) 527–6546.

New York, N.Y. 10007, 41st Floor, Federal Office Bldg., 26 Federal Plaza, Foley Sq. (212) 264–0634.

Philadelphia, Pa. 19107, Jefferson Bldg., 1015 Chestnut St. (215) 597–2850.

Phoenix, Ariz. 85025, 5413 New Federal Bldg., 230 N. First Ave. (602) 261–3285.

Pittsburgh, Pa. 15222, 2201 Federal Bldg., 1000 Liberty Ave. (412) 644–2850.

Portland, Oreg. 97204, 217 Old U.S. Courthouse, 520 S.W. Morrison St. (503) 226–3361.

Reno, Nev. 89502, 2028 Federal Bldg., 300 Booth St. (702) 784–5203.

Richmond, Va. 23240, 2105 Federal Bldg., 400 N. 8th St. (703) 649–3611.

St. Louis, Mo. 63103, 2511 Federal Bldg., 1520 Market St. (314) 622–4243.

Salt Lake City, Utah 84111, 3235 Federal Bldg., 125 S. State St. (801) 524–5116.

San Francisco, Calif. 94102, Federal Bldg., Box 36013, 450 Golden Gate Ave. (415) 556–5864.

San Juan, P.R. 00902, Room 100, Post Office Bldg. Phone: 723–4640.

Savannah, Ga. 31402, 235 U.S. Courthouse and Post Office Bldg., 125–29 Bull St. (912) 232–4321.

Seattle, Wash. 98104, 8021 Federal Office Bldg., 909 First Ave. (206) 583–5615.

PASSPORT OFFICES

Boston, Mass. 02203, Room E 123, John Fitzgerald Kennedy Bldg., Government Center. (617) 223–2946.

Chicago, Ill. 60604, Room 244–A, Federal Office Bldg., 219 S. Dearborn St. (312) 353–5426.

Honolulu, Hawaii 96813, Room 304, Federal Bldg. (808) 546–5748.

Los Angeles, Calif. 90012, Room 1004 Federal Office Bldg., 300 North Los Angeles St. (213) 688–3283.

Miami, Fla. 33130, Federal Office Bldg., 51 Southwest First Ave. (305) 350–5395.

New Orleans, La. 70130, Medallion Tower Bldg., 344 Camp St. (504) 527–6161.

New York, N.Y. 10020, Room 270, 630 Fifth Ave. (212) 541–7700.

Philadelphia, Pa. 19108, 401 North Broad St. (215) 597–7482.

San Francisco, Calif. 94102, Room 1405, Federal Bldg., 450 Golden Gate Ave. (415) 556–4516.

Seattle, Wash. 98101, 1410 Fifth Ave. (206) 583–7941.

Washington, D.C. 20524, Passport Office, Federal Bldg., 17th and H Sts. N.W. (202) 783–8200.

The State Department is also expanding a program whereby post offices handle passport applications. The service is currently available in major cities in Massachusetts, New York, California, and Minnesota. If the experiment is a success, passports will be available in a growing number of post offices across the United States.